MURDER ON SHADES MOUNTAIN

MURDER ON SHADES MOUNTAIN

THE Legal Lynching
OF Willie Peterson
AND THE Struggle FOR
Justice IN Jim Crow
Birmingham

Melanie S. Morrison

DUKE UNIVERSITY PRESS   DURHAM AND LONDON   2018

Designed by Heather Hensley
Typeset in Garamond Premier Pro by Westchester Publishing Services

Library of Congress Cataloging-in-Publication Data
Names: Morrison, Melanie, [date] author.
Title: Murder on Shades Mountain : the legal lynching of Willie Peterson and the struggle for justice in Jim Crow Birmingham / Melanie S. Morrison.
Description: Durham : Duke University Press, 2018. | Includes bibliographical references and index.
Identifiers: LCCN 2017039036 (print)
LCCN 2017056838 (ebook)
ISBN 9780822371670 (ebook)
ISBN 9780822371175 (hardcover : alk. paper)
Subjects: LCSH: Peterson, Willie, 1896–1940—Trials, litigation, etc. | Trials (Rape)—Alabama—Birmingham. | Birmingham (Ala.)—Race relations—History—20th century. | African Americans—Crimes against—Alabama—Birmingham.
Classification: LCC KF224.P48 (ebook) | LCC KF224.P48 M677 2018 (print) | DDC 345.761/02532—dc23
LC record available at https://lccn.loc.gov/2017039036

Cover art: Boulders on Shades Mountain. Photo courtesy of Alabama Department of Archives and History.

To all who fought for racial justice
in Jim Crow Birmingham
and kept hope alive

To accept one's past—one's history—is not the same as drowning in it; it is learning how to use it. An invented past can never be used; it cracks and crumbles under the pressures of life like clay in a season of drought.

—JAMES BALDWIN, *THE FIRE NEXT TIME*

CONTENTS

How does a white man born in 1918 and raised in Birmingham, Alabama, become so passionate about racial justice?

Growing up in East Lansing, Michigan, in the 1950s and '60s, I frequently heard this question put to my father by friends and acquaintances who were perplexed by the strength of his antiracist fervor. It could have been one of my father's sermons that provoked the inquiry. Or his leadership in the campaign to abolish the restrictive real estate covenants that barred people of color from obtaining mortgages or purchasing homes in our university community until 1968.

My father believed racism is a white problem and that he, as a white man, would be held accountable by his Creator for what he did or failed to do to confront, name, and mend this deep wound in the soul of America. As he was fond of declaring from the pulpit: "To love God you must work for justice, and justice cannot be realized in this country until racism is eradicated!"

His response to the question of how he had become so passionate about racial justice usually came in the form of short stories about people who made a deep impression on him as a young person. His childhood mentor and pastor, the Rev. Henry Morris Edmonds, topped that list. Founder of Independent Presbyterian Church in downtown Birmingham, Edmonds was a prominent and sometimes controversial figure during his tenure as senior pastor from 1915 to 1942.[1]

"As a teenager in the 1930s," my father recalled, "I sat on the front pew of Independent Presbyterian Church every Sunday, come rain or come shine. I took copious notes as Rev. Edmonds held forth on the great issues of our day, including racism. Seeing that kind of courage and clarity modeled by a white man made a deep impression on me."

My grandparents were members of Independent Presbyterian Church, along with many of the white elite from the Mountain Brook suburb of Birmingham where my father was raised. As the only son of a wealthy entrepreneur, my father—Truman Aldrich Morrison Jr.—was being groomed to take over the family business from his father, who owned gas stations and tire companies all across the city. His father—Truman Aldrich Morrison Sr.—was an ardent segregationist. I grew up hearing stories from my father about the racial apartheid of his youth, the Jim Crow laws that enforced it, and the racist public officials whom my grandfather so admired, including police commissioner Eugene "Bull" Connor. Years later, Connor became a national icon of white supremacy when, in 1963, he ordered his men to unleash police dogs and fire hoses on peaceful black demonstrators marching with Dr. Martin Luther King Jr.[2]

There was one story that stood out above all others. As my father told it, two sisters and a friend from prominent white Birmingham families went for a ride on Shades Mountain, on the southeastern edge of the city. What began as a pleasant drive on a summer's afternoon in 1931 ended in a nightmare, with two of the women killed.

The sole survivor, Nell Williams, was eighteen years old. She told police that a black man wielding a gun had jumped on the running board of the car and demanded they drive to a secluded wooded area. In the struggle that ensued, Nell's sister, Augusta Williams, was mortally wounded, and their friend Jennie Wood died a few days later in a Birmingham hospital. My father's telling of this story was especially riveting to my three siblings and me, not only because my father was intimately acquainted with some of the people involved, but also because those events proved to be cataclysmic in his young life.

I vividly remember knocking on the door of my father's study as a young teenager, imploring him to tell me once more about the murders on Shades Mountain. When working at home, my father always wore a faded blue cardigan with ink stains on the pockets that sagged from the weight of assorted pens, lozenges, and keys. It was the storyteller as much as the story that I longed to hear. My father was fully present when he told this story, undistracted by the ubiquitous pastoral duties and deadlines that usually held him captive. He invited me into an intimate domain where few others were granted entrance. Being entrusted with the whole story made me pulse with pride and feel suddenly older than my years. He never said, "It was those events that changed my life forever." He did not need to. His story told me.

"No one knows for sure what happened on that fateful day in August 1931," he usually began, leaning back in his chair, crossing his long legs and gazing out the study window.

I leaned forward, impatient for details. He looked through the window as if he saw the three young women in the distance moving toward him.

"Nell Williams, her older sister Augusta, and their friend Jennie Wood had gone for a ride up Shades Mountain . . . just to take in the sights. It was a beautiful vista atop that mountain."

I pictured three girls laughing and talking as they drove up the winding mountain road with a sheer dropoff to the left, like the roads we took through the Smoky Mountains on our way to visit our maternal grandmother in Virginia. I had no memories of the vistas or the valleys in Birmingham. The estrangement between my father and his father prevented us from taking family trips to see my paternal grandparents.

"Only Nell survived to tell the tale."

"What happened on the mountain, Dad?"

No matter how many times I had heard the story, I did not want him to skip any part of it.

"Back in those days, automobiles had what we called running boards. Sort of a step into the car. . . . Autos were higher off the ground back then. Nell Williams said that a Negro appeared suddenly, jumped on the running board of their car, held them at gunpoint, and made them drive to a secluded spot off the beaten track."

He reached for his pipe and turned the pipe bowl upside down over the green enameled ashtray. He tapped it gently to dislodge old ashes.

"Tragically, Augusta and Jennie died of gunshot wounds." He unzipped the plaid vinyl pouch and rubbed the moist new tobacco between his fingers. I wondered if he was stalling for time.

"Only Nell lived to tell the tale." He shook his head, while transferring three small pinches of tobacco into the pipe bowl.

"Poor Nell. She lost her sister and her best friend that day."

We sat in silence while he held a flame above the pipe bowl and sucked in short staccato breaths to start the smoke flowing. I don't remember that he ever offered a physical description of Nell or that I asked for one. I simply imagined her looking like our former babysitter, Angela: tall and slender, with dark brown shoulder-length hair pulled back from her face with copper-colored barrettes.

"Nell was under so much pressure to identify the assailant. Weeks went by. Suspects were rounded up. But Nell couldn't identify any of them as the culprit. You can't imagine how tense things were in Birmingham. Everyone was on edge."

I actually had some inkling about the tension because of other stories my father had told me about the brutality of Southern white supremacy.

"Poor Nell," he said again. "It's no surprise she finally cracked under the strain. Weeks after the killings, she and her mother were driving downtown, and she pointed at a Negro walking nearby. 'That's him!' she shouted, pointing at poor Willie Peterson, a black man in the wrong place at the wrong time."

Poor Nell Williams. Poor Willie Peterson. Closing my eyes today, I see my father shaking his head and hear the empathy tinged with pity in his voice.

"Willie Peterson didn't resemble the description Nell had earlier given the police. Except for the fact that he was a Negro. But she never wavered. She insisted he was the man."

My father told me how the white citizens of Birmingham were more than ready to pronounce Willie Peterson guilty without a trial. Some wanted to lynch him on the spot, needing no further proof than Nell's assertion that he was the assailant.

"In all of Birmingham, there were very few people who dared go against the tide. But my mentor and pastor, Rev. Henry Edmonds, was one of them."

He did not need to add those identifiers. I knew full well who Henry Edmonds was. I had heard so many stories about this man. Besides, his portrait hung directly above my father's desk, and my youngest sister was named in his honor: Stephanie Edmonds Morrison.

"Henry Edmonds condemned this rush to judgment, imploring his fellow citizens to behave with decency, insisting that Willie Peterson deserved a fair trial." Quoting Edmonds, my father's voice assumed the tenor and modulation he himself used when preaching.

"What about Genevieve?" I asked. "How come you haven't mentioned her yet?"

"I'm getting to that," he said, smiling. "I'm impressed you remember Genevieve."

How could I forget Genevieve Williams? She was Nell and Augusta's younger sister and my father's first love. The idea that my father had been romantically involved with someone besides my mother thoroughly captivated me.

"She was a lovely young woman. The belle of the ball . . . and highly sought after by my contemporaries, I might add." He winked at me and glanced over his shoulder to see if my mother was within earshot. "But, mind you, beautiful as she was, Genevieve could never hold a candle to your mother."

He told me that Henry Edmonds's advocacy for Willie Peterson enraged Genevieve's family. It insinuated Nell was either delusional or lying.

"I experienced their ire on more than one occasion. Genevieve and I spent many summer afternoons on the back porch of the Williamses' house in Redmont. As fate would have it, their house was perched on a hill overlooking the Edmondses' home."

At this point in the story, my father always stood up, put his hands behind his back, and walked in a circular fashion around the room, mimicking Henry Edmonds's habit of composing his sermons by walking the circumference of his backyard.

"So there I was, sitting with Genevieve and her family on Saturday afternoons. Drinking iced tea, looking down at the man whom I respected above all others. But the Williams family couldn't bear the sight of him. In their eyes, he was a traitor."

"What did you do?" I asked.

"I was torn up inside. I identified with the Williams family in many ways. They'd lost Augusta. Nell had suffered terribly. And I was in love with Genevieve. On the other hand, I felt such allegiance to Henry Edmonds, whom

I deeply admired. His integrity was above reproach. And it weighed heavily on me that Willie Peterson might very well be innocent."

"So, what did you do?" I asked again. He seemed not to hear me.

"Worst of all, I had to endure the ranting of Dent, Genevieve's older brother. He shamelessly bragged about going to the jail shortly after Willie Peterson's arrest and shooting him point blank with a pistol. Dent's only regret was that he hadn't succeeded in killing him."

That part of the story always stunned me: the fact that Dent Williams could just brazenly walk into the jail and shoot Willie Peterson. When my father reached that point, I interrupted and voiced my outrage and disbelief, as though my indignation could alter events that transpired decades before.

"Wasn't anyone guarding Willie Peterson?" I shouted. "How could the police let that happen?"

"Oh, they let a lot of things happen in those days, Melanie. And they caused their own share of violence and mayhem."

A Three-Time Traitor

Torn by conflicting loyalties to his girlfriend and his mentor, my father's parochial white world began to come apart. He became obsessed with the possibility that Willie Peterson was innocent. Whenever he attempted to voice this concern at home, his father reacted with rage and his mother changed the subject. I learned years later from my Aunt Harriet that, much to the amazement of most everyone at the time, my father suddenly stopped dating Genevieve and became sullen and reclusive.

"Mother and I were utterly baffled when Truman ended the relationship," she told me. "He was head over heels in love with Genevieve. They were perfect together, and she was as sweet as they come. It was like Truman suddenly became a different person. He was a Beau Brummel one day and a recluse the next. He shut himself off from the family, locked in his room, reading the Bible and all those other books."

Inspired by Rev. Edmonds to pursue ministry and a call to racial justice work, my father eventually left Birmingham to attend seminary in Chicago. When my father left the South, my grandfather considered him a three-time traitor, betraying his class, his region, and his race. This estrangement between father and son is one of the reasons I only met my grandfather twice before he died at age eighty-four.

Later in life, when asked how and why he had become so passionate about racial justice, my father often hearkened back to the murders on Shades Mountain and the arrest of Willie Peterson. "That's where it started," he explained. "I began to recognize the disparities between what my white world had taught me and the ravaging inequities of segregation and Jim Crow racism. Those inequities had been there all along, but I hadn't seen them. I began to see them when every white person in my world except Henry Edmonds pronounced Willie Peterson guilty despite the evidence pointing to his innocence. I also began to see it when those same people defended Dent Williams tooth and nail, saying he'd only done what any respectable white man *should* do to avenge the honor of his sisters."

It was on the Williamses' porch, holding Genevieve's hand and hearing Dent brag about trying to kill Willie Peterson, that my father knew he could not straddle both worlds any longer. The chasm had grown too wide, too deep. He would have to choose: stay with Genevieve, take over the Morrison family business, and live out the privileged destiny in Mountain Brook that his parents and Genevieve's envisioned for them. Or break with everything familiar and give himself to a wholly different kind of work. On that porch, the foundations of his white and privileged world had been shaken by this event of seismic proportions. Rather than try to patch them over and continue on, he broke rank with most of the people in his world and began to align himself with Christian socialists and racial justice activists. In the solitude of his upstairs bedroom, he fervently prayed that God might use him to help repair the devastation and inequities that his ancestors had wreaked. Already in his teenage years, he had the inkling that he would spend his lifetime trying to repay this grievous debt.

The Roots of a Legacy

For many years, I retold the Shades Mountain story just as it was handed down to me. It was one way of accounting for the legacy of antiracist activism I inherited from my father. I have always known that my passion for racial justice and my work as an antiracist educator were seeded by the stories my father told and the life he modeled for me. He was a pastor, but the work of dismantling racism was his deepest calling; it is what got him out of bed in the morning and kept him up late at night.

My father was an avid reader of literature about the black freedom struggle. He could not contain his enthusiasm for certain books and was impatient for me to reach the age when it would be developmentally appropriate for him to hand me James Baldwin's *The Fire Next Time* or Lillian Smith's *Killers of the Dream*. Whenever he lent me a volume from his sacred canon, he would always preface this act with the same words: "Melanie, I can guarantee that you won't be the same when you finish this book. You'll wonder how you ever lived without it and say to me, 'Dad, why didn't you show me this before!'" In the stories he shared, and the books we read and discussed, my father wanted me to know that white people have a critically important role to play in the struggle for racial justice. Most of all he wanted me to hear, *You are of consequence in this struggle.*

Two years after my father's death in 2006, I took a three-month sabbatical from my work as a racial justice educator and headed to Durham, North Carolina. Being my father's daughter, I packed every book I owned about racism and white privilege. I did not want to be 750 miles from home, regretting that I had left behind the one book I needed most.

I began my sabbatical by reading *An Enduring Ministry*—a recently published biography of Henry Edmonds written by Marvin Yeomans Whiting, former chief archivist at the Birmingham Public Library. I devoured the biography, searching for evidence that might corroborate the stories we had heard about my father's mentor. When I came upon six pages of single-spaced narrative in a footnote, all of it pertaining to the Williams/Wood murders in 1931, I felt a rush of adrenaline akin to what archaeologists must feel when they unearth the precious remnants of an ancient city. Here in print were details of the incident that rocked Birmingham and proved to be so formative in my father's young life. Whiting stated that he initially intended to include a detailed account of "this largely ignored event in Birmingham history" in the main text, but space and balance had prevented it.[3]

Curious as to why a case of this magnitude had been largely ignored, I launched an online search for other books and articles about the Willie Peterson case. I was surprised at how little I found, in contrast to the preponderance of literature about the Scottsboro trial that had begun a few months earlier in 1931, when two white women claimed they were raped by nine young black men aboard a freight train in northeastern Alabama.[4] I was excited that historian Robin D. G. Kelley addressed the Williams/Wood murders and the arrest of Willie Peterson in *Hammer and Hoe*. His analysis of the fierce competition waged between the Communist Party and the National Association for the Advancement of Colored People (NAACP) for control of Peterson's defense intensified my desire to read everything I could about this case.[5]

In the sources I discovered, I was surprised that none featured the role Henry Edmonds played in the Peterson case. I knew my father's adoration of his mentor might have given way to hyperbole in his telling of the story, but why was there no mention of Edmonds whatsoever in these sources? More significant still, these sources highlighted the reign of terror carried out by law enforcement and white vigilantes in the aftermath of the murders on Shades Mountain. My father never mentioned those harrowing events. He had not told me that white vigilantes burned black-owned businesses to the ground and fired shots at a group of black people who stood peacefully talking on a Birmingham street corner.[6] Nor did my father tell me that the NAACP and the Communist Party launched campaigns in defense of Willie Peterson.

I doubt that my father forgot those parts of the story or chose to keep them from me. I suspect he never knew those things as a teenager living in his insular white enclave of Mountain Brook. Discovering these gaping holes in my father's story, I became intensely curious about what else I might unearth were I to undertake a serious and sustained study of this case. In November 2010, I made my first field trip to Birmingham, compelled to learn more about the Williams/Wood murders and the arrest of Willie Peterson, as much by what my father did not tell me as what he did.

Discoveries on the Journey

During that first visit to Birmingham, spending time in the archives and seeking out people who might know about the murders, two things dawned on me with great force. More than ever I felt compelled to research and write about this extraordinary case, and I wished that I had begun this journey twenty years earlier. Almost eighty years had passed since the attack on Shades Mountain, and it was no longer possible to find and interview people who were old enough in 1931 to remember that event or its significance. In subsequent trips, I spoke with elders in Birmingham's black community one generation removed who might have heard from their elders about the murders on Shades Mountain or the arrest of Willie Peterson. None recalled the Peterson case, but several informed me that such gross miscarriages of justice were all too common in Jim Crow Birmingham. As one man put it, "I'm surprised to learn Willie Peterson wasn't lynched by a white mob during his first night in jail."

On numerous trips to Birmingham and other cities that housed archival materials, I sought to recover every newspaper article, editorial, letter, diary, trial transcript, city directory, sermon, photograph, census record, map, and manuscript collection of the organizations related to this case. I soon discovered that extant primary source material provided far more documentation about the white women attacked on Shades Mountain than about the black man accused of being their assailant. The reasons for this imbalance are manifold, with race and class being two decisive factors. Nell Williams, Augusta Williams, and Jennie Wood were daughters of affluent white families that possessed the resources to send all three to college. Willie Peterson, born into a sharecropping family in rural Pike County, Alabama, worked as a child in the cotton fields and never learned to read or write. After moving to Birmingham in 1919, Peterson worked in the mines for subsistence, nonunionized wages, and struggled like most black miners to make ends meet.

Significant events in the lives of the Williams sisters and Jennie Wood— such as an engagement to be married or a debutante ball—were noted in Birmingham newspapers. By contrast, Willie Peterson's name did not appear in newspapers, white or black, until he was arrested for the Shades Mountain murders. Even then, no journalist spoke with Peterson or his family members directly, as they did with Nell Williams and her family members. Nell Williams's lengthy and largely uninterrupted testimony about the events of August 4, 1931, can be found in the grand jury transcripts. Willie Peterson's recollections of that day and night are recorded as responses to belligerent attorneys seeking to coerce a confession, confuse the witness, or discredit what he remembered.

From the start, I resolved to write a historical narrative that would be true to primary sources. I vowed to resist the temptation to cross the line into fiction when writing about the thoughts and feelings of people in this book. Every quote, unless otherwise indicated, can be traced back to a primary source such as a trial transcript or newspaper article. The relative dearth of information about Willie Peterson proved to be a daunting and agonizing challenge as I sought to write about him and his wife, Henrietta, with as much detail and complexity as I wrote about Nell Williams and her family. I considered interviewing the descendants of the key subjects in this case to supplement the written primary sources. When I discovered that Willie Peterson had no descendants, I decided to abandon that avenue of investigation, fearing that I would replicate another form of imbalance in my sources.

Nevertheless, I have sought to render Willie Peterson the subject he deserves to be in this story, not simply the object of white supremacist injustice. As I researched this case, I came to see more clearly the difference between radical disenfranchisement and actual silencing. Willie Peterson's community of family, neighbors, church members, and friends risked all manner of abuse, harassment, and violence as they stepped up to offer support and testify on his behalf. And in the face of a system that sought to rob him of every form of human agency, Willie Peterson refused to be broken.

Eight years ago, I set out on a journey to learn everything I could about the murders on Shades Mountain and the fate of Willie Peterson. As I researched these events, discovering time and again how partial and inadequate my father's knowledge had been, I was compelled to tell a fuller, truer, and far more complicated story about the social and economic forces at work in Jim Crow Birmingham as well as the individuals and movements at the heart of this case. Recognizing that every historical narrative is shaped by the narrator's choices and social location, I have sought to write about this tumultuous and fertile era with honesty, empathy, and complexity.

PART I

DANGER IN THE MAGIC CITY

one

AUGUST 4, 1931

Nell Williams came down the mountain alone in the dark. She did not have the strength to lift her wounded sister Augusta into the car. Their friend Jennie Wood was lying nearby, spine shattered in the dew-wet grass.

"Go, Nell," Augusta pleaded. "Go get help."

Nell came down the mountain alone in the dark with a tire blown flat by a stray bullet. She shifted gears with her left arm while steadying the wheel with her knee, her right arm pressed against her side to stanch the bleeding.

Go, Nell. Go get help. Go get help.

Nell came down the mountain alone in the dark desperate to find a house with a front porch light on. Would she be greeted by a welcoming, soothing presence? Or someone who would berate her for being so reckless as to sit on those rocks at the crest of the mountain, ignoring what she had been told since childhood: No matter what time of day, don't go to secluded places. It's not safe. They prey on girls like you.

Go, Nell. Go get help. Go get help. Go get help.

Mrs. G. B. McCormack was sitting on her porch in Mountain Brook at 8:00 p.m., enjoying the cool evening breezes. She stood up when she heard an automobile coming up the driveway and the car door open. She could not make out the figure moving toward her, stumbling across the lawn. With one hand on her front door she called out, "Who is it?" Out of the shadows a young white woman with bloodstained clothes staggered onto the porch. Clutching her bleeding arm, Nell Williams asked to use the phone and pointed up the road.[1]

"My sister and my friend are up there off Leeds Highway. They've been shot. . . . I've been shot . . . by a Negro."

Some people shut down after experiencing severe trauma, making it difficult for police and reporters to gather information while it is fresh. Nell had a need to talk. Maybe as a way of externalizing the horror, hoping if she shared the agonizing memories they would not stay locked inside forever.

Sitting near Mrs. McCormack as she dialed the police, Nell told how "the Negro" had come out of nowhere, held them hostage for four hours, then shot all three of them before disappearing into the woods. Standing on the road in front of the McCormack house waiting for the ambulance, Nell told her story to officer C. A. Nollner of the Mountain Brook police.[2] Sitting in the front seat of the ambulance, she told the driver, Lewellyn John, and his assistant, Paul Sutter, as she led them back to the spot where Augusta and Jennie lay waiting in the dark.[3] On the operating table, she told Dr. J. M. Mason and his team of nurses as they worked to remove the bullet lodged in her arm.[4]

She told Jefferson County marshal W. W. Kilpatrick that the man was coal black and talked like he was well educated.[5] She told Fred H. McDuff, Birmingham's chief of police, giving him a full description of the assailant.[6] And early Wednesday, "between hysterical sobs and shudders," she told Marie Parks, reporter for the *Birmingham Post*.[7]

"We had been to a show and were driving around before going home. We were going slowly and it was not yet dark when the negro jumped on the running board and pointed a gun at us demanding money. We offered him what we had but he forced me to drive into the woods. I was frightened and didn't know what to do so I followed his orders. When we got in the woods, he began to say insulting things."[8]

As Nell described the ordeal to doctors, nurses, and reporters, she stressed how the assailant had lectured them and subjected them to continuous insults.

"He seemed to be making a speech and appeared to be an educated negro. He insulted us time and again, while we begged him to let us go. He blamed the white race for the negro's conditions and declared the white people are forever heaping injustice on the negro."[9]

Nell said his "radical" diatribe grew so "ugly" and "sickening" she could not bear it any longer. That's when she grabbed at him, hoping the three of them could wrest the gun from him. But he started shooting, and eight rounds later all three women had been wounded. Augusta was shot in the abdomen, just below her rib cage. A bullet struck Jennie's neck, severing her spine. Nell was wounded in her upper right arm. All three women lay perfectly still until the man left on foot through the woods. Nell estimated he had held them hostage for four hours.[10]

"I knew our only salvation would be for me to pretend I was dead. I lay there for what seemed an age, as he walked around us—at last he left. I thought he would never go."[11]

When Nell's father came running through the doors at St. Vincent's Hospital, Augusta Williams was still alive. Her body was covered with blankets, her face bloody and pale. Three doctors were working to save her, but she had lost too much blood. Clark Williams watched helplessly as his daughter drew her last breath.

Hoping to shield Nell from additional trauma, her father said Augusta was resting comfortably. After she recovered her strength, there would be plenty of time for truth telling. Nell herself could have bled to death, doctors said. The bullet had pierced her brachial artery. They feared at first that they might have to amputate Nell's arm, but gangrene infection did not occur. It was Friday before Nell learned she had lost her beloved sister.[12]

The prognosis for Jennie Wood was not good. She had been shot through the cervical spine. Chances were negligible that Jennie would survive her wounds. If she did, she would most likely be paralyzed. Only family members were permitted to see her. Mrs. Wood refused to leave her daughter alone in the hospital despite pleas from her husband and children to get some rest. She held vigil outside Jennie's room as friends came in shifts to comfort her.[13]

All night and into the day on Wednesday, posses of officers and armed citizens combed the woods and fields of Shades Mountain in search of the suspect. The Jefferson County sheriff had called for assistance from the

Birmingham police department. That night they deputized 250 white men. Other men, acting as self-appointed vigilantes, poured into the countryside. During the night, the homes of black residents in Birmingham were raided, people pulled out of bed, and a total of twenty local suspects arrested. As the *Birmingham Post* reported, "Feeling ran high in the exclusive Mountain Brook section Wednesday and posses representing every section of the city joined the manhunt."[14]

No trace of the assailant was found that night except possibly one footprint, announced in the *Birmingham Post* as "belonging to the Negro." The scents and trails detected by bloodhounds turned out to be those of officers and bystanders.[15]

"Above the Smoke and Dust of the City"

In the world that Clark and Helen Williams had worked so diligently to create for Nell, Augusta, and their two other children, a tragedy such as this was never supposed to happen. When a new subdivision of elegant homes was being developed on the crest of Red Mountain for Birmingham's white, wealthy, and upwardly mobile families, they had jumped at the chance to be among the first residents of the Redmont neighborhood.

The year was 1916 and Nell was only three years old. The bliss of being the baby in the family would soon be interrupted by the birth of her little sister, Genevieve. Clark Williams had a lucrative job as an attorney in a city that was growing at a phenomenal pace. Expecting their fourth child, the Williamses decided to move from their Phelan Park home that was now too small. Besides, like so many Birmingham residents, they longed to escape the industrial grime and stifling fumes pouring from the steel mills and factories. An ad for the new Redmont subdivision boasted that the development was "above the smoke and dust of the city, yet within walking distance."[16]

Only white people had the option of moving up the mountain to Redmont. Black workers who labored in the city's blast furnaces and coke ovens had no way of escaping the toxic fumes or the debilitating health hazards resulting from those fumes. Many of Birmingham's black residents were relegated to company-built "quarters" near the furnaces or to racially segregated neighborhoods deemed undesirable by white residents—along railroad tracks, creek beds, or alleys.[17]

Nell and Augusta grew up playing with the children of Birmingham's wealthiest families. The offspring of George W. Connors, president of Connors-Weyman Steel Company, were close friends and classmates. The Williams sisters rode ponies belonging to the great-grandchildren of Henry F. DeBardeleben, one of Birmingham's preeminent industrial magnates and a founder of the city.

It is likely that the only black people Nell and Augusta came to know personally were the servants and chauffeurs employed by white families in the neighborhoods where they were raised. Lucy Taylor was a widowed black woman in her sixties when she began working as nursemaid to the four Williams children. When Clark and Helen Williams moved to Redmont, Lucy Taylor went with them, living in the home on Aberdeen Road and working as their private nurse well into her seventies.[18]

After graduating from Phillips High School, Augusta and Nell attended college. In August 1931, Augusta was a recent graduate of Ward-Belmont College in Nashville, Tennessee, regarded as one of the South's most prestigious finishing schools. Nell was on summer break from Birmingham-Southern, a private liberal arts college located on 192 acres of rolling hills on the western edge of Birmingham.

The Williams sisters may have come to know their friend Jennie Wood through Highlands Methodist Church. At age twenty-seven, Jennie was five years older than Augusta and nearly ten years older than Nell, but they had formed a close bond that transcended the age difference. Like Nell and Augusta, Jennie had two sisters and a brother. Jennie's parents owned a spacious two-story home in Birmingham's Forest Park, and her father enjoyed a healthy income as a produce dealer. After graduating from Birmingham-Southern in 1928 and attending Randolph-Mason College in Virginia, Jennie returned to Birmingham and threw herself into two activities she was passionate about: teaching children in the Highlands Church Sunday School and playing tennis. She had been a debutante, presented by the Redstone Club at its lavish Christmas Ball.[19]

As Nell would later tell it, they had gone to a matinee picture show that Tuesday afternoon in early August. It was a beautiful day, so on a whim they decided to extend their leisurely afternoon by taking the Leeds Highway up Shades Mountain. It was not yet dinnertime and they would be back long before dark. There was room for all three of them in the spacious front seat of the Woods' seven-passenger LaSalle. Jennie drove slowly as they climbed the two-lane dirt road toward the crest of the hill, where an outcropping of boulders stood. They had been to those rocks for an Easter sunrise service and knew firsthand how stunning the view could be. That's all they wanted to do, Nell said. Simply sit on those rocks in the stillness of the late afternoon. Look out over the vast expanse of Shades Valley. Then pile back into Jennie's blue sedan and head for home.

"He Talked as if Well Educated"

When residents of Birmingham opened their Wednesday newspapers, they found a full-page spread featuring large photographs of the Williams sisters and Jennie Wood surrounded by column after column of Nell Williams's harrowing account. The *Birmingham News* devoted a full page to describing the crime scene. A photo showed four white men standing in a semicircle, holding flashlights trained on a grassy spot. Wearing suits, ties, and hats, they appeared to be men vested with authority. A fifth white man, more casually dressed in rolled-up shirtsleeves and a cap, crouched to examine the ground that the other four had illumined. Under a large bold heading—LONELY ROAD LEADS TO DESOLATE SPOT ON EDGE OF PRECIPICE MARKED BY TRAGEDY—the reporter described the crime scene:

> The little road, leading along the top of a high ridge, finds its way over to the edge of a sheer rocky cliff from which a beautiful view of the valley is presented toward the west. Strewn cigarette packages, pickle bottles and paper plates mark its use as a picnic ground. Large slabs of rock, some clean and some lichen covered, add to the wild beauty. Yet one must be careful. So precipitous is the cliff that a false step would send one to instant death below. Vines and underbrush grow thickly thereabouts. Black ashes testify to campfires. A sunset from this place should be beautiful. Dusk and twilight should stress the quietude and peace of the spot.[20]

A description of the suspect was released Wednesday morning by Birmingham police chief Fred McDuff. It ran in all the papers and was broadcast by radio throughout the day: "The girls described the negro as being black, about 5 feet 10 inches, mustache, 150 pounds, dressed in light overalls, felt hat and rubber-bottom shoes. He talked as if well educated, the girls said."[21] On Thursday, the *Birmingham News* printed an amended description of the assailant: "The negro is reported to have been without a mustache and clean shaven . . . the negro's age as 30 to 35; height, 5 feet 10 inches; weight, 135 to 150 pounds; black; face broad at temple and thin at chin; dressed in blue overalls with white stripes; torn on back; old gray hat turned up on sides and down in front; sole of right shoe torn so toe will show."[22]

How and why the description changed was not reported. Perhaps reporters got the first one wrong. Perhaps Nell changed her mind or remembered new details. A third and far more detailed description would later be released to the public in the form of a circular. Thousands of copies were distributed to law enforcement officials throughout the South and as far away as Chicago and New York. The circular included additional descriptors provided by Jennie Wood when Chief McDuff interviewed her two days after Nell first described the assailant. Jennie said "the Negro" had gold between and behind his lower front teeth, in what she considered as "an extra good dental job."[23]

$3300 Reward

Offered by the Citizens and Civic Clubs of Birmingham, Alabama,
for information leading to the arrest and conviction of negro Murderer,
wanted in Birmingham for the murder of Miss Williams and Miss Wood,
committed night of August 4, 1931.

The following is a description of the Negro.

Black—35 years old.

Height—5 ft. 8 or 10 inches.

Weight—135 or 145 pounds.

Large pop eyes, starry look.

Some gold inlay dental work behind lower front teeth,
overlapping top slightly. (Suggest that investigate for evidence
of this gold inlay having been taken out since the murder)

Cheeks slightly sunk in.

Medium voice, southern accent.

A pimple similar to a mole just below right corner of mouth.

Ready talker with southern accent, but uses bad grammar.

When last seen was wearing blue Union-alls
with white stripe, sleeves worn off at elbow.

Gray felt hat badly torn.[24]

These descriptions may have guided the posses combing the mountainside and fanning out into black neighborhoods. But it is more likely that rage propelled their search and the acts of revenge they meted out. They may have cared less about the suspect's height, weight, and clothing than about Nell's assertion that "the Negro" was well educated, delivered disgusting radical diatribes about the white race, and threatened to get even. Those images were relayed by word of mouth on the telephone, in grocery stores, in bars, in barbershops, and over back fences.

In Nell's first accounts of the kidnapping, she did not speak of sexual assault or rape. Nevertheless, rumors of rape raged through Jefferson County and propelled the posses that stormed through the city and surrounding regions. It was inconceivable to most white Southerners that a black man would hold three white women hostage for any length of time without sexually assaulting them. Black men were viewed as rapists who preyed on white women. That self-generated fear often led white men to inflict terrifying and terrorizing reprisals on black men in the name of "protecting white women."[25]

Doubts Begin to Surface

From the start, editors of black newspapers in different parts of the country expressed doubts about Nell Williams's story. Both her description of the assailant and the attitude he allegedly displayed seemed highly suspect to people in black communities. Noting that she made frequent reference to the abductor's insulting remarks, the *Pittsburgh Courier* said, "Many statements made by a white person in the south to another white person, as between equals, become insults when uttered by a Negro, who is considered an inferior."[26] The *Norfolk New Journal and Guide* reported that the black community felt Nell Williams's story was riddled with discrepancies, and they suspected the full story had not yet been told.[27] The *Afro-American* speculated that the slayer might have been a white man masquerading as black "to throw the burden of his heinous crime upon the shoulders of some poor innocent colored man."[28]

It is likely that a considerable number of both white and black residents in Birmingham harbored doubts about certain aspects of Nell's story. It was highly unusual for a black man to be wandering on foot with a loaded gun in that part of Jefferson County. Nearby homes were owned by white people who possessed the means to build on the wooded slopes of Shades Mountain. Had they spotted a black man walking on their property or the road, they would have notified authorities. That section of Leeds Highway was not a route taken by black men on their way to or from work in the mines. If a black man were to go hunting, he would have been carrying a rifle, not a pistol, and he would not have chosen that section of Shades Mountain as his hunting ground.

Nell alleged that the gunman had ordered them to drive more than a mile on Cherokee Road in Mountain Brook to the Leeds cutoff road. With cars passing by in broad daylight, the sight of a black man in the backseat of their car would surely have raised suspicions. Why would a black man choose to hold the three women hostage in a wooded area known to be a place where white lovers and friends held picnics? He would be taking an enormous risk to harangue and insult the women for hours when they were never more than a hundred yards from a public road.

If the assailant was black, he surely knew the risks. Black men who committed far less egregious crimes could expect to be hunted down and brutally murdered in Jim Crow Alabama. Lynch mobs were mobilized if it was rumored that a black man had made eye contact with a white woman in a manner deemed offensive or insubordinate.

"A Negro Did It"

As the manhunt stretched on and dozens of black men were arrested, detained, and brought before Nell Williams for examination, rumors began to circulate in black neighborhoods that the women had gone to Shades Mountain for reasons other than Nell stated. The source of those rumors may have been black women who worked in white homes throughout the city and regularly overheard conversations at white dinner tables that did not make it into the press. The black chauffeurs who drove their white employers to work also caught fragments of conversations that wafted from the backseat. Black people knew through personal experience and from the wisdom conveyed by their elders that the surest way for a white woman to avoid being caught or suspected of taking part in a morally perilous situation was for her to say, "A Negro did it." If she wished to protect herself or another white person complicit in a compromising affair, the most accessible and reliable scapegoat was a black man. If a physical or sexual assault occurred and a white woman of Nell Williams's social class and standing said, "A Negro did it," white men were honor bound to avenge this gravest of violations using any means necessary.[29]

two

A CITY BESET BY FEAR

The attack on Shades Mountain sent a tidal wave of panic through white Birmingham and the industrial elite, already beset by the twin fears of imminent economic collapse and the growing presence of "outside radical agitators."

The 1929 stock market crash devastated Birmingham. By August 1931, the steel mills had all but ceased to operate. Unemployed workers struggled to stave off homelessness and hunger. Just months before the crash, the Sixth World Congress of the Communist International declared that black people in America's South were the potential vanguard of the Marxist revolution in the United States, and the party chose Birmingham as its headquarters for this new campaign. Birmingham's industrial leaders feared that these outside agitators would instigate a new round of union organizing, something that Birmingham's corporate elite had sought to curtail and suppress for decades. Furthermore, the Communist Party advocated "social equality" between the races, a belief that was anathema to most white residents of Birmingham. The black assailant that Nell Williams and Jennie Wood described had not only committed heinous acts of violence; his diatribes suggested that he endorsed this radical notion of social equality.

Rooted in Racial Apartheid

In August 1931, Birmingham was still a relatively young city. Just sixty years earlier, in 1871, a small group of investors founded Birmingham with an eye to developing an iron and steel industry based on the coal, iron ore, and limestone deposits found nearby. From its inception, the industrial elite stoked white racial fears and maintained segregated work and housing facilities as ways to divide white and black workers and prevent unions from forming. At the time, black workers from rural Alabama languished in slave-like conditions as sharecroppers on former plantations. Attracted by work in Birmingham's mines, mills, and factories, black workers began pouring into the city. By exploiting that nonunionized labor pool and bolstering the mechanisms of white supremacy, the industrialist founders hoped to avoid the costs and headaches that their competitors faced as unions made inroads in the North.[1]

In its first two decades of existence, Birmingham grew exponentially, earning the name the Magic City, and boasted the largest black population of any city in the South. According to an 1886 report of industrial development in Birmingham, 40 percent of the residents were black and accounted for 90 percent of the workers employed by the furnaces near Birmingham and the vast majority of labor employed by manufacturing industries, foundries, and rolling mills.[2] Birmingham's industries also flourished through the use of the convict lease system. In 1900, ten thousand black convicts worked in the thirty coal mines owned by the Pratt Mines complex, fourteen of which were on the outskirts of Birmingham.[3]

In the early 1900s, Birmingham grew to become the chief industrial city in the South. As new workers flooded into the city, officials annexed surrounding neighborhoods and villages. The 1920s saw a particularly dramatic influx as Birmingham experienced a 45 percent growth rate, increasing from 310,054 residents in 1920 to 431,493 in 1930.[4]

As the black population grew, the white power elites saw a pressing need to reinforce the already strict Jim Crow norms and practices of racial apartheid. Carl V. Harris states that the large majority of white people in Birmingham viewed black people as a necessary but menacing presence in their white-controlled communities: "In short, three notions about the Negro loomed large in the minds of Birmingham whites and made the whites believe that government control of Negroes was necessary. The whites believed, first, that the Negro was a useful, indeed necessary, menial laborer; but, second, they regarded him as an irresponsible and unreliable worker; and, third, they considered him menacing, prone to commit crime."[5]

Undergirding these racist stereotypes was the dominant white conviction that black men were an ever-present danger to white women because they could not control their sexual appetites. The races must therefore be strictly and permanently separated.

In the 1880s and 1890s, Birmingham's economy flourished with the construction of new blast furnaces and the expansion of coal and iron industries. The racial dividing lines were impenetrable. Skilled craftsmen were white and unskilled workers were black. The craftsmen had unions; the black workers did not.[6] As steel mills were introduced in Birmingham at the turn of the century, the need for semiskilled workers expanded due to increased mechanization of those mills. The steel mill owners and managers launched an all-out campaign to keep this new industry free of unions and make Birmingham an open-shop city. Their campaign was largely successful because the steel companies adopted a widespread and firmly enforced policy of hiring only white workers for their skilled and semiskilled positions. By utilizing this racial wedge, the interests of white workers were protected, thus ameliorating their pressing need for a union.[7]

In the mid-1920s, Birmingham officials developed a comprehensive system of planning and zoning to guarantee that white and black neighborhoods would remain separate in perpetuity. By 1931, Birmingham's black residents lived in racially zoned neighborhoods that were undesirable to working-class and upper-class white people.[8] The areas designated by law for black residents had substandard sanitary conditions and lacked adequate street lighting, police protection, and other city services available in white neighborhoods. The majority of dwellings in black-zoned areas had no bathing facilities or running water, and more than 80 percent used kerosene for lighting.

To ensure that racial segregation would remain inviolate, Birmingham officials also formulated new ordinances outlawing racial mixing of any kind. Even though Alabama's constitution, adopted in 1901, firmly enshrined white supremacy as the central governing principle of the state, Birmingham's white power structure wanted to reinforce that principle with a battery of local provisions. As Charles E. Connerly notes, "By 1930, Birmingham had adopted ordinances preventing the mixing of races in dice, dominoes, or checker games, as well as in restaurants, pool rooms, railroads and street rail facilities, street cars, or toilet facilities. Just in case this list was not sufficiently exhaustive, Birmingham also prescribed segregation in 'any room, hall, theatre, picture house, auditorium, yard, court, ball park, public park, or other indoor or outdoor place.'"[9]

As the Great Depression reduced revenues from industry and commerce, the owning-class families of Birmingham, whose sprawling mansions dominated the Redmont and Mountain Brook suburbs, feared unions and the growing influence of communist radicals, who threatened to drive up labor costs and undermine Birmingham's social and economic system.

The Communist Party Sets Up Shop

Birmingham's industrialists had good reason to fear that the Communist Party was gaining traction in the city's black community. Its popularity was increasing proportionate to the spiking unemployment, foreclosures, homelessness, and hunger that Birmingham's poor and working classes faced in the early 1930s.[10]

On March 23, 1930, the Trade Union Unity League, a communist labor auxiliary, called its first mass meeting in Birmingham. Two hundred people attended, most of them black. The Communist Party's adamant call for black self-determination as well as social and economic equality impressed many in attendance and served as an effective recruiting tool. By fall 1930, the party had grown to more than a hundred members in Birmingham—with many more regularly attending meetings and demonstrations organized by the party.[11] Unlike the National Association for the Advancement of Colored People, which catered to the relatively few middle-class black people living in Birmingham in the 1930s, the Communist Party gave voice and visibility to poor and working-class black people.

Despite strict city ordinances that forbade interracial meetings and "criminal anarchy," Communist Party–sponsored demonstrations demanding relief for unemployed workers drew hundreds of black and white protestors in the spring and summer of 1930.[12] Just weeks before the assault on Shades Mountain, the party held a series of demonstrations in North Birmingham. Organizers criticized the inadequate relief efforts of the Red Cross and demanded that free utilities be granted unemployed workers, free lunches be given to public school children, and all people, no matter their race, be permitted the right to vote.[13]

Scottsboro and Camp Hill

The significance of the attack on Shades Mountain and the massive manhunt that followed in its wake cannot be fully understood apart from another alleged crime that occurred only five months earlier in rural Alabama, about a hundred miles northeast of Birmingham. Were it not for the communist weekly the *Southern Worker*, the arrest of nine young black men on the charge of gang rape might have gone unnoticed. James Allen, editor of the *Southern Worker*, made the plight of those nine men the centerpiece of his fledgling newspaper by covering their trials in Scottsboro, Alabama, in late March 1931.[14]

The nine defendants, who became known as the "Scottsboro Boys," were traveling as hoboes on a train when they allegedly raped two white women, Ruby Bates and Victoria Price, who had also hopped the train. As the trials got under way, thousands of white people from all across the state poured into Scottsboro and surrounded the courthouse. Fearing the angry crowd could erupt into a lynch mob, Governor Benjamin Meek Miller deployed the National Guard for the duration of the trials. The defendants were represented by a court-appointed lawyer who was granted no time to prepare an adequate defense. Within four days, eight of the nine defendants had been convicted and sentenced to die.[15]

At the conclusion of the trials, Communist Party representatives met with the families of the defendants and offered to appeal the convictions through their legal arm, the International Labor Defense (ILD). When the families accepted the offer, ILD leaders hired a Chattanooga attorney and vowed to do everything in their power to secure the young men's freedom. The Communist Party also launched an international campaign to free the Scottsboro defendants that raised money for the appeals, publicized what the ILD termed an egregious "legal lynching," and encouraged supporters to flood Governor Miller's office with petitions and letters protesting the convictions.[16]

The ILD's campaign to free the Scottsboro defendants shone a bright light on Jim Crow injustice by garnering national and international attention in the press. Just weeks after the guilty verdicts were announced in Scottsboro, five thousand people marched in New York City in support of the accused men. In the months that followed, Scottsboro demonstrations occurred at American consulates in Europe, South Africa, and Latin America.[17]

The campaign to free the Scottsboro defendants also earned the respect of many in Birmingham's black community as the ILD worked to expose the racist maneuverings of the Alabama judicial system.[18] On July 10, 1931, one of the defendants, Haywood Patterson, was granted a stay of execution as the ILD appealed his case to the U.S. Supreme Court. This news was received with jubilation in Birmingham's black community. Among many white residents of the city, it proved to be one more cause for alarm.

While making significant inroads in Birmingham's black community, the Communist Party was also helping to organize black tenant farmers and agricultural workers in rural communities under the aegis of the Croppers' and Farm Workers' Union (CFWU). In Tallapoosa County, ninety miles southeast of Birmingham, the CFWU formulated seven demands that they planned, over time, to present to white landlords. The demands included a minimum wage of one dollar per day, the right of sharecroppers to sell their own crops, a nine-month school year for children, and food advances. When landlords learned that the CFWU was gaining momentum and growing in membership, they enlisted the help of local law enforcement to break up union meetings and arrest union organizers.[19]

On July 15, 1931, the Tallapoosa County sheriff deputized a group of white vigilantes to raid a meeting in Camp Hill, Alabama, viciously beating the men and women in attendance. Undeterred, 150 black sharecroppers met the following evening in an abandoned house on the edge of Camp Hill. The sheriff returned, this time with a larger cadre of local law enforcement officials, and gunfire was exchanged. Over the next few days, scores of black men were arrested, and white vigilantes carried out attacks on black share-croppers in Camp Hill, killing dozens of people and driving many families from their homes. In the aftermath, rumors raged across the state, warning that groups of armed black men were roaming the Alabama countryside seeking to avenge the deaths of their Camp Hill comrades by raping white women.[20]

"Radical Agitators Sought for Questioning"

With news of Scottsboro and Camp Hill filling Birmingham papers, and Communist Party–sponsored neighborhood councils steadily gaining adherents in Birmingham, anticommunist fears had reached near hysteria in some quarters by the summer of 1931. On July 18, the *Birmingham Age-Herald* carried a story headlined "Negro Reds Reported Advancing," announcing that eight carloads of black communists from Chattanooga were traveling to Alabama to help their comrades in the Camp Hill Sharecroppers Union.[21]

Not surprisingly, rumors of communist conspiracy also fueled the investigation of the Shades Mountain attack. On August 6, the *Birmingham Post* ran a front-page story with this three-part headline:

KIDNAP PLOT LED TO GIRL'S MURDER, OFFICERS BELIEVE,
Radical Agitator Is Sought for Questioning,
As Communistic Propaganda Is Blamed for Attack[22]

The *Birmingham News* ran an editorial on August 6 condemning the heinousness of the assailant, who lectured the young women on communistic ideals: "If this is one of the outgrowths of Communism on these shores; if this is the aim of propagandists of that doctrine, then Southerners and all Americans whatsoever who understand the inequalities of races— Southerners who are white and Southerners of dark skins as well—must by every means possible lance out of the . . . body this infamous and unnatural teachment."[23]

The attack on Shades Mountain became the pretext for intensifying efforts to arrest anyone suspected of being a radical. Deputies raided homes and offices, seized organizational files, and arrested white and black people believed to be communist sympathizers. On August 10, sheriff James F. Hawkins announced he had added five officers to the Jefferson County police force in "an intensive and determined campaign to break up radical activities and apprehend agitators who are organizing Communist groups and distributing red literature in this section." Hawkins was reported as saying that he hoped "to put an absolute end to the movement before it . . . made any more headway and to ferret out the leadership."[24]

The Scottsboro trials and the Camp Hill violence had many in Birmingham's white community on edge, fearing that it was only a matter of time before something as horrific would befall the Magic City. Nell Williams's story of what occurred during those terrifying hours on Shades Mountain was the culmination of their worst fears. In many ways, the violence perpetrated on August 4 was more frightening and repugnant to Birmingham's social elite than that of either Scottsboro or Camp Hill. Unlike Ruby Bates and Victoria Price, the victims on Shades Mountain were white women from the most refined and prominent families in Birmingham. If they could not be protected, no one was safe.

Furthermore, Nell Williams contended that the Shades Mountain assailant delivered "ugly diatribes" against social inequality. She said he had the "disgusting" audacity to insist that black people were as good as white people. The dreaded doctrines of social equality and race mixing were precisely what enraged the editors of the *Birmingham News* when they lashed out against the communist propagandists. As historian Nell Irvin Painter explains, in Jim Crow parlance, social equality was a decidedly negative concept and term: "It meant people of two races, usually including black men, sitting down together at table or on a train, sharing a smoke at a club, or belonging to the same organization on a footing of equality."[25]

For many white people raised in Jim Crow Birmingham, social equality would lead to moral chaos akin to the nightmare enumerated by Georgia's former senator Tom Watson: "[The Negro] grows more bumptious on the street. More impudent in his dealings with white men; and then, when he cannot achieve social equality as he wishes, with the instinct of the barbarian to destroy what equality he wishes, he lies in wait . . . and assaults the fair young girlhood of the south. . . . It is time for those who know the perils of the negro problem to stand together with deep resolve that political power shall never give the negro encouragement in his foul dreams of a mixture of races."[26]

"The Negro" that Nell Williams and Jennie Wood described bore every characteristic that Watson decried. He was, by Jim Crow standards, the epitome of a dangerous and "uppity" black man. His straightened hair and gold teeth were symbols of newfound wealth and emancipation from white control. He talked as though he was an educated Northerner who had come to the South to stir up trouble. Showing no deference whatsoever to white women, he had the nerve to talk down to them as he delivered lectures. Dressed in union overalls, he espoused radical ideology and harangued his captives about the crimes that white oppressors had perpetrated against the black race. He sought to enact revenge by preying upon innocent white women in a place where they had no access to white male protection. After holding the women captive for hours, he shot them and then escaped without a trace to terrorize his next unsuspecting victims.

The portrait of the Shades Mountain assailant—fed by circulars, rumors, headlines in the white press, and Nell Williams's stories—was in many ways a composite sketch of the aggregated fears of white Birmingham in the grasp of the Great Depression.

three

REIGN OF TERROR IN THE BLACK COMMUNITY

In the aftermath of August 4, fear of another attack blazed through the white community. A killer whom Nell Williams described as vicious, boastful, and revengeful was on the loose.

In Birmingham's black neighborhoods, violence was not only feared; it was a daily and nightly occurrence for weeks following the attack on Shades Mountain. Posses of armed white men roamed the city streets harassing and apprehending any black man, woman, or child they decided was suspicious or deserving of punishment. The same *Birmingham News* editorial that called on Southerners to use "every means possible" to "lance out" the dangerous doctrines of the Communist Party also called upon white and black citizens to "pursue relentlessly" the murderer who was probably still "in hiding in Jefferson County—perhaps in Birmingham." The editorial gave implicit license to raid black homes, declaring, "It would not be surprising if some Negro family were entertaining this black devil unaware."[1]

After counseling "colored people" to show loyalty by sharing whatever they might know with police, the editors declared that it was the duty of citizens as well as law enforcement "to comb the woodland country with armed posses; to leave no territory in the country unsearched . . . to find the brutal murderer."[2]

It is doubtful that the 250 men that were specially deputized on the evening of August 4 needed any encouragement to carry out what the editors of the *Southern Worker* called a "reign of terror" in the days to come.[3] The night of the attack, teams of men armed with guns and bloodhounds scoured the woods, ravines, and hillsides of eastern Shades Valley. Other teams fanned out to train stations and roads throughout the county in an attempt to apprehend black people leaving the area. Any black person traveling by car, train, or foot came under suspicion. Law enforcement agencies around the state were put on alert to be on the lookout for black people traveling through their communities from the direction of Birmingham. Crews on the railroads leading into or out of Birmingham were also told to report anything suspicious. During the first night, at least twenty suspects were arrested in Birmingham but only three detained for further questioning.[4]

Wednesday morning, August 5, Rufus Austin was taken from a freight train in Anniston, Alabama, sixty miles from Birmingham. Police chief S. O. Smith said Austin "fitted the description" and was carrying a gun that had been discharged once. Austin was brought to Birmingham for questioning. There he was charged with vagrancy and held on a $5,000 bond. Officials planned to take him to St. Vincent's Hospital so that Nell Williams could view him.[5]

That same day, deputies obtained bloodhounds from Lovick prison camp in Jefferson County and set out for Jasper, Alabama, approximately forty miles from Birmingham. They searched the woods near Jasper for a black man who was seen leaving a train coming from the direction of Birmingham. Witnesses said he ran into the woods. The search failed to turn up anyone.[6]

Black-owned businesses were targeted by vigilantes, and random attacks on black people occurred as angry mobs charged through black neighborhoods left especially vulnerable by a city-imposed curfew that turned off the lights in black neighborhoods by 10:00 p.m.[7] Shortly before midnight on Wednesday, Virgil Berry, the black owner of a grocery store and restaurant on Georgia Road, was awakened by two loud explosions in rapid succession. Running outside, he saw shattered glass strewn on the sidewalk. The walls and windows of his building had been blown out and the interior badly damaged. Berry told detectives that he believed two charges of dynamite had been thrown, one from the Georgia Road side of the building and another on the other side.[8]

Thursday morning, Birmingham's riot squad was sent to 305 Sixth Avenue South after receiving a report that a drive-by shooting had occurred. A group of black people stood talking outside a black-owned grocery store when passengers in an unidentified automobile sped by and opened fire on them. No one was seriously injured.[9]

Deputies and special officers raided the homes of anyone they believed had any connection with communist organizers in Birmingham. Police could hold those suspects under the auspices of the Criminal Anarchy Ordinance passed by the Birmingham City Commission the previous year. Thursday morning, August 6, three black men in their twenties—Eugene Braxton, Daniel James, and John James—were arrested in a house on Sixteenth Street in Birmingham. Deputies said they found communist literature in the house, and they had good reason to believe the three men might be the trio that a witness said she saw driving near the location on Shades Mountain where the attack took place.[10]

That witness was most likely Mrs. J. M. Gillespie of Mountain Brook, who told authorities that around 4:00 in the afternoon on August 4 she had seen three black men "wandering aimlessly" in an old automobile in Mountain Brook. On Thursday, police revealed that additional witnesses reported they had seen black men headed in the direction of the spot where Nell said the assailant jumped on the running board of their car. The stories of those witnesses led police to develop a theory they considered plausible enough to share with the press. Chief deputy sheriff R. E. Smith announced that they believed the suspect was hiding in the home of Birmingham communists and there were likely three radical agitators involved in the kidnapping; two had dropped the assailant off for several hours and then circled back to pick him up. That would account for the fact that posses had been unable to detect footprints in the surrounding woods.[11]

Sheriff Hawkins reported that this theory was given additional credence during a Wednesday morning raid on the Communist Party headquarters in downtown Birmingham when authorities found the office closed and literature removed. Clearly, the sheriff said, this was an indication that they knew what had transpired the day before. Smith launched a countywide search on Friday for the "rickety, worn-out" Chalmers touring car that police believed the three "radical suspects" drove when they trailed the blue sedan in which the three women rode.[12]

Reports started flooding in about white vigilantes posing as police or railroad agents accosting and sometimes killing black men in Birmingham and neighboring communities. On Thursday, August 6, police were called to Hillman Hospital, where Charlie Horton was lying wounded and in critical condition. Still conscious, he said that two white men claiming to be police had pulled him out of his bed at 3:00 that morning. They announced he was under arrest, carried him to a dark place a half block away, and shot him in the neck with a bullet that went through his spine. Doctors said his recovery was "speculative." When investigators searched his home, they claimed to have found communist literature and a newspaper clipping that reported a threat made against City Commission president Jimmie Jones. The police denied having attacked Horton, but they failed to investigate the crime.[13]

In a similar incident, James Bennett of Route 1, Bessemer, was roused from his sleep by two men claiming they were policemen. After shoving him in their car, the assailants drove a short distance from his home, shot Bennett three times, and left him by the roadside. He was taken to the hospital at 3:00 Friday morning by three black men who heard him crying for help. When the *Birmingham Post* reported the assault, Bennett was near death. Investigators said that those responsible for the shootings were not real officers.[14]

On Friday afternoon, August 7, two young cousins, James and William Edwards, were shot while traveling on a freight train as it approached the Irondale section of Birmingham. William Edwards, age sixteen, jumped from the train in Irondale. He had bullet wounds in his left arm and leg. His cousin James had been shot in the head but clung to the train for three more miles. When he could not hold on any longer, he rolled off the train to his death. William Edwards sought help at a friend's home in Irondale, who notified authorities. He told officers that three white men were standing on the Southern railroad tracks, and one of them inexplicably opened fire on them with a rifle as their train passed by. A witness corroborated Edwards's account, saying the men had told him they were railroad agents.[15]

Fearing additional reprisals and violence, a number of prominent black leaders urged black churches, businesses, and civic organizations to contribute to the Reward Fund that sought information about the Shades Mountain assailant. The Fairfield Colored Civic League held a large gathering on August 6 with A. G. Gaston presiding. Several resolutions were adopted condemning the violence, pledging cooperation with police in tracking down the assailant, and making plans for raising money for the reward fund.[16] Black employees at the general offices of Tennessee Coal and Iron wrote the following letter to Sheriff Hawkins:

> "We, the undersigned colored employees of the general office of the Tennessee Coal & Iron Railroad Company, located in the Brown-Marx Building, wish to contribute $50, which we wish to be added to the reward offered for the capture and prosecution of the person, or persons, guilty of the offense upon these young ladies a few days ago. We wish to go on record as being against any lawless acts committed by a member of our race or any other race.
>
> "We wish you to know that any information we are able to gather that will aid you in the capture of the criminal will promptly be brought to you, and that no criminal nor his deeds will be harbored by anyone whose name is signed below.
>
> "This letter was signed by the following employees, C. H. Freeman, W. L. McAlpine, Daniel McGuire, A. LeGrande, Otey Hancock, John Simpson, William Jenkins, Alexander McCray, W. L. Toney, Shirley M. Mason, William Webb, Joseph Lawson, William Shephard, Brady Richardson, Sandy Harris and George Allen."[17]

On Thursday, black suspects from Birmingham and surrounding towns were brought to St. Vincent's Hospital, where Nell Williams was recuperating from her wounds. Police were anxious for her to identify the assailant. It was likely an enormous stress for her to begin the identification process so soon after the trauma she had experienced just two days before. It may be that her family continued to shield her, as her father wished, from the news that Augusta was no longer alive. In fact, the afternoon that Nell began viewing suspects at St. Vincent's, funeral services for Augusta were held at the family home in Redmont. Dr. W. R. Hendrix from Highlands Methodist Church officiated.[18]

Within three days, the violence unleashed on black people and black businesses had reached such a fever pitch that Birmingham's white newspapers published editorials calling for peace and calm. The editors of the *Birmingham Age-Herald* condemned the "guerillas" that used this occasion "for a wholesale imperiling of innocents." They called upon authorities to arrest the "white desperadoes" who were capitalizing on the city's grief and horror as a means for expressing their hatred.[19]

Likewise, the editors at the *Birmingham News* decided to publish a rejoinder to the blistering editorial they had published the previous day, encouraging citizens to "relentlessly pursue" the brutal murderer. In the rejoinder, the editors condemned the "sporadic outbreaks" of "race hatred" perpetrated against "the persons and property of Negro citizens." They also expressed their hope that this "blind passion for revenge" was already "cooling."[20]

Unfortunately, neither law enforcement officials nor the self-appointed white vigilantes heeded the recommendations set forth in these editorials. The black community continued to experience an unmitigated reign of terror, and there was little if any attempt to thoroughly investigate the violence or hold people accountable. The discovery of communist literature became a pretext for blaming the victim of an attack rather than pursuing the attacker, as in the case of Charlie Horton. The coroner who examined James Edwards determined that he had not been killed by a bullet but had suffered fatal injuries when he fell from the train. And because his cousin's injuries were not life threatening, authorities did not attempt to apprehend the three white men who opened fire on the two black men.[21]

On August 6, a joint meeting of the Jefferson County Sheriff's Department and the Birmingham Police Department was held to discuss the strategies for apprehending the Shades Mountain assailant. It was agreed that efforts would be coordinated through the sheriff's office with chief deputy R. E. Smith in charge. Birmingham's chief of police, Fred H. McDuff, pledged to work closely with Deputy Smith. Later that day, Deputy Smith announced that the search for an old car had turned up no clues, and officials had pretty much abandoned the theory that three men were involved in the kidnapping. He also acknowledged that several residents of Shades Valley and Mountain Brook had complained about deputies entering their homes and taking their servants for questioning. Smith stated that the information gained from the servants had been valuable but the practice would be halted.[22]

Thousands of circulars with a description of the assailant had been sent to police departments throughout the South and to major northern cities including Chicago and New York. County deputies made trips to Chattanooga and Knoxville, Tennessee, to view suspects being held in both those cities.[23]

Each day, headlines in the city newspapers announced another possible lead in the case: an old gray hat was found near a cave in the vicinity of the slaying; a physician treated a black man who fit the description of the assailant; a man named Charles Hollis was arrested in Bluffton, Alabama, a hundred miles from Birmingham, after being noticed walking alone on the highway; a black man hauled from the swamps near Selma confessed to authorities that he had walked four days and four nights from Birmingham.

Every day the press reported that new suspects were paraded before Nell Williams, but so far she had rejected them all as too tall or too short, too dark or too light. Daily updates were released about Jennie Wood, saying she remained in critical condition.[24] And reports continued to reach police about beatings or shootings perpetrated by white vigilantes at railroad stops. One week after the attack on Shades Mountain, Willie Lawton from Fort Valley, Georgia, was taken to Hillman Hospital after being assaulted by two white men near the Seaboard Railway tracks in Birmingham. Lawton told officials that he had first been fired upon, but the shooters missed their mark. His injuries were reported as "not serious," and no investigation was undertaken.[25]

First-Person Narrative

Hundreds of black men were apprehended, detained, questioned, and sent to Birmingham in what was heralded as the "largest manhunt in the history of Jefferson County."[26] Many who lived through those interrogations likely bore emotional and physical scars that took years to heal, if they ever did. The newspapers reported only slivers of stories, snatches of accounts, and brief descriptions of the black men being hauled out of swamps, hunted down in woods and caves, pulled off trains, snatched from their beds, and thrown into jail. And none of these accounts described the suffering inflicted on suspects while in police custody.

There is, however, one extant source; an extensive narrative published in 1937 by Angelo Herndon, one of the first black men arrested and interrogated by deputies in Birmingham, who considered him a prime suspect in the communist conspiracy and kidnapping. Angelo Herndon was only eighteen years old when he was apprehended by Birmingham authorities. The Jefferson County Red Squad had been keeping a close eye on Herndon in the wake of the shootout at Camp Hill. He was an idealistic and energetic new member of the Communist Party who had recently come to Birmingham from Ohio to work in Tennessee Coal and Iron mines.

Herndon would later achieve significant notoriety after being convicted of inciting insurrection in Fulton County, Georgia, when he organized a hunger march and demonstrations by black and white workers at the Atlanta Courthouse in July 1932. His case was appealed all the way to the U.S. Supreme Court, which granted him freedom in 1937. That same year, he published an autobiography titled *Let Me Live*, in which he devoted an entire chapter to describing the ordeal he suffered at the hands of Birmingham detectives.[27]

Herndon began his narrative declaring that the chronicler of his times would surely mark the day when three white women were shot near Birmingham as "one of the most tragic events for American Negroes." On that day, Herndon was forty miles from Birmingham organizing coal miners. Returning home, he discovered that someone had broken in, smashed his furniture, and thrown every pamphlet and book he owned out the window into the gutter.[28]

Later that night, detectives entered the house through the window and hauled Herndon and two of his friends from their beds. The mother of one of the men came running into the room and asked the police why they were handcuffing and arresting the men. The detective struck her with the butt of his gun and screamed, "Shut up, you nigger wench!"[29]

The three men were taken to the Birmingham jail, where a detective sat across from Herndon, a rubber hose in his hands. He shouted obscenities and threatened to kill Herndon. Each time Angelo refused to say, "Yes, sir" or "No, sir," the deputy struck him in the head. Unable to break him, the detectives took Herndon twenty miles out of town into a wooded area, where they chained him, still handcuffed, to a tree.

"We don't give a hoot and a damn about your little old Communist Party," the leader screamed. "What we want to know is: Who shot Nell

Williams and the other two white girls? If you didn't do it yourself you know damn well who did. Now come across and pipe up or else you won't leave here alive."[30]

Herndon answered with all the calmness he could muster: "I know nothing about the shooting. I have nothing to confess."

For thirty minutes, two detectives wielding rubber hoses delivered blows to Herndon's body in rapid succession: "The rubber hose rose and fell with a hiss, rose and fell again in tireless monotony. I no longer listened nor heard what my tormentors were saying."[31]

Seeing they could not beat a confession out of him, they threw him in the car. All the way back to the jail, they kicked and punched him while threatening to lynch him. He was thrown in solitary confinement without a mattress, food, or water: "Huddled on the floor of my cell I fell into a sickly slumber, terribly ill in body and in mind. My nightmare experience had taken all the spirit out of me. I slept like one dead."[32]

The next morning, they led Herndon into the jail yard and claimed that his two friends had squealed on him after they had been beaten in the same woods where he had been chained to the tree.

"They told us everything, Angelo, and it's no use of you pretending any further. They even told us where to find the gun with which you did the shooting. Here it is. Do you recognize it?"

The officer was laughing while he held the gun in front of Angelo, proud to have caught him in a snare. Herndon shook his head. He did not recognize that gun. The officers locked him up again. This was only one of several traps the police used to try to convince each of the three suspects, one by one, that the others had turned on him, accusing him of being the perpetrator.[33]

After being locked up for more than a week, the three men were led to the visitor's pen, where two detectives stood talking to a woman who was later identified as Nell Williams. She shook her head and whispered "no" when the officers nodded in the direction of Herndon and his friends. When the police finally decided to drop the murder charges, they charged the three men with vagrancy.[34]

Herndon devoted pages to describing "the reign of terror" unleashed on black neighborhoods in Birmingham, painting a vivid and frightening picture of the pall that hung over those sections of town for more than a month:

Negroes dared not show their faces on the streets. They hid in their houses, scared beyond words, their doors and windows tightly shut and barred against any possible attackers. Not only were the streets deserted by Negroes, but the houses gave the impression that no one lived in them. No Negro dared make a sound, for fear of attracting the attention of the white hoodlums, the vigilantes and the American Legionnaires who prowled through the streets like beasts of prey with shotguns and revolvers in their hands. Negro mothers sternly hushed their babies when they cried. The sinister word "lynch" was heard in tragic whispers on every side. Few Negroes slept during those eventful days and nights. They waited, waited with bated breath and constricted hearts for something terrible to happen. And it did, day after day, night after night.[35]

The Rape of Black Women

Angelo Herndon estimated that as many as seventy black people of both sexes were killed in the weeks following August 4, 1931.[36] The exact number of deaths is difficult to document, but the enormity of suffering borne by Birmingham's black community cannot be overstated.

Significantly, Herndon directed attention to one gaping hole in newspaper accounts of the violence: black women were also victims. In those weeks when white men were hunting for a suspected black murderer, black women were more vulnerable than ever. The caricature of black men as insatiable rapists was a dominant feature of white supremacist culture, but the primary victims of interracial rape in Jim Crow Birmingham, as throughout the South, were black women. As historian Danielle McGuire has documented, white men in the Jim Crow era "abducted and assaulted black women with alarming regularity. White men lured black women and girls away from home with promises of steady work and better wages; attacked them on the job; abducted them at gunpoint while traveling to and from home, work, or church; raped them as a form of retribution or to enforce rules of racial and economic hierarchy; sexually humiliated and assaulted them on streetcars and buses, in taxicabs and trains, and in other public spaces."[37]

It is not surprising that incidents of sexual assault and rape perpetrated by white officers, deputies, and vigilantes during the reign of terror in August 1931 remained glaringly unaccounted for in newspaper reports or police records. As Nell Irvin Painter noted when researching the rape of black women at the beginning of the twentieth century, "According to commonplace assumptions of the time, rape was a crime whose only victims were white women."[38] Given the sense of entitlement and impunity that white males possessed in Jim Crow Birmingham, rape was undoubtedly another form of terror meted out to the black community in the aftermath of August 4.[39]

four

FEAR, LOATHING, AND OBLIVION
IN THE WHITE COMMUNITY

Feature-length stories about the manhunt dominated the front page of Birmingham's newspapers for nearly two weeks after the attack. Descriptions of the assailant, theories of communist conspiracy, daily updates on Jennie Wood's condition, and reports about the latest arrests kept the city's attention riveted on this gruesome tragedy. The *Birmingham Age-Herald* reported that "thousands of persons" came to view the crime scene in the week following the attack. Especially during the weekend, long lines of automobiles clogged the road leading to the spot where the women were held and killed.[1]

On Friday, August 14, two-inch headlines announced that, after a nine-day battle, Jennie Wood had succumbed to her devastating wounds. The *Age-Herald* ran a large front-page photo that could have been taken from Jennie's college yearbook. Her dark hair was coiffed in gentle curls. She wore an elegant string of pearls. Her eyes were hauntingly sad. The photo was framed on the right with a column of words that read, "Miss Jennie Wood, society girl here, died Thursday, the second victim of a negro killer who shot her and two others the night of Aug. 4."[2]

As the manhunt stretched on with no apparent breakthroughs, reports about the investigation moved to the second page of the *Post*, *News*, and *Age-Herald*. The killings were still a vital topic of conversation in bars, barbershops, and other social gathering spots, but the daily challenges of coping with the Great Depression once again took center stage in most white households. The severity of economic distress varied from household to household, but no one was immune from the widespread dislocation that the stock market crash of 1929 unleashed in Birmingham. Thousands of white workers were laid off or cut back to part-time employment. Many in Birmingham's wealthy owning class were woefully overextended when the crash hit, having borrowed and invested huge amounts of capital during the prosperous bubble of the 1920s. Government officials were under tremendous pressure to provide relief to the unemployed, and industry leaders were struggling to keep their companies afloat in the face of an abrupt decline in the demand for steel.

The stress of the Depression and the insularity of racial segregation meant that many white families in Birmingham remained unaware of the breadth and depth of terror unleashed on the black community. Reports of the arrests, shootings, and murders of black victims were customarily brief and seldom front-page news unless the authorities wanted to broadcast their success at apprehending suspects. The trauma suffered by the victims was not reported. In contrast to extensive coverage of the anguish suffered by the Williams sisters and Jennie Wood, there were no in-depth portraits of the black men and women who had been wounded, killed, raped, or disappeared by avenging vigilantes and deputies. The emotional impact of the weeks-long manhunt on family members, neighbors, and the wider black community was never mentioned in Birmingham's white newspapers.

Dent Disappears for Days on End

Life may have moved on for many white families in Birmingham by late August and early September, but that was not true for the Williams family. Clark Williams could not stop rehearsing the minute-by-minute sequence of events that had occurred on that terrible afternoon in early August. He berated himself for not realizing sooner that his daughters were in mortal danger.[3] He and his wife, Helen, were concerned about whether Nell would heal from the trauma of being the sole survivor. The weeks-long search for the murderer was taking a frightful toll on her, both physically and psychically. They were also deeply worried about their twenty-four-year-old son, Dent, who had not been the same since August 4.

Helen Williams was afraid Dent would do harm to himself. Clark Williams worried that his son might exact revenge from someone else, especially since learning that Dent had gone to Augusta's grave and spoken a pledge aloud: "Sister I will get him or else I will never do anything more."[4] Dent disappeared for days on end, heading east to Anniston or south to Montgomery, following up on leads he had read about in the papers. Other times Dent just headed out with the belief that he could smoke out the killer's hiding place. Coming home at all hours of the day or night, he kicked doors open and slammed his fist into walls. When his father tried to talk with him and calm him down, Dent turned and left the room. One night after Dent came home in a rage, Clark crawled into bed with him and slept beside him all night, holding him tightly as his son's body jerked ferociously for hours.[5]

In the weeks following the attack on Shades Mountain, deputies frequented the Williams home in Redmont. They came to question Nell and gather additional information about the case from family members. Dent's behavior was a constant topic of conversation among the deputies after those visits. It was disturbingly erratic and agitated. While they questioned Nell, Dent paced back and forth. He looked like a man who had not eaten or slept in weeks. And they learned from Clark Williams that Dent had been all over Alabama searching for the assailant.[6]

Two Emergency Meetings Convened

One of the religious leaders in Birmingham's white community deeply concerned about the murders on Shades Mountain was Rev. Henry Edmonds, pastor of Independent Presbyterian Church, a large congregation in the heart of the city. The Williams family did not attend the church, but they were neighbors in Redmont. The Edmonds home was just down the hill on a street that ran parallel to Aberdeen Road. Having counseled people who had suffered unspeakable trauma, Edmonds felt deep compassion for Nell and her family, knowing the weight of sorrow they were carrying.

Edmonds was also keenly concerned about the impact these killings were having on the wider community. Fearing that radical elements were bound to use this tragic incident to sow discord between the races, he decided to convene a statewide emergency meeting of the Commission on Interracial Cooperation (CIC), to be held August 11 in Birmingham. Edmonds had been elected chair of the Alabama branch of the commission the previous year, and he believed the CIC could play a calming, mediating role in a city besieged by fear, racial tension, and economic hardship.

The CIC was founded in Atlanta in 1919 by white Southerners concerned about the resurgence of white mob violence in the aftermath of World War I. While condemning the most egregious forms of racial violence such as lynching, many CIC members approved of segregation and rejected radical efforts to dismantle Jim Crow laws and practices. The membership was predominantly white, but it also attracted conservative black leaders. Many of its eight hundred state and local committees had interracial boards and meetings.[7]

Henry Edmonds was well suited to chair the Alabama chapter of the CIC. He was an outspoken critic of the Ku Klux Klan, and he used the pulpit to issue strong condemnations of lynching. At the same time, Edmonds defended the segregationist doctrine of "separate but equal." He did not believe that the system of segregation was inherently unjust or stacked against black people. Through education, moral suasion, and charitable programs, Edmonds believed gross inequities could be addressed and the "disadvantaged" could be given opportunities to live healthier and more wholesome lives.[8]

The statewide meeting that Edmonds convened one week after the attack on Shades Mountain was an interracial gathering of Alabama clergy, educators, and businessmen. It focused on the threat posed by the Communist Party at a time when Alabama residents, white and black, were facing severe economic hardships. Those in attendance agreed that mounting tension between the races could be laid at the feet of foreign agents intent on sowing discord and fomenting violence. A subcommittee was appointed to prepare a special investigative report exposing the sinister motives and operations of these outside agitators. That report, titled "Radical Activities in Alabama," was approved at a subsequent meeting held September 14 and released to the press and affiliate organizations throughout the South.[9]

The report stated that black Alabamians in the forefront of communist organizing had been duped by "sinister alien influences." These "apostles of revolution" only pretended to care about the welfare of black people like the Scottsboro defendants. The report alleged that radicals were actually hoping the Scottsboro defendants would be executed so that their "unseemly assaults" on the "honor of the state" might be vindicated.

Nothing in the report suggested that Jim Crow racism or economic exploitation of black workers might be the cause of black resistance and efforts to bring change to the region. No criticism was leveled against the white posses that fomented violence in Scottsboro and Camp Hill. Nor did the report mention the vigilante violence occurring in Birmingham when the August and September meetings took place. According to the authors, the sole source of racial tension so evident in Alabama was the radical outsiders who had infiltrated the state, bringing with them "able leadership, tireless energy, worldwide organization, and apparently unlimited money."[10]

Prime Suspects

After weeks of arrests and interrogation, investigators in Jefferson County were desperate to discover solid clues leading to the Shades Mountain assailant. Chief McDuff's patience was wearing thin. He sympathized with Nell Williams, knowing she was under enormous pressure to positively identify one of the many suspects they had brought to her. He did not want to contribute to her duress in any way, but he could not help feeling impatient and even distrustful about her indecision. At times he wondered if she still had the capacity to conclusively identify the assailant, given the ways her descriptions changed over time.

McDuff was particularly disgruntled about how things had gone awry with the first prime suspect they had apprehended just days after the murders on Shades Mountain. He had been confident that this was the man—a strong, large young black man with long hair and gold inlay in his lower teeth. Nell was still in the hospital when she and her father examined the man. They held him there for thirty minutes while Nell asked him to walk back and forth in front of her. When she grew uncertain that he was the assailant, her father warned her not to make a hasty decision. Nell responded,

"Well, Daddy, you know I told you that the Negro did not get there 'till just about dark and during the time he was there for the most part he sat in the automobile behind me where I could not see him and during the most of the other time he was there it was dark so that I could not see him to pick out particulars of a description to any considerable extent."[11]

After a few more minutes of discussion and examination, Nell said she could not identify this black man as the party. McDuff had no choice but to let the man go. Not twenty minutes later, Clark Williams called and demanded that he hold the man; Nell had changed her mind. When McDuff said he had released him, Williams responded, "For God's sake, catch him again." McDuff dispatched his deputies to hunt for the suspect, but he had vanished.[12]

Another prime suspect surfaced later that month in Montgomery County. Deputy Ed Taylor contacted Dent Williams, who was in Montgomery at the time, and told him they had someone who fit the description of the Shades Mountain murderer. Dent told Taylor to hold the man until he could bring Nell to Montgomery to view him. When Nell and Dent arrived in Montgomery, Sheriff Stearn asked Nell—before seeing the suspect—what characteristics would be most important for her in positively identifying the assailant. Nell said his voice would be key; she could never forget that voice. Sheriff Stearn then asked Nell to sit in front of a screen that hid the suspect in question. The sheriff instructed Nell to listen carefully as the man repeated statements that the sheriff voiced. Nell nodded and said that she recognized that voice.

When they pulled the screen away, Nell wept. Gazing at the black man standing before her, she began to express doubts. She could not be absolutely certain. She thought he was the man but she needed more time. The suspect was held for a week and then released when investigators discovered that he had been working on August 4 at the Montgomery Airport, and his coworkers could testify to that fact. Before his release, neither Nell nor Dent called authorities to say that Nell was positive he was the man.[13]

The *Birmingham News* reported the next breakthrough on August 14. Authorities were investigating an anonymous letter that had arrived shortly after the attack. It was addressed to Sheriff Hawkins, postmarked Chicago, and written by a man who boasted of being "the negro" that committed the crime. Taunting authorities, he gave the name of a dance hall in

Chicago where he could be found. He dared the police to come find him. Little credence was initially accorded this strange epistle until police discovered another letter written in the same handwriting and on the same paper in the home of a black woman in Irondale. When questioned, the woman said the Irondale letter had been written by her son. He had been visiting from Chicago and left town the day after the shooting.[14]

The officers offered no explanation of how the Irondale letter had been unearthed. It may have been discovered during one of their raids on the homes of suspected communists. Chief Deputy Sheriff Smith wired Chicago police, asking them to check the address and arrest any black men they thought suspicious. The Chicago police acted with dispatch and wired Sheriff Hawkins that they were holding Elijah and Leroy Thompson. Hawkins asked them to send fingerprints and pictures of the men.

When Nell was shown photographs of Elijah and Leroy Thompson, she saw a resemblance between Elijah Thompson and the assailant. But she could not be absolutely certain. She would need to see the man in person. Authorities set to work obtaining requisition papers from Montgomery. They intended to travel to Chicago as soon as possible and bring Thompson to Birmingham.[15]

The Thompson brothers were arraigned in a Chicago court on August 20 and then detained while Chicago authorities awaited extradition papers from Alabama.[16] For weeks, Elijah Thompson appeared to be the most viable suspect. Just in case Thompson did not pan out, Sheriff Hawkins released a statement asking every white man in Shades Valley to "check up on his negro employees and if possible check their whereabouts the night of the shooting. If there is any question at all about the whereabouts of any negro servant, the sheriff's office should be notified."[17]

The anticipated trip to Chicago was delayed when Elijah Thompson retained an attorney and fought extradition. He told authorities that he and his brother, Leroy, had indeed been in Birmingham earlier that summer but had left on August 2. They had receipts proving they had taken the ferry across the Ohio River on August 3, and their lawyer had collected sworn affidavits from fourteen witnesses prepared to testify that Elijah Thompson was in Chicago the night of August 3.

On August 26, officials announced that the trip to Chicago had been called off and efforts to extradite Elijah Thompson abandoned. Chicago police had sent a new batch of photos. After carefully examining the pictures, Nell Williams decided Thompson did not resemble the assailant after all.[18]

The manhunt continued as summer gave way to autumn. Well into September, law enforcement officials throughout the South continued to apprehend suspects and send word to Jefferson County, confident that "this one perfectly [fit] the description." One by one, the men were brought to Nell Williams. Day after day, to the consternation of the investigators, Nell shook her head and said, "No, that's not the Negro that murdered my sister and my friend."

PART II

TRIALS AND TRIBULATIONS

five

THE ARREST

September 23, 1931

The simmering heat of the sidewalk could be felt through the soles of Willie Peterson's shoes as he walked toward Beamon's Cafe on Birmingham's Southside. The avenues and paved side streets had been baking for days as temperatures soared to record-breaking highs seldom reached in late September.[1] The nights, thick with dense and unrelenting humidity, brought no relief.

By four in the afternoon, Willie's blue overalls and long-sleeved jumper were so soaked with sweat he wondered if he should have heeded his wife's plea and stayed home. She had tried to talk him out of going because he got so tired in the afternoons. She also worried for his safety.[2]

"If you're going downtown, Willie, be home long before dark," she said. "Negroes can't be too careful these days."

He knew Henrietta was right. The city had been on edge for weeks. Willie could not remember the exact date or all the sordid details, but he knew it was early August when those white ladies were attacked up on Shades Mountain. Two of them died, and the young one who lived to tell about it said a black man had committed the crime. Willie had seen reward posters with a description of the suspect nailed to telephone poles and taped to store windows.

Rumors had rippled through Willie's neighborhood in Woodlawn soon after the murders. Some said it wasn't any kind of Negro at all. Those white girls had been "up to no good" on that mountain. Things had gotten out of hand. Willie didn't know what to think. He was just thankful that Henrietta was safe and he had not lost any friends or neighbors to the white vigilante violence that followed.

Willie had taken the streetcar from Woodlawn to his mother-in-law's rented room on the Southside. He wanted her to know that Henrietta had been sick in bed for the past three days. She was slowly gaining strength and might even be up and around by tomorrow, but they had no way of calling her mother, and Willie felt she should know that Henrietta had been through a rough patch.

Willie often lay awake at night worrying about Henrietta and the extra load she had been carrying for the past two years. She worked so hard and had so little time for herself. She was fortunate to still have a job when so many of their neighbors were being laid off from the mills and the mines. The family she worked for were decent white people, but Henrietta was working longer hours for the same amount of money she had been paid before the Depression hit so hard.[3] It weighed on Willie that he could not contribute anything except a meager disability check from the Veterans Administration. His tuberculosis had steadily weakened him, and he had lost so much weight his bosses at the Ruffner Mine told him he was no use to them anymore. He had been unemployed and chronically ill for two years. He was only thirty-eight, but most days he felt like a man in his seventies. That worried him too, seeing as how Henrietta had just turned twenty-four.

After kissing his mother-in-law goodbye, Willie headed east on Avenue G toward Fourteenth Street where his first wife's uncle, Lee F. Beamon, ran a café. Whenever Willie was in this neighborhood, Lee and his wife insisted on giving him generous helpings of leftovers like cornbread and collard greens. It made Willie happy to think of taking delicious treats home to Henrietta that day. He had promised her he would be careful and not overdo. He would rest at her mother's, then sit for a spell with Lee Beamon at the café before taking the trolley back to Woodlawn. He would be home well before dinnertime.

Yearning for some cornbread and a tall glass of sweet iced tea, Willie had turned onto Fourteenth Street when he noticed a car driving slowly beside him and three white people looking in his direction.

"Maybe they're lost," he thought. Avenue G was a main east-west thoroughfare in the city, but it was unusual to see white people driving on the side streets in this black neighborhood unless they were giving a ride to someone who worked for them as a nursemaid, cook, or chauffeur. Willie turned to his right to see what the car's occupants might be looking at. Turning back toward the car, he realized all three passengers were staring directly at him. The auto slowed and came to a stop. The man at the wheel, who appeared to be about twenty years of age, called to Willie.

"Boy, come over here."

As Willie walked toward the car, he saw a young woman, about the same age as the driver, in the passenger seat and an older lady seated in the back. As he leaned toward the open window, he averted his eyes, knowing that he should not make eye contact with the women.

"Can I help you, sir?"

The driver said nothing. Willie spoke a little louder but was careful not to shout.

"Sir, what can I do for you?"

Again, the driver did not respond, but the woman next to him said, "Buck, I am sure that is the Negro."

Willie did not dare look directly at the woman, but he felt certain he had never seen her before. What could she mean, he was "the Negro"?

"Just stand there and let this girl look at you," the driver said, reaching for his handgun.

Willie stood upright. He wanted to run, but he kept his feet firmly planted on the red-hot pavement beside the car.

"What's your name, boy?" The driver was now holding the gun on his lap.

"Willie Peterson, sir."

"This is the man," the young woman said with an eerie calmness.

"Are you certain, Nell?" the driver asked.

"Yes. It's him. I *know* it's him."

Willie had no idea who this woman was or why she thought she knew him, but he knew he could not contradict her. He stared at the car door, praying to God that someone in the car would realize she was mistaken and the driver would put the gun down.

"Step back two feet and then don't move an inch or I'll shoot you," the driver bellowed. He opened the car door and told the older woman to come sit in the driver's seat.

"I'll get in the back with the darky while you drive us to the police station," he said, never taking his eyes off Willie.

"Oh no, I can't drive," she said. "I'm too nervous. My hands are shaking."

The driver got out and stood beside Willie. He told the women to go find a phone and call the police. As they headed off in the direction of Beamon's Cafe, he called to them to be careful and remember where they were. Then he ordered Willie to get in the backseat. Standing beside the car, the driver continued to interrogate Willie, pointing his gun through the open window.

"Where do you live, boy?"

"Woodlawn."

"Do you own a car?"

"No, sir. I used to, but I don't now."

Willie thought it was a strange question. Why did the man care? Willie had not driven a car in two years. When he could no longer afford gas or tags, he had given his old secondhand Model T Ford to a friend.

"Where were you on August 4?" the driver asked.

August 4? August 4? Willie repeated the date to himself, frantically searching his memory. How in the world could he remember where he was two months ago? Days ran together, each one just like the other, now that he did not work. But chances were he stayed close to home on August 4 just as he did most days, so he could lie down to rest in the afternoon.

"I was home sick, sir," Willie said.

"Who's your doctor?"

"Dr. Ferrell of Woodlawn."

Willie wanted to take off his hat and wipe the sweat from his forehead, but he did not want to make any sudden moves.

"Do you know anything about the killings on the mountain?" the driver asked.

"No sir, I don't," Willie replied.

The white man's voice had hardened as he spit that last question at Willie. When the man said "the killings on the mountain," the pieces began to fall into place for Willie. Apparently that young lady who was sitting in the front seat thought he had something to do with those murders. *Great God in heaven*, Willie prayed silently, closing his eyes, trying hard to breathe. *Lord Jesus, look down on this your servant and protect me.*

Willie turned to see if he could escape out the other door, but the man shouted at him to turn back and face him.

"Don't do anything stupid, boy," the man screamed, cocking the gun. "If you do, I'm going to kill you."

Willie sat back against the seat and folded his hands in his lap. Just then, a car came screeching around the corner and pulled up right behind them. Three police officers, with guns drawn, came running up on either side of the car. One of them reached through the window and struck Willie in the face, slamming his head against the back of the front seat. Another officer stepped onto the sideboard and grabbed Willie by the arms, pulled him out onto the road, and dragged him toward the police car. While shouting epithets, the third officer threw Willie against the hood, handcuffed him, and shoved him into the backseat.

As they drove to the station, one of the men sat beside Willie with his gun drawn. The two men in the front seat were jubilant that the Shades Mountain murderer had finally been apprehended, but they shook their heads in disbelief that he was so scrawny, weak, and pale.

Willie could feel a trickle of blood flowing from just above his right eye. He stared straight ahead and said nothing when the officers taunted him with questions and accusations. *How can I get word to Henrietta?* Willie wondered. *She'll be so worried. Maybe I can reach Rev. Matthews. It's Wednesday evening Bible study night at New Morning Star Baptist Church. Maybe Rev. Matthews can go see Henrietta and let her know I'm alive.*

A block from the jail, one of the officers predicted that a lynch mob was bound to gather that night.

"You've got the wrong Negro," Willie said. "I didn't kill anyone."

Lee Beamon was an uncle-in-law to Willie Peterson. He loved to sit in front of his café in the late afternoon and read the paper before the dinner crowd arrived. Wednesday afternoon, the twenty-third day in a hot September, he had hoped for a breeze as he stepped outside, but the temperature still hovered in the upper nineties. Fortunately, the café was on the west side of Fourteenth Street, so he could set his chair in the shade. Hot as it was outside, it was more stifling still in the café. He had just finished reading that

U. S. Steel was threatening to cut wages once again when two white women came running toward him.

"Does this café have a telephone?" the younger one asked.

"No, ma'am, but there's one next door." The women seemed not to hear him and headed off in the direction of the beauty shop the next block over.

It was then he noticed a commotion down the street. He could see a white man standing on the pavement talking to someone in a car. He could not make out what they were saying. A police car rounded the corner and screeched to a halt. Three officers jumped out and rushed to the stopped car. One of the deputies reached through the rear window and slapped the man in the car. A second officer yanked him from the backseat, threw him against the hood, and handcuffed him.

"Good Lord, that's Willie Peterson," Beamon shouted into the café.

Mary Beamon emerged, wiping her hands on a towel. Shading her eyes, she watched with her husband as the police car hurtled toward Avenue G.

Lee and Mary Beamon had known Willie Peterson for more than two decades. Willie's first wife was Lee Beamon's niece. She was married to Willie for eight years before she died, suddenly and far too young. Lee and Mary were very fond of Willie and his new wife, Henrietta. When he got too sick to work in the mines, they told him to stop by the café and get leftovers anytime he was in the neighborhood.

"You're family, Willie," is what they had said. "And kinfolk got to take care of each other, 'specially in these times."

After the police drove away, Lee Beamon approached the driver and asked if he knew the man who had been taken away in the police car. "No," he replied and turned away.

Lee Beamon had no way of knowing that he was addressing Edward M. "Buck" Streit, a neighbor of the Williams family, who was driving Nell and her mother to Elmwood Cemetery that afternoon to place fresh flowers on Augusta's grave. Beamon was tempted to tell this white man that he had known Willie for twenty-three years, and he could vouch for him being an honest man, as good and kind as they come. Beamon wanted to point to his café, just a few yards away, and tell this stranger that Willie was probably headed there to get something to eat. There was so much Lee Beamon could have said if the man had only looked at him, but he knew better than to press the point or ask any questions.

A Lynch Mob at the Jail

As news of the arrest spread, crowds began to gather outside the Jefferson County Jail in downtown Birmingham. By nightfall, 1,500 people were milling in the alley. Sheriff Hawkins and Chief McDuff were in complete agreement that they must do everything in their power to keep the prisoner safe and defuse the angry mob. The last thing they wanted was a lynching. Ever since the onset of the trials in Scottsboro, Alabama officials were being held up to a new level of scrutiny. Reporters from all across the country had come to fill the courtroom in Scottsboro and write about the constant threat of lynching that hung like a storm cloud over the town. Birmingham's civic leaders had a strong investment in projecting a very different image of their city. They wanted Birmingham to be known as "a city upon a hill"; a civilized, cosmopolitan metropolis where everyone is deemed innocent until proven guilty.

Hawkins and McDuff were also worried that Dent Williams had been pacing the jailhouse halls since Peterson was apprehended. Their officers had warned them that Dent had been threatening for weeks to kill his sister's murderer if he ever laid eyes on him. Weighing their options, McDuff and Hawkins decided they could not risk keeping Peterson in Birmingham. Under cover of night, they took the prisoner out a side door and escorted him in a caravan of police cars to Kilby Prison in Montgomery. Sheriff Hawkins rode in the car with Peterson for safekeeping.[4]

After Peterson had left the jailhouse, officer W. M. Burge took Dent aside, sat him down, and extracted a pledge that he would not interfere with law enforcement or harm the prisoner in any way. Burge was pleasantly surprised when Dent offered no resistance and promised not to inflict or incite violence. The officer then explained that Peterson had been taken to Kilby for fear that the crowd might storm the jailhouse. Burge was again surprised when Dent volunteered to go into the alley, address those assembled, and help de-escalate the situation.

"They have taken him out of the city," Dent told the crowd. "I'm satisfied we have someone. Nell has positively identified him. This means more to me than to you—she is my sister. We don't want any trouble."[5]

With news that the suspect had been taken from the jail and the Williams family wanted "no trouble," the crowd began to disperse.

"Providence Led Me to Him"

Willie Peterson bore little resemblance to the description Nell had given earlier save for the fact that he was black. Peterson was light-skinned and weighed no more than 125 pounds. His hair was cropped close to the scalp and he would never be described as "well educated." Nevertheless, Nell told reporters that the minute she heard him speak, she knew beyond all doubt that this was the man. His voice and his eyes were the two characteristics she recognized immediately. Nell noted that when Buck Streit called "the Negro" over to the car, he did not appear at all frightened. She was certain he did not recognize her at first. After all, it was dark on the mountain and he had three people to remember; she had only one. But when she returned to the car after calling the police, he looked paler, almost sick. It was then she noticed that he would not look directly at her: "He seemed to keep shifting his eyes. That's just the way the negro did that afternoon on the mountain."[6]

She told reporters that when she first saw "the Negro" that day she felt no fear at all. When they got up closer to him and she knew he was the one, she was "just terribly pleased and happy." When asked if she planned to go to the jail and confirm her identification, Nell said there was no need, none at all. She had never been more certain of anything. Willie Peterson was the man, and she believed Providence had led her to him.

"I knew I would see him some day. Something inside me just told me I would, and that was my only hope. For weeks I have been accustomed to looking into the faces of dozens, and now mother and I both feel that Providence pointed out this one."[7]

The First Round of Interrogation

Two days after the arrest, solicitor George Lewis Bailes, assistant solicitor James McKenzie Long, and a court reporter traveled to Kilby prison to interrogate Willie Peterson. Assistant Solicitor Long did the talking for the team. With no defense attorney present, he was able to ask Peterson a host of questions with the intent of getting him to name people, places, and circumstances that could later be used against him. Long had access to the police files and was fully informed about law enforcement's theory that the shooter was a communist who had possibly spent time in the North and who probably had been dropped off on Leeds Highway by two comrades.

Long also had access to the information police had obtained about Peterson since his arrest two days before.[8]

Long seized upon the fact that Peterson had been stationed "up north" in a military camp in Iowa when he served in the armed forces. He asked Peterson how often he associated with white people, and white women in particular, while he was in the north, adding that "up there . . . white and negroes go together." Peterson said he stayed with people of his color all the time and knew nothing about that. Long pressed the point, saying that Peterson surely visited sporting houses when he got a pass to leave the camp.

"You knew that white women were in those places up there?"

"No sir, I don't know sir. I never did visit them at all," Peterson responded.

Long quizzed Peterson about associations and lodges that he belonged to, claiming that Peterson must have attended meetings where they talked about how badly black people were treated and how they weren't accorded their fair share. Peterson denied attending any such meetings and explained that his only affiliation was with the Christian church.

"You had been to meetings where they said the negroes were as good as white people and ought to be treated like white people?" Long asked, as if echoing something Peterson had admitted doing.

"You told those women over there on the mountain that negroes were as good as white folks, didn't you?"

Peterson again denied any such affiliation and said he never talked to those women.

Knowing that Peterson once worked in the ore mines near Irondale, Long suggested that he must have frequently walked over the mountain on foot from his home in Woodlawn. Peterson said he took the Gate City car when he had enough money to pay the fare; when he didn't, he would walk to the mines with his brother-in-law and an old miner. He was puzzled by Long's repeated suggestion that he was well acquainted with Leeds Highway. Yes, the Gate City car took him on the Irondale mountain road. Yes, the car stopped at Leeds Highway, and, yes, he had to walk the rest of the way to the ore mine, but, no, he had not walked up and down Leeds Highway. No, he was not familiar with that highway.

Throughout the lengthy interrogation, Peterson insisted he was nowhere near Shades Mountain on August 4 and did not kill anyone. He was too ill to leave home most days, he explained. Long paid no attention to these explanations and denials. He kept circling back, asking Peterson to give him names of the people he had seen during the afternoon and evening of August 4. While pretending to be concerned about Peterson's welfare, Assistant Solicitor Long explained that the only way Peterson would escape a death sentence was if he could recall the names of people he had talked with on August 4.

"It is important that you have somebody that will go in court and swear ... where you were every hour and minute of [August 4] between twelve o'clock and midnight that night. It is important that you have witnesses to tell that, because this lady, the one that you shot in the arm, Miss Williams, you didn't kill her, you didn't know but what all of them were dead, did you?"

"I ain't shot nobody. I never killed nobody in my life," Willie said.

Long leaned in and doubled down: "Well, you know this lady has accused you of it and said that you were the boy that did the shooting.... When she goes to court and tells the jury that, you know that you have got to get something to prove different?"

"Yes sir," Peterson said, voicing agreement with the second part of Long's statement.

"Well, put your thinking cap on now and tell me the names of the people that you can prove by where you were from twelve o'clock August 4 the day those young ladies were shot."

Peterson tried to conjure up what might have happened that day and who he might have spoken with, but he could not be absolutely certain of times and people. He had no precise memory of Tuesday, August 4. Long was not satisfied with "maybes" and "probably on that day." He pressed for full names and exact times as though he was a benign coach who wanted to assist Peterson in preparing an airtight alibi.

"Now, tell me the names of the witnesses to prove where you were, to offset what that young lady is going to swear to. Just as fast as you think of them just tell that young man [pointing at the court recorder] and he will write them down."

"I'm trying to think of them now," Willie replied. "All of those colored people I know."

Pressured by Long, Peterson began to name his neighbors and acquaintances and give times that would best fit when they usually stopped by to talk with him on the porch or waved to him as they passed by the house. He paused periodically, saying he did not want to "tell narry story" because he was not guilty of the crime. Peterson was fearful he might be stepping into traps laid by Assistant Solicitor Long, but he also did not want to give the appearance of being evasive. He insisted he had nothing to hide; it was just impossible to remember that day above all days. By the time the interrogation ended, Peterson had given Long names and times. Each one could potentially be used against Peterson when those witnesses testified in court if Long and his team were able to establish enough discrepancy in time and place and thereby weaken Peterson's credibility.

A Gray Hat, a Gold Tooth, and Religious Fanaticism

While Assistant Solicitor Long and Solicitor Bailes were in Montgomery interrogating Willie Peterson, Sheriff Hawkins issued a warrant charging Peterson with murder. The next scheduled week for trying capital cases in criminal court was to begin October 12, preceded by a grand jury hearing on October 5. With only a few weeks to spare, Chief McDuff and Sheriff Hawkins's team of deputies set to work gathering evidence to corroborate Nell Williams's identification of the slayer.

Two days after the arrest, Birmingham newspapers announced that investigating officers had been successful in their endeavors. Searching Peterson's home, they discovered an old hat that they suspected might fit the description given by Nell Williams. When they brought it to her, she declared that it was indeed the hat her assailant had worn that fateful night. Peterson had a gold tooth, one of the identifying marks of the slayer. Investigators also told reporters that Peterson's father-in-law was a preacher and stated, "Peterson is a religious fanatic whose wife has threatened several times to leave him because of his religious activities." According to investigators, these discoveries confirmed what Nell had previously told reporters: the assailant had endlessly lectured the women about religion. The deputies also said that Nell had revealed a new fact about the assailant: he bragged about being the son of a Birmingham preacher.[9]

The *Birmingham News* reported that Peterson's home was only one and a half miles from the crime scene off Leeds Highway on Shades Mountain.[10] The paper failed to mention that this distance was as the crow flies. By car, the distance was closer to seven miles. It would take extraordinary stamina and willpower to walk the rugged terrain of a one-and-a-half-mile route from South Woodlawn to Old Leeds Highway. A traveler on foot would have to ford creeks and find his way through woods before scaling Shades Mountain.

Dent Williams told the press that his family was more than satisfied that these discoveries corroborated Nell's positive identification, and he told Solicitor Bailes to "get it over with as soon as possible."[11] Solicitor Bailes concurred that there was no need for additional corroborating evidence. "As far as I can see," he said, "if Miss Williams positively identifies the negro, there is nothing else to it."[12]

Had Willie Peterson's friends or neighbors been asked about his character, background, and proclivities, a very different portrait would have emerged. But news about "the negro suspect" was largely filtered through Nell Williams's accounts of the day he was arrested and through statements by the white doctors, attorneys, reporters, and law enforcement officials that treated or questioned him. It would be weeks before Peterson would have an attorney to advise him or launch investigations on his behalf.

six

ATTEMPTED MURDER

Despite the evidence gathered by investigators, police chief Fred McDuff had serious doubts that Peterson was a viable suspect. His physical stature did not match Nell Williams's description of the assailant. It seemed to him highly improbable that a man suffering from tuberculosis could have held three women hostage alone for four hours. Unable to shake those misgivings, McDuff decided to bring Peterson back to Birmingham and arrange a secret meeting at the county jail with Clark Williams, Nell Williams, and Willie Peterson. If Nell had another chance to see Peterson up close and experience how frail he was, perhaps she would change her mind.[1]

Clark Williams jumped at the chance to meet with Peterson, hoping the prisoner would confess and spare Nell the agony of a protracted trial. Williams did not understand why Chief McDuff and Sheriff Hawkins had taken Peterson to Kilby Prison in the first place. He felt certain they could have gotten a confession out of the prisoner the first night. Instead, they foolishly sent "the Negro" to a facility where he would have access to a host of hardened criminals who could coach him on how to be evasive and lie.

Williams was relieved that McDuff had had a change of mind and was bringing Peterson back to Birmingham for an interrogation.[2]

Peterson was returned to Birmingham under cover of night for a meeting on Friday, October 2. As news of this conference spread among officers and reached Solicitor Bailes's office, the number of people attending grew substantially, and Chief McDuff decided to use the largest space available at the county jail—a room just off the jail yard that was sleeping quarters for deputies on late-night duty. Even so, it would be a tight squeeze for a group that had grown to include six law enforcement officers, two prosecuting attorneys, Jennie Wood's father, and Nell Williams, accompanied by her father, mother, and brother.[3]

After announcing that no guns whatsoever would be allowed in the conference room, Chief McDuff asked everyone to disarm. He led the way by placing his own gun on the warden's desk. One by one, the men in the room removed their guns. After Clark Williams stepped forward, his son, Dent, pulled a gun from his waistband and placed it on the warden's desk. Before leaving the warden's office, Clark Williams asked officer W. A. Disheroon to frisk Dent to be certain he was not carrying another pistol. The officer did a thorough search and found no weapon.

As people filed into the fifteen-foot-square room, they squeezed onto benches lining the walls or sat on one of the two single beds. Willie Peterson was seated at the foot of the other bed. He had no one present to represent or support him. Officer Burge sat nearby to guard him.

Solicitor Bailes began the interrogation. In response to every question about the attack on Shades Mountain, Willie Peterson replied, "You have the wrong Negro." After several minutes of questioning, Solicitor Bailes rose to his feet and suggested that all the sheriff's deputies leave the room. Nell Williams wanted to ask some questions, and Solicitor Bailes felt that "clearing the room a bit" might make that process easier for her.

When the deputies left, Nell stared at the prisoner but asked no questions. Solicitor Bailes turned to deputy E. L. Hollums, suggesting he take a turn at examining the suspect. Hollums asked Peterson how many times he had been married and how many children he had fathered. When Peterson replied that he had no children, Nell Williams interrupted and demanded that Peterson tell everyone what he had told her: that he had ten children.

"No, lady," Peterson objected. "I haven't told you anything at all."

Nell moved closer to Peterson and looked him in the eye.

"You are the man."

"No, I ain't, Miss. You've mistaken me for some other Negro."

Nell's father then took a turn, hammering Peterson with questions designed to trick or cajole him into confession. When that proved unsuccessful, assistant solicitor James Long moved his chair closer to Peterson's cot and reminded him they had talked soon after his arrest. Long encouraged the suspect to stand, stretch, and walk a few steps in front of the bed. He hoped Peterson's movement might give Nell a better view and reveal distinguishing physical traits that could be useful information for the trial. Peterson had difficulty standing upright. He walked a few paces on legs that appeared stiff and weak. Long told him to sit again and place his hands on the table.

"What's the matter with that finger?" Long pointed at Peterson's little finger on his right hand. It was severed at the top and shriveled.

"I broke it a long time ago."

Long asked Willie to turn his hands over so everyone in the room could get a better look at the injured finger. He especially wanted Nell to see it in case that might shake loose memories of other physical traits of the assailant on the mountain.

When Long resumed his interrogation, Sheriff Hawkins and Chief Deputy Sheriff Smith entered the room for the first time. One of their deputies, Officer Parrish, had been watching the examination through a hallway window and grew concerned that no one from the sheriff's office was present. He called Sheriff Hawkins and encouraged him to come as soon as possible.

"Willie, do you remember me talking to you last week?" Long asked, referring to the interrogation at Kilby Prison.

Peterson stared, blinking, and shook his head.

"There's so many talked to me I don't know."

Long leaned in and raised his voice.

"Well, to make it clear in your mind who I am, I told you that the young lady had pointed you out and said you were the one that killed her sister and that she was going in the courtroom and swear to that and that nothing in your life was ever as important to you as it is now to know where you were from 12 o'clock on the day of the killing until 12 o'clock that night."

"Yes, sir, I remember that."

Long then repeated every detail of that conversation, placing special emphasis on the things that Peterson had failed to remember at Kilby about

August 4, suggesting once again that Peterson had no good alibi. Long did his best to confuse the prisoner with an avalanche of questions and statements but made no progress in coercing a confession.

After a full hour of questioning, chief Fred McDuff sensed the group had grown restless and weary. He was just about to announce that they would bring things to a close when gunshots rang out.

"Lord, have mercy," Willie moaned, folding his arms across his chest.

Dent Williams, standing six feet from the bed, had fired five shots. Three entered Peterson's body—two in the chest and one in his arm. In the chaos that ensued, Chief McDuff grabbed Dent, who willingly surrendered the gun, saying, "I'm not going to do any more. I'm through."

Peterson slumped over on the cot and said softly, "White folks, you are killing an innocent Negro."

No one rushed to stanch the flow of blood, but Deputy Hollums did respond to Dent's request that "somebody catch Mother." When Hollums moved to support Mrs. Williams, thinking she might faint, she said, "I am all right."

Convinced that Peterson was about to expire, Assistant Solicitor Long decided to increase the intensity of his interrogation. In sworn testimony, Sheriff Hawkins would later refer to Long's behavior as "the worst grilling [he] ever heard." Hoping to use the fear of God and imminent heaven as a means of coercing a confession, Long leaned over Peterson, who was now lying on his side.

"You are dying, Willie. You can't die with a lie on your lips," Long bellowed. "I am awfully sorry this has happened, but you deserve to die. You murdered two women."

"No, sir, I didn't," Peterson protested. "I want to talk with my wife."

Saying there was not time to fetch her, Long promised he would personally deliver Peterson's message to his wife.

"Tell her to meet me in heaven," Peterson whispered.

Feigning misapprehension, Long reiterated the request: "Tell her you wronged her? Tell her you killed those white women?"

"No sir," Peterson said.

The bloodstains on Peterson's shirt grew more visible. He drew his legs up in a fetal position to lessen the pain. Assistant Solicitor Long knew that Henrietta Peterson had told law enforcement officials that her husband was impotent. Four years of battling tuberculosis had left him lethargic and weak. Moving closer to Peterson, he demanded to know how long it had been since he had intercourse and how often he had intercourse with white women. When Peterson insisted that "black men are for black women and white women are for white men," Long changed the subject to Peterson's preacher in the hopes of setting a different trap.

Nell Williams had told investigators that the assailant, during his diatribes on the mountain, had spoken with appreciation about Brother Bryan, a well-known preacher in Birmingham. Long asked Peterson if he wanted to see his preacher, hoping he would mention Brother Bryan. Peterson exclaimed, "Yes, sir, get my preacher, Rev. Matthews."

Reiterating that Peterson would be dead before the preacher could get there, Long asked what message he should give Rev. Matthews.

"Tell him to keep on preaching the word," said Peterson.

"What word?" Long asked.

"The word of God."

Pretending not to hear, Long continued, "Tell him to keep preaching that Negroes are better than white folks?"

"No, sir, no, sir, that is wrong." Peterson was lying on his side, doubled up, holding his stomach.

Clark Williams interrupted, reaching over the table and motioning to Willie: "Look at me, boy, look at me. One of these women you killed told you she had a father and he was a good man."

"Captain," Peterson said, looking up at Williams, "I haven't killed anybody."

"I am the girl's father and I am a good man," said Williams. "I tell you, you can't afford to die without telling the truth. You did kill my daughter, didn't you?"

"No, sir, I didn't kill her," Peterson uttered one last time before the ambulance arrived.

As Peterson was taken out on a stretcher, Nell Williams approached Assistant Solicitor Long, saying she knew that "the Negro" would never confess before dying.

"I would know him in sixteen hundred people," she declared. "He lied."

Dent was right behind Nell, asking if he could get a bond. His father joined in, insisting he did not want his boy to spend the night in jail.

"Can't we fix a bond for him?" Clark Williams asked.

"You might, Clark," Long replied. "I have no charge against him."

Dent Williams went home to sleep in his own bed that night. Willie Peterson was taken, bleeding profusely, to Hillman Hospital, where he was not expected to live.

In the corridor outside the interrogation room, Chief McDuff informed Assistant Solicitor Long that Sheriff Hawkins had called the governor and asked him to deploy the National Guard to surround the hospital and protect Peterson.

"It looks to me, Fred, like they better call out the United States Army!" Long rocked back on his heels and laughed. "It's a hell of a come-off that a Negro can't get protection in a county jail when you've got the chief of police, the sheriff, and other officers in the room."

"Well, there is many a man that would go in and cut that Negro's throat if he could," McDuff replied.

Long leaned in again and shook his head: "That Negro ain't no more guilty than I am."[4]

Chief McDuff was clearly out of sorts and more than a little worried that he might come under fire for allowing this conference to take place when it was rumored that Dent Williams was not to be trusted. McDuff and Hawkins had taken special precautions to protect the prisoner after his arrest—to no avail. Should Peterson miraculously survive his wounds, things might only get worse. McDuff felt certain there were more than enough white citizens in Birmingham who would relish the thought of taking him from his hospital bed and hanging him in the public square.

McDuff's fears were not groundless. That night, crowds estimated between 1,200 and 1,600 people filled the streets around Hillman Hospital. County and city police guarded the entrances to the hospital and blocked traffic from the nearest streets. Brigadier general John C. Persons, commander of the 167th Infantry of the Alabama National Guard, readied fifty guardsmen at the headquarters on Third Avenue. Another fifty-six men were assembled at the cavalry headquarters at Roberts Field in case additional support proved necessary. The weekend passed without incident, but Willie Peterson lay near death at Hillman, and attending physicians were pessimistic about his recovery.[5]

When news broke of Dent Williams's attempt to murder Willie Peterson, it was Jefferson County sheriff James F. Hawkins who bore the brunt of criticism because the conference took place at the county jail. Having learned there was a movement afoot to impeach Sheriff Hawkins for neglect of duty, the governor dispatched attorney general Thomas Knight to make a thorough investigation. Sheriff Hawkins told the press that the decision to bring Peterson back to Birmingham had been Chief McDuff's, not his.[6]

Dr. D. J. Coyle examined Peterson at Hillman Hospital on Sunday, October 4. He reported that the patient was showing no signs yet of recovery and was in "very critical" condition.

"One wound was in his left forearm," Coyle told the press, "but the more serious wound was abdominal. The bullet penetrated his lower chest, went downward and outward and ruptured his liver among other abdominal injuries."[7]

Peterson had not lost consciousness, so Solicitor Bailes stopped to see him on Sunday. In their brief conversation, Bailes reiterated the question Assistant Solicitor Long had asked two days before while Peterson lay bleeding on the cot in the county jail.

"If you thought you were going to die would you want to say anything?"

"Nothing except that I am an innocent man," Peterson replied.

"A Dangerous Frame of Mind"

Clark Williams wasted no time making a case for Dent's defense in the court of public opinion. While doctors worked around the clock to save Willie Peterson, reporters were invited to the Williams home to hear a detailed, emotionally charged description of Dent's state of mind at the time of the shooting. The Birmingham papers were happy to play into his hand. It was the kind of story their white readers devoured.[8]

"Since boyhood, Dent has been his sisters' protector," Clark Williams told reporters. "They thought he could whip anything alive."

Describing how Dent had worked himself into a "dangerous frame of mind," Clark Williams said he had tried his hardest to withhold from Dent the whole story of what transpired on Shades Mountain. According to Williams, Nell had heard Augusta praying while they were held captive. She implored God "to send Dent—her hero and protector—down the lane to her rescue." Williams told reporters that he could not bear to tell Dent about this prayer for two weeks after the murders. When at last he revealed how Augusta had "appealed to Divine Providence," pleading that her brother be sent, Williams said his son's body seemed to quiver, and the next day "he began a plight of personal vengeance."[9]

With breathtaking brevity, the *Birmingham Post* reported, "Dent Williams went into many sections of the state, searching for the Negro." Apparently, this revelation did not cause the reporter to wonder whether Dent's thirst for revenge might provide clues to the recent spike in deaths among black men. Instead, the reporter focused on the pain and suffering of the Williams family. Quoting Clark Williams, the article noted that Dent's disappearance and determination caused additional anxiety for his "prostrated mother."

"While he was out at night looking for the slayer of his sister," Clark Williams said, "naturally we lived in fear for his life and safety. Several times, he has gone without food and sleep for days."[10]

With the headline "Father Says Shot Fired in Answer to a Prayer," the *Birmingham Post* likened Dent's violent attack in the county jail to honor killing. A photo of Dent and Nell Williams accompanied the article with a cutline explaining that the picture had been taken in happier years before tragedy struck the Williams family, tragedy that culminated in Dent's shooting of Willie Peterson. The last few words of the byline read, "After the shooting, Dent made his way to Nell and embraced her."

The *Birmingham News* reported that Clark and Helen Williams were so concerned about their son's state of mind that they tried "to elude" him when they were departing for the jailhouse on October 2, but Dent discovered that Peterson was in town and insisted on being present for the interrogation. Clark told reporters that he and his wife had insisted that officers frisk their son for weapons, not once but twice.[11]

In an editorial that appeared a week later in the *Birmingham Post*, the call to impeach Sheriff Hawkins for failure to protect a prisoner in his charge was dismissed as "grossly unfair and unjustified." In defense of the sheriff, the editorial explained that Clark Williams, a longtime neighbor and friend of Hawkins, had given the sheriff his word that neither he nor his son would do anything to harm the prisoner.[12]

So Many Unanswered Questions

In stark contrast to the *Post*'s sympathetic portrait of Dent Williams, black newspapers asked probing questions about Williams's motives for the shooting and why no one was being held accountable for having placed Willie Peterson in such jeopardy. The October 17 edition of the *Pittsburgh Courier* ran this headline: "WAS VICTIM SHOT TO SEAL HIS LIPS? Birmingham Affair Cloaked in Mystery . . . Many Angles in Case Unexplained."[13]

The *Courier* noted that the manhunt came to an abrupt halt when Nell Williams identified Willie Peterson as the lone black killer of Nell's sister Augusta and her friend Jennie Wood. From that moment on, the police dismissed as "rumor" the story "that an outraged white woman had traced an erring husband up the same road the young women had decided to travel to catch the cooling breezes of a hot August afternoon." The *Courier* reported that "colored men and women" abruptly lost their jobs if they repeated stories told by their white employers; they were warned in no uncertain terms "that they must cast no aspersions on the virtue and veracity of the young white women involved."

Even prior to Peterson's arrest, law enforcement officials failed to follow up on leads in the case if they did not align with Nell Williams's story. In their initial investigation of the crime scene, police found cigarette butts, paper plates, and remnants of a campfire. *The Birmingham News* reported those discoveries the day after the shootings.[14] From that time forward, however, no mention was made of those items by white reporters or police investigators.

Black papers like the *Pittsburgh Courier* questioned why authorities failed to ask whether a party might have taken place the night of August 4. More disturbing still, why had the police failed to disclose that they had gathered fingerprints from Jennie Wood's car? There were so many unanswered questions about the police investigations. How could 250 men with bloodhounds fail to discover one shred of plausible evidence on the mountain? How could the sole footprint found be summarily described as "the Negro's footprint"? Had fingerprints been taken? If so, did they match Willie Peterson's? According to the black press, everything—including Dent's attempted assassination—pointed to a cover-up aimed at protecting the reputation and social status of the three white women attacked on Shades Mountain.[15]

Miraculously, Willie Peterson survived the shooting. When he regained consciousness, he was heard to whisper, "I didn't kill the girls."[16]

seven

GRAND JURY TESTIMONIES

On Wednesday, October 7, 1931, a grand jury was convened with the dual purpose of hearing testimony about the shooting of Willie Peterson and about the slaying of Augusta Williams and Jennie Wood. Nell Williams appeared before the grand jury to give an account of what occurred on Shades Mountain.[1] The story that Nell told that day was, in some respects, different from the one she told on the night of August 4, after the shooting.

Nell told the grand jury that she and her sister Augusta, along with their friend Jennie Wood, had gone for a ride up Shades Mountain after seeing an afternoon matinee in downtown Birmingham. At about 5:30 in the afternoon, the three women climbed large rocks to enjoy the spectacular view of the valley below. When they returned to their car and began to head back to Redmont, "a Negro" approached the car from the south, jumped onto the running board on the passenger side, and pointed a gun at them. Demanding they stop or he would shoot them, he entered the rear door of the car and ordered Jennie to drive to the woods. Jennie asked what he wanted and he replied, "I want your money."

Jennie drove a little way into the woods and stopped the car. The women emptied their handbags and pockets and gave him a total of two dollars and fourteen cents. Then he asked their age, and, when they pretended to be schoolgirls, his mood softened. He announced he would let them go if they drove a little farther and turned around.

"He was perfectly friendly," Nell explained. "He helped Jennie get the car turned around and then said, 'Stop and I will get out here.' But he didn't move."

When Jennie reminded him that he said he would get out, he grabbed the keys to the car and demanded Nell get in the backseat so he could sit in front.

"I have never let a white woman go," he said, "and I will not let you go before one of you goes with me."

Nell said that all three women were resolute in their refusal to go with him.

"Then none of you are going home," he said. "The last woman I attacked said she wouldn't tell, and she had a whole mob after me."

Nell described to the grand jury how he kept lecturing them, saying it was foolish for them to look down on him simply because of his skin color.

"He told us, 'I am just as good as you are. White men have done worse than this and get by with it.' We didn't say anything, but we were perfectly disgusted, of course."

Nell and Augusta said that their father was a preacher, hoping that would dissuade him.

"That's nothing," he replied. "My father is supposed to be a preacher. They are all hypocrites anyway. Brother Bryan is the only good man in Birmingham."

When it was dark, he removed the backseat of the car.

"One of you get out and lay on this," he demanded. The women didn't move. He reached over the seat and threw open the back door, yelling for one of them to get out and lie on the seat cushion. Again they refused.

"All right, I will shoot all three of you," he shouted, starting to exit the car.

Nell and Augusta jumped him, trying to wrestle the gun away. He fired twice in rapid succession, and Augusta fell to the ground beside him. During the struggle, Jennie got out of the car and was coming around the front. He pointed the gun at her and asked, "Are you going to do what I said or am I going to shoot you, too?"

Nell paused. "Must I go on?" she asked.

"Just tell it all," Solicitor Bailes responded.

With difficulty, Nell continued, explaining that Jennie went with the assailant because she wanted to get Augusta to the hospital.

"I got up and started toward her," Nell said, her voice shaking. "He saw me coming and shot again, and I fell down like I was dead." Nell surmised that the bullet fired at her must have been the shot that punctured the tire of Jennie's car.

"I saw that Jennie was going to fight," Nell told the grand jury, crying, "and the only thing I could do was to lay and pretend that I was dead. . . . I heard Jennie ask, 'Are you through?' He said, 'Yes,' so she walked to the car and was about to get in when he shot her. She fell right beside Augusta."

Just before the man turned to leave the scene, he fired a "parting shot" at Nell that struck her arm.

"We lay there until we thought he was out of hearing," Nell continued. "And I said, 'Augusta, are you dead?' and she said, 'No,' and I said, 'Jennie, are you dead?' and she says, 'No, but I can't feel anything. I am paralyzed.'"

Nell tried to lift the two women into the car, but she could not use her right arm because the bullet was lodged in it. Concluding she had no choice, she had to leave the two women bleeding on the mountain as she drove to Mountain Brook in search of help.

The description of the assailant Nell gave the grand jury was, in several respects, different from the description she had given law enforcement officers the night of the attack and the following morning. Initially, officer C. A. Nollner of the Mountain Brook police had asked Nell if the man was wearing a hat. "No," she told him, "I saw no hat."[2] In her grand jury testimony two months later, Nell not only remembered a hat, she recalled it in vivid detail: "He was wearing a gray felt hat pulled up in a point and turned up in the back. . . . Sometimes he would pull it back and scratch his head."

On the night of the attack, Nell told Officer Nollner that "the Negro" was "black," with long hair that he kept brushing back with his hand. When the grand jury prosecutors later asked about his hair, Nell said that she had not paid much attention to his hair except that he would pull his hat back and scratch his head from time to time.[3]

Nell also told Officer Nollner that the man could have been a Northerner because he did not talk like the black people in Birmingham, and he seemed well educated. Her speculation that the assailant could have been a well-educated Northerner was reported in all the white Birmingham newspapers on August 5, fueling rumors that he was a communist.

At the grand jury hearing, when asked if the man talked "just like an ordinary Negro," Nell responded, "Yes, sir, I knew he was a Southern Negro."

"Didn't talk like an educated Negro?"

"Oh, no, sir."

"Say anything about communism?"

"No, sir, except the Negroes being as good as the whites."

The night of the attack, while Nell lay in the operating room at St. Vincent's Hospital, she told the attending doctors and nurses that she was driving the car as they made their way up Shades Mountain earlier that afternoon. She also said that "the Negro" had jumped on the running board as they were passing a bridge and ordered them to drive a mile and a half down Cherokee Road onto Leeds Highway before forcing them to turn into the wooded area where the attack occurred.[4]

To the grand jury, Nell gave a very different account of when and where the assailant jumped onto the running board of Jennie's car. In that account, Nell, Augusta, and Jennie had just returned to the car after sitting atop boulders by Leeds Highway. Jennie was at the wheel, backing away from the spot where they parked near the boulders. She had the car in low gear when "the Negro" came "from the right," jumped on the running board, pointed his gun inside the car, and ordered them to drive to a little road that led into the woods, about a hundred yards from the rocks.

Nell's grand jury testimony was also at odds with what Chief McDuff remembered from interviewing her at the hospital the morning after the attack. According to McDuff, she had said "the Negro" was five feet nine or ten inches in height, black in color, and clean-shaven with no moustache. His face was broad at the temples and thin at the chin, and he had long eyelashes curled up at the ends.[5]

In her grand jury testimony, Nell chose not to describe the assailant by way of height, color, eyelashes, or other distinguishing features, and prosecutors did not ask follow-up questions about his physical appearance. It could be those physical details had become blurred for Nell with the passage of time. It is also possible that she did not want to draw attention to the fact that the man she ultimately identified as the assailant did not bear those physical characteristics. Willie Peterson was light skinned, did not have a broad temple or narrow chin, and had worn a moustache for years. His eyelashes were not unusually long or curled, and he was at least three to four inches shorter than the man Nell described.

The State of Alabama v. Dent Williams

In the case of the *State of Alabama v. Dent Williams*, the grand jury heard testimonies from fifteen individuals who were present the day Dent Williams fired five shots at Willie Peterson. The issues at stake had to do with premeditation and whether Dent Williams acted alone or had an accomplice. Considering how many witnesses were present at the time of the shooting, there was no question that Dent Williams was the person who fired bullets at Willie Peterson. The questions asked of the grand jury witnesses had to do with whose gun Dent used in the shooting, when he took possession of it, and whether someone gave it to him.

Several grand jury witnesses testified that all the men were ordered to surrender their guns to the warden before the interrogation got underway at the Jefferson County Jail on October 2. After Dent Williams placed a little derringer on the warden's desk, Clark Williams pulled Deputy Sheriff Disheroon aside and asked him to frisk Dent. He wanted to be certain his son was not hiding another gun. Disheroon thoroughly searched him and found nothing but a wallet. No one asked Nell Williams or her mother to surrender guns that day.[6]

Chief McDuff testified that he was approximately six feet from Dent when the shooting started. Just prior to hearing the shots fired, McDuff remembered that Dent was standing very close to Nell, and the two seemed to be conferring. Dent fired in such rapid succession that McDuff could not get to him before five bullets had been discharged. McDuff grabbed Dent's arm and kept hold of him even after Dent handed him the gun. He feared Dent might pull a knife and try to finish Peterson off by slitting his throat. Solicitor Bailes came from the other side, grabbed Dent's right arm, and pushed him out the door. McDuff said Dent evidenced no regret. The only thing that seemed to worry him was whether he would have to spend the night in jail.[7]

Officer E. L. Hollums said that Dent had seemed for some time like "he wasn't alright" and could not be trusted. If the opportunity presented itself,

Hollums feared Dent would try to kill Peterson. When asked why Dent was allowed to go into the cell, Hollums replied, "We figured he didn't have any pistol; it was just to satisfy the family."[8]

Clark Williams testified that a friend had given Nell a nickel-plated 32-caliber revolver after the attack on Shades Mountain and told her to carry it with her always. She often kept it in the glove compartment of the car. Clark Williams felt certain his son had pulled that revolver from the glove compartment that day when no one was watching and concealed it under his clothing.[9]

Chief deputy sheriff R. E. Smith and several other officers had a different theory about where Dent got the gun. They believed Nell slipped her gun to Dent while they were standing close together in the crowded room. Smith remembered that Nell was wearing a dark dress "with a kind of coat effect" in which she could easily have hidden a gun.[10] Deputy sheriff W. M. Burge testified that Dent was standing near his sister. She reached over and whispered something to him just before the shots rang out. Burge could not hear what Nell whispered or see the gun, but he suspected Nell handed it to her brother.[11]

Deputy Orville Haynes confirmed that theory. He was standing in the hall outside the room and could see the interrogation through a window. Nell, Dent, and Mrs. Williams were sitting together on a bench. Dent and Nell stood up while the interrogation was winding down. Haynes thought they were getting ready to leave when Nell came and stood very close to Dent. She opened her coat and whispered in his ear. Next thing Haynes knew, there was gunfire. He strongly suspected Nell had been carrying the gun under her coat.[12]

When Haynes was asked if he had ever heard Dent Williams threaten to kill Peterson, he told the grand jury that Dent had made a threat that very day:

Q: What was said?
A: [Dent Williams] asked when the negro would be brought back for trial.

Q: When was that?
A: Over in front of the H & M Bonding Co. and he tried to get me to tell him the negro was in town.

Q: What did he then say?
A: Just said they were going to bring him back, he understood, for the preliminary, and I understood he waived the preliminary, and I didn't think he was in town and didn't think they would bring him back. . . .

Q: How did he say he was going to kill him?

A: He said he would kill him if he had to get him in the courtroom.[13]

When Solicitor Bailes asked Haynes why he failed to report the threat, Haynes said he did not know that they had brought Peterson back for questioning.

Sheriff Hawkins was the last person to testify before the grand jury. He had come into the October 2 interrogation just a few minutes before the shooting began. When the shots rang out, he was conferring with Assistant Solicitor Long. Because Peterson did not collapse immediately, Hawkins thought at first that someone was firing blank cartridges to scare the prisoner. He did not see anyone pass a gun to Dent because he was focused on his conversation with Long.

Hawkins testified that Dent Williams had come to his office an hour before the grand jury hearing got underway. "I am sorry that my acts have caused you any trouble," Dent told Hawkins, "and anything I can do for you now I want to do it." When asked if Dent expressed remorse for having shot Peterson, Hawkins said he had not; he was only sorry for the inconvenience he had caused Hawkins.[14]

ILD Offers to Defend Willie Peterson

On October 9, the grand jury issued two indictments. Willie Peterson was charged with the murders of Augusta Williams and Jennie Wood. The charge against Dent Williams was assault with the intent to murder in the shooting of Willie Peterson. Nell Williams was not named as an accomplice. Sheriff Hawkins was absolved of any wrongdoing in the jailhouse shooting.

Soon after the indictment, an ILD representative approached Henrietta Peterson and offered to represent her husband. He assured her they had already secured the services of Rosenthal and Rosenthal, an outstanding husband-and-wife attorney team from New York, and the ILD would cover all of the legal fees. He also promised that the ILD would do everything in their power to win Willie's freedom and then safely usher him out of the South. They would organize public support nationally and internationally, just as they had done for the Scottsboro defendants. Henrietta Peterson was greatly relieved, considering her husband was on disability, and she earned a minimal salary as a domestic worker. With gratitude and the first glimmer of hope, Henrietta signed the ILD retainer.[15]

True to their word, ILD officials working in tandem with the Rosenthals began to organize support committees in Birmingham and Chattanooga, Tennessee. They set about gathering evidence, talking with prospective witnesses, and raising funds for Peterson's defense. They issued hundreds of leaflets in the black communities of Birmingham and Chattanooga informing residents that a new case resembling Scottsboro required their support and active involvement.[16]

One of the local members of Birmingham's Communist Party who joined the effort to free Willie Peterson was a new recruit to the party who had quickly gained the attention and trust of ILD leaders. Hosea Hudson was a tall, thin black man in his mid-twenties who worked as an iron molder in the Stockham Pipe and Fitting Company. On September 13, ten days before Willie Peterson was arrested, Hudson attended his first Communist Party meeting at the urging of a former coworker. Impressed by the party's defense of the "Scottsboro Boys" and its uncompromising advocacy for worker justice, Hudson joined the party before the night was out and was appointed unit leader at Stockham.[17]

As unit leader, Hudson recruited new members and organized workers to press for demands from company bosses, including an eight-hour workday, safer working conditions, and the abolition of Stockham's piece-rate pay system. The unit's first issue of the *Red Stockham Worker* newsletter, published in November 1931, ran an article titled "Free Willie Peterson." Hudson and his comrades charged that Peterson's arrest and Dent Williams's attempted homicide sought to divert attention away from rumors that the women were killed at a "society" party on Shades Mountain. The newsletter encouraged Stockham workers to support "Peterson Defense Committees" and demand his immediate release.[18]

Communist organizers like Hosea Hudson spoke of the violence perpetrated by law enforcement and vigilantes as "legal lynching." They criticized the NAACP and CIC for failing to boldly condemn these lynchings and for cooperating with officials who carried out raids on the black community. The ILD was especially harsh in its condemnation of individuals and organizations in the black community that contributed to the Reward Fund and went to the police with names of possible suspects in the hope of receiving the reward money.[19] According to the *Southern Worker*, Willie Peterson's arrest was a "frame up" designed to terrorize the black working community.

"Willie Peterson, tubercular miner, now lying in the hospital suffering from bullet wounds inflicted upon him by a white lyncher, is to be placed on trial on a murder charge. . . . The Birmingham legal lynching gang, that is to say the police, the courts and all the 'law enforcing' machinery are preparing to stage a legal lynching of the Negro worker as part of their campaign of terror against the entire Negro working class population of Birmingham."[20]

eight

THE NAACP COMES TO LIFE

After seeing patients all day, Dr. Charles A. J. McPherson had wanted to come home, put his feet up, and read the newspaper. But that would have to wait. He had to write Walter White that night. He did not want someone else to break this urgent news to the executive secretary of the NAACP. That was his job. Walter White needed to know that Nell Williams's brother, Dent, had tried to kill Willie Peterson in the jailhouse and National Guard troops had to surround Hillman Hospital to keep the white mob at bay. The city once again felt like a tinderbox waiting for a match to be thrown. Tensions were back to the level they had been right after the shooting on Shades Mountain in early August.

Charles McPherson had been scrupulously writing reports to the national offices of the NAACP for years as secretary of the Birmingham branch, an office he assumed in 1921, two years after he moved to Birmingham to start his private practice as one of the few black physicians in the city.[1] Just one week earlier, he had written a lengthy report to Walter White, giving him the blow-by-blow account of how an emaciated tubercular black man had his life abruptly upended when Nell Williams pointed at him and said, "That's the man who attacked us on Shades Mountain."

As soon as he had heard about the arrest, McPherson smelled a frame-up and vowed to do everything in his power to secure adequate legal representation for Peterson. He knew it would be an uphill battle. He feared that Birmingham's lawyers would be reluctant to defend a black man accused of such a heinous crime. Branch funds were limited, especially with the Depression bearing down, and NAACP membership in Birmingham had been declining for years. When Charles McPherson was elected branch secretary ten years earlier, Birmingham was a flourishing chapter with 975 members on the rolls. Today, October 4, 1931, there were only six dues-paying members.[2]

McPherson was convinced that the decline in membership was directly attributable to the Ku Klux Klan's resurgence in the 1920s. Klan violence, coupled with the brutality of the Birmingham police, terrorized the black community.[3] McPherson believed that many members had distanced themselves from the NAACP because they wanted to assume a lower profile in the community. Other members let it be known they were leaving for the opposite reason. They wanted the NAACP to assume a higher profile in Birmingham and adopt a more confrontational style in challenging overt acts of racial discrimination. The branch had gotten off on the right foot, those critics argued, when it organized a parade in 1919 to welcome black soldiers returning from World War I.[4] But they felt that early boldness had faded with time as NAACP leaders seemed more concerned about alienating sympathetic white people than meeting the needs of Birmingham's black community.[5]

The exodus of members left Dr. McPherson to function as president, secretary, and treasurer in the latter half of the 1920s. He had worked hard to keep the organization afloat. Although often tired and dispirited, he could not let the branch go under.[6] McPherson had been a fervent and devoted member of the NAACP since 1910. Just months after the national organization was launched, he had attended a meeting in New York City called to introduce the NAACP to the public. McPherson was mesmerized that night by the passionate and erudite oratory of founding luminaries like Professor W. E. B. DuBois, the first African American to be awarded a Ph.D. at Harvard University. McPherson was also deeply impressed by the NAACP's ambitious goals to outlaw lynching and combat discrimination in housing, education, and the judicial system.[7]

Eleven years later, he still believed in those goals. Birmingham's black community needed the NAACP now more than ever, and the plight of Willie Peterson was proof of that need. McPherson rubbed his eyes, took a deep breath, and continued typing. He told Walter White that Willie Peterson was in critical condition, but still hanging on. The enclosed newspaper clippings reported that Peterson declared his innocence as he lay bleeding on the jailhouse cot. Rumors of all kinds were flying around town. Some said Sheriff Hawkins would be impeached. The most persistent rumor within the black community was that those white women did not want people to know why they were up on Shades Mountain or what actually happened that night. People were angry about the violence that the police and vigilantes had unleashed, but so far there were no organized protests.

McPherson was very worried that the communists might step in and take charge of Peterson's defense, the way they had with the "Scottsboro Boys." Some people were saying that Willie Peterson's wife, Henrietta, had already retained lawyers. McPherson hoped they were not communist-backed attorneys. He promised to investigate the matter and then ended his letter:

> Should anything develop I will reach you by telephone, as you suggested, and in the meantime keep you informed by letter and newspaper clippings. I am,

> Yours very sincerely,

> Charles A. J. McPherson, M.D.[8]

A Wake-Up Call for the NAACP

In early October 1931, Walter White was still under fire from NAACP members in different parts of the country for his failure to organize a campaign for the Scottsboro defendants. He had been appointed executive secretary of the national NAACP just one month before the young men were arrested. He came into office having played a leading role in the NAACP's antilynching campaign. As a light-skinned black man with blue eyes, he was able to cross the color line and pass as an undercover investigator who gained access to local citizens, white and black, where lynchings had taken place.[9] In his first month as national secretary, he had hesitated to assist in the Scottsboro campaign. In the meantime, the International Labor Defense (ILD), the legal arm of the American Communist Party, launched a nationwide campaign protesting the "legal lynching" of the nine young men.[10]

Criticism of the NAACP's slow response began pouring into the national office. When it reached a boiling point, White decided to intervene. He contacted his branch officials in Chattanooga and Birmingham, visited the Scottsboro defendants in Kilby Prison, and sought to retain counsel for them. By the time he intervened, the ILD was viewed in the mainstream press as the central organization championing the case. In December 1931, the ILD had gained authorization from the parents and defendants to move forward with the appeal process for all nine defendants. This was a bitter defeat for Walter White and the NAACP. Through the deft and daring campaign led by the ILD, the Scottsboro case gained national and international attention.

The black press was merciless in its criticism of White's failure to act more swiftly and decisively. Black editors expressed their suspicion that he only got involved out of fear that the ILD would gain favor among black people in the South. The editor of the *Washington World*, Eugene Davidson, declared, "If [the NAACP] now feels that fighting the spread of communism is more important than fighting white Southerners who will lynch, massacre and slaughter and expect to get away with it," then "it has outlived its usefulness."[11]

The Scottsboro case proved to be a wake-up call for the NAACP and Walter White. As the Communist Party gained substantial numbers of both admirers and adherents, the NAACP experienced significant decline in membership and near bankruptcy at the dawn of the Great Depression.[12] At the urging of Charles Hamilton Houston, vice dean of Howard University Law School, White began to pay more attention to so-called legal lynchings, where black people were accused of significant crimes on the basis of flimsy evidence, tried without adequate representation, and sentenced to death. The case of Willie Peterson was a prime example. Both the Birmingham branch and the national leadership of the NAACP resolved to organize a campaign for Peterson, hoping to prove that they, too, could win freedom for a black man that many believed was not guilty as charged.[13]

New Lawyers for Peterson

Despite this resolve, history threatened to repeat itself when Charles McPherson discovered that Henrietta Peterson had already turned to the ILD for legal assistance. After getting wind of this, McPherson paid her a visit on October 24. Her husband was still recuperating from gunshot wounds at Hillman Hospital. Henrietta was staying with her mother so she could be closer to the hospital.

Two local white attorneys, J. R. Johnson and J. T. Roach, had approached Mrs. Peterson, saying they were convinced of her husband's innocence and wanted to represent him. She told McPherson that she did not trust them any more than she trusted other Southern white lawyers. They were asking $1,000 and she felt they were interested purely in the money. The ILD representative, on the other hand, had promised to protect her husband, cover all the legal fees, and organize public support.[14]

Charles McPherson warned Henrietta Peterson that the people associated with the ILD were considered "Reds" from Russia and she would be courting trouble by publicly associating with them. In an already prejudiced environment, that would only work to her husband's disadvantage. Furthermore, the fact that her lawyers were Jewish would mean that jurors would be doubly prejudiced against them. If she wished "to get the support of the best colored people and white people in Birmingham," she would need to terminate the services of these communist lawyers.

"You see Mrs. Peterson, the newspapers came out saying that your husband was a 'Red.' They said that your husband was an agitator. Now you allow them to take the case, they will say that proves it."[15]

As evidence of the many ways the ILD alienated whites and "the best colored people," McPherson showed Mrs. Peterson a pamphlet that the ILD was distributing throughout the city, hoping she would find its language provocative and inflammatory.

"That kind of literature will make the white people in Birmingham mad," Charles McPherson advised. "They may go to the hospital and lynch him and we don't want that to happen. . . . You may be railroading your husband to the electric chair if you follow them."[16]

McPherson said that unlike the ILD, the NAACP believed in law and order and in giving everyone a fair trial. Had they known she needed a lawyer, they would have been to see her sooner. But now, they stood prepared to help her and her husband. Listening intently to everything McPherson was saying, Henrietta Peterson grew agitated and uncertain.

"I do not know anything about law," she said, beginning to cry. "It just keeps me worry all the time. Just worry me to death." She wiped her eyes and looked away. "I don't know what to do. I am trying to do the best I can for my husband to save him."

McPherson assured Mrs. Peterson that he would take her husband's case to the NAACP for their assistance, but she would have to agree to break off contact with the ILD. Henrietta Peterson was swayed by McPherson's arguments. She terminated the services of Rosenthal and Rosenthal and, with the assistance of the NAACP, retained Johnson and Roach. Through local and national sources, the NAACP was able to raise $2,000 in legal fees.

J. R. Johnson and J. T. Roach were not law partners and most likely had never worked together before joining forces to defend Peterson. The way Roach would later tell it, Johnson had approached him not long after Peterson's arrest, saying he had an opportunity to defend Peterson and was eager to do so on one condition: that Roach come aboard as co-counsel. Considering the severity of the crime, Roach felt he could not agree to work on the case unless he was confident Peterson was innocent, and that would require further investigation. When Johnson returned a couple weeks later and reiterated the invitation, Roach consented, saying he believed Peterson was indeed innocent.[17]

Disagreements began to surface between the men as they worked to prepare the case. They found it difficult to reach accord on the line of defense they should take, and Roach considered withdrawing from their nascent and friction-filled partnership. Because the first trial date was so near at hand, he decided it would be unconscionable to abandon Peterson in this manner. He was also consoled by the fact that Johnson had agreed to let Roach serve as lead counsel.[18]

In early November, attorneys Roach and Johnson issued a public statement urging Birmingham residents to withhold judgment until all the facts of the case could be presented in a court of law. What caused them to take this rather unorthodox measure is open to speculation. They may have wanted to take preemptive action, knowing that an all-white jury would bring an ingrained bias against their black client. They may have been the targets of threats by people who angrily accused them of being "Negro lovers." They might have been capitalizing on the notoriety this case was sure to bring them. Whatever their motivation, Birmingham's black newspaper, the *Birmingham Reporter*, ran their statement:

> We have been employed by Willie Peterson to defend him against the very serious charge of killing two white girls. After giving the matter a thorough investigation we have an abiding faith in the innocence of our

client. We took this case more from a humane standpoint than anything else. We earnestly beg the public to withhold passing judgment until the matter has been heard by a court of justice. We feel sure, regardless of the fact that our client is a Negro, that he will be vindicated of this charge when all facts pertaining to his defense shall have been heard. We are not Negro lovers but we do feel, as many other good citizens of the south feel, that it is just as much our duty to vindicate the innocent as it is to convict the guilty. This certainly should guide us in dealing with the Negro of the south.—ROACH & JOHNSON, 308 Bankers Bond Bldg., City.[19]

"He Bears a Good Name"

In preparing an alibi for their defendant, Roach and Johnson interviewed Willie Peterson's neighbors, family, and fellow church members, as well as former employers and supervisors. In all the stories and information shared, the man who emerged was a far cry from the assailant that Nell Williams and Jennie Wood described in the wake of the attack. Everyone who knew Peterson consistently named him as kind, soft-spoken, self-effacing, and affable. As his uncle-in-law, Lee Beamon, put it, "[Willie] bears a good name in this country. . . . I never knew him to carry a short-gun or speak of doing anything harmful to anybody."[20]

Peterson was born in south Alabama near Troy and moved to Birmingham in 1920 seeking work in the mines. Before contracting tuberculosis, Peterson had worked steadily in the Valley View, Ruffner, Lewisburg, Virginia, and Sloss One mines. The people for whom he worked described him as a hardworking man who got along well with others on the job. A former supervisor, Oscar L. Cardwell, told Attorney Roach that Peterson had worked two years for him at the Lewisburg Mines until a physician, Dr. Payne, diagnosed him with tuberculosis. Cardwell said Peterson was inclined to be religious and avoided the company of the other miners "when they indulged in telling ruff and smuttie jokes. He was considered by me and also by the white folks and the negroes as one of the best negroes who worked on that job."[21]

His friends and family never knew him to own a gun or threaten to physically harm anyone. Nor was he ever in trouble with the law before being arrested for the murders on Shades Mountain. Willie Peterson was a World War I veteran. While stationed near Fort Dodge in Iowa, he came down with typhoid fever and was given a medical discharge.[22]

He had been married to Henrietta Peterson for five years. They had no children. Two and a half years into their marriage, Willie had to quit work because of his tuberculosis, a weak heart, and high blood pressure. Many days, he would be up and around for only a few hours before having to take to his bed again utterly exhausted. When he was arrested, he was strikingly thin and gaunt, weighing no more than 125 pounds. Henrietta did not want to leave him alone for days on end. She worried about his failing health and feared he might have a bad spell while she was gone. But they depended on her income as a domestic worker, meager as it was, and her employers preferred that she spend several nights a week at their house.

Willie Peterson was devoted to his church and felt a deep kinship with the people who worshipped there. He had been a deacon before becoming chronically ill. New Morning Star Baptist Church was located up the hill and one street over from the house that Willie and Henrietta Peterson rented. Even when he was not feeling well, he would get himself to church most Sundays.[23]

New Morning Star was likely one of the many small black Baptist churches established in Birmingham in the 1920s by poor and working-class black people who had migrated from the Black Belt of Alabama. Churches like New Morning Star served as neighborhood centers and "a shelter in the storm" for black people who suffered daily indignities in Jim Crow Birmingham.[24] Willie Peterson was called "John" or "nigger" on the street, and "boy" or "uncle" in the places he worked. At New Morning Star, he was known as "brother" or "Mr. Peterson," and his leadership abilities were recognized when he was appointed deacon.[25] It was not surprising to those who knew Willie Peterson that he called for two people as he lay bleeding in the Jefferson County Jail—his wife and his pastor.

A Tuscaloosa Barber

After being shot by Dent Williams, Willie Peterson hovered between life and death. While he was still under the care of doctors at Hillman Hospital, two officers and the prosecuting attorneys brought a black man named Henry Wilson to Peterson's hospital room. After getting a good look at the patient, Wilson said, yes, that was indeed the man who had come to his Tuscaloosa barbershop shortly after August 4 and boasted about shooting the white women on Shades Mountain.

News that a black Tuscaloosa barber was the state's key witness spread like wildfire through Birmingham. Peterson's attorneys did not buy Wilson's story. That Willie Peterson would travel an hour to Tuscaloosa to get his hair cut struck them as ludicrous. Most days their client was too sick with tuberculosis to get out of bed. Willie had not left the city of Birmingham in the past year except to make two trips to see physicians in Furman, Alabama, so that he could qualify for VA disability payments.[26] Attorneys Johnson and Roach vowed to get to the bottom of this Tuscaloosa barber story. They hired a white private detective, H. W. Fuller, to investigate Henry Wilson's background and credibility as a witness. Charles McPherson, the NAACP secretary, shared their suspicions and helped raise funds to pay the detective.[27]

On the basis of information supplied by the private detective, Roach and Johnson felt confident they could discredit Henry Wilson's testimony. A black domestic worker in Tuscaloosa informed Detective Fuller that "Henry Wilson" was actually Tom Sheppard, an ex-convict who worked as a dishwasher. He neither owned a barbershop nor worked in one. She explained that Sheppard had accepted a bribe to assume a false identity and lie about meeting Willie Peterson.[28]

During the evening of November 4, Peterson was returned from Hillman Hospital to the Jefferson County Jail, this time in a caravan of five police vehicles containing fifteen officers. His trial was scheduled for December 7. Charles McPherson and Peterson's attorneys sent the detective back to Tuscaloosa to gather more information about "Henry Wilson," so they could prepare an airtight case about his real identity and impeach his testimony during the trial. The detective returned from Tuscaloosa with a significant new piece of information: the alleged bribe came from two white women who had driven to Tuscaloosa by automobile to meet with Wilson and Officer Robinson from the Tuscaloosa force. Their identities were not yet known, but these women were expected to return to Tuscaloosa before the trial was scheduled to begin.[29]

nine

MOUNTING THE DEFENSE

The day of his arraignment, Willie Peterson was brought into the court-room seated in a chair carried by two black trusties and surrounded by twenty-five white deputy sheriffs. He pleaded not guilty to the state's accusation that he had murdered Augusta Williams.[1] That Peterson was only being tried for the murder of Augusta Williams was perhaps attributable to prosecution fears that Jennie Wood's description of the assailant differed significantly from the description given by Nell Williams. Should that discrepancy be revealed in court, it might be difficult to convict Peterson for either murder. Furthermore, Jennie Wood's father, Wade Wood, had come to doubt that Peterson was the assailant, and the prosecution could not present him as a prosecution witness.[2]

The trial got under way Monday, December 7, with Judge J. Russell McElroy presiding.[3] An estimated 1,500–2,000 people showed up to witness the proceedings, but only 150 were allowed entrance. One side of the court-room was reserved for white people; the other side, for black people. As a precaution, Judge McElroy ordered three deputies to search all the men outside the courtroom for weapons. Despite the lingering suspicion that

Dent Williams shot Willie Peterson with a gun hidden in Nell Williams's coat or handbag, Judge McElroy declined to have the women frisked. Everyone who entered the courtroom, however, women as well as men, was searched.[4]

On the second day of the trial, Nell Williams took the witness stand and told the all-white jury much the same story she had told the grand jury. Because Willie Peterson was standing trial for the murder of Augusta Williams and rape was not among the charges, she did not testify that Jennie Wood had been sexually assaulted, and she was not questioned about it. Nell Williams was the principal witness for the prosecution. Her father, Clark Williams, also testified for the prosecution, as did Buck Streit, the Williamses' friend and neighbor who was driving when Nell first identified Willie Peterson as the assailant. After less than three hours of testimony, the state rested its case.[5]

Defense attorneys Roach and Johnson called twenty-eight witnesses to the stand, both white and black. Peterson's alibi rested on three main arguments: (1) On August 4, he was nowhere near Shades Mountain; (2) he was too ill to have perpetrated the crimes described by Nell Williams; and (3) he did not resemble the man whom Nell had described to authorities shortly after the attack. Among those who testified to the third discrepancy were Birmingham's Chief of Police McDuff and officer C. A. Nollner of the Mountain Brook police force. Nollner, who had answered Williams's call for help that night, testified that the description Nell gave on the witness stand was significantly at odds with the description she gave hours after the assault. Among the points of contention were the length of the assailant's hair, the hue of his skin, his height and weight, and the issue of whether he was wearing a hat. On the evening of August 4, Nell said the assailant was hatless. On the witness stand, she insisted that he was wearing a gray felt hat. This gray hat became a critical part of the prosecution's case because it was the only tangible piece of evidence they could produce to corroborate Nell Williams's witness testimony.[6]

Willie Peterson's white former supervisor from the Virginia Mines testified as a character witness. His white physician offered reasons why a man in Peterson's physical condition would not have been able to commandeer a moving vehicle or hold three women hostage. A white cosmetic saleswoman testified that she had seen Peterson in his Woodlawn neighborhood the afternoon of August 4. Her testimony was corroborated by the eyewitness accounts of numerous black residents from Peterson's neighborhood and church who swore they had seen and talked with the defendant on August 4. Even Jennie Wood's father was called as a witness by the defense. They hoped to show that Jennie Wood's description of the assailant differed from the one Nell Williams had given in her testimony. The judge disallowed Wade Wood's testimony, ruling that it was inadmissible hearsay.[7]

Henrietta Peterson was present in the courtroom each day. According to the *Birmingham News*, she had to obtain permission from the attorneys to remain in the courtroom during the trial. At the start and close of each session, she came inside the rail, rubbed Willie's back, and offered quiet encouragement.[8]

Tuesday night, after the court had recessed for the day, Charles McPherson and Peterson's attorneys met with the defense witnesses. Feeling hopeful about the mood in the courtroom and the outcome of the trial, Attorney Johnson announced he would bet any amount of money that Peterson would be acquitted or a mistrial would be announced. He went on to boldly proclaim that 75 percent of the white people in Birmingham did not believe that Peterson committed the crime, 50 percent did not believe a black man committed the crime, and he himself believed that a white person committed the crime.[9]

When the trial got under way Wednesday, the prosecution had not yet put Henry Wilson, the alleged barber from Tuscaloosa, on the stand. Reporters conjectured that the state was withholding his testimony until the rebuttal phase, after the defense rested its case.[10] That same day, Charles McPherson wrote Walter White and shared a bombshell about the white women whom investigators believed instigated the bribe of Henry Wilson: "These two women are believed to be Nell Williams and her mother. Henry Wilson was promised $50, ten of which was paid at the time and the balance was to be paid after Peterson's conviction. These people also told Henry Wilson to get another Negro to swear the same thing and they would give him $25.00."[11]

Peterson's lawyers stood ready to reveal the whole plot if the prosecution put Henry Wilson on the stand. The "other Negro," having turned on Wilson, was willing to testify for the defense and tell how he had been offered a bribe through Wilson. Four other witnesses were prepared to reveal Henry Wilson's real identity and his less than stellar reputation.[12]

Willie Peterson took the stand that afternoon, the fourteenth defense witness of the day. He testified he had never laid eyes on Nell Williams prior to September 23 when he was arrested. He was home all day on August 4 and did not own a gun, and the hat found in his home by police belonged to his brother-in-law.[13]

Johnson and Roach asked Peterson to roll up his pant legs and shirt-sleeves to prove that he was too emaciated and weak to have walked from his home to the crime scene on Shades Mountain as the state had asserted. When the prosecution objected, the court overruled the objection. Solicitor Long then accused the defense of "having the defendant carried around in a chair" as a theatrical device to win the jury's sympathy for Willie Peterson. Defense attorney Johnson made a motion for a mistrial based on this flagrant accusation. When the judge denied the mistrial, he ordered Long's remarks stricken from the record.[14]

Before the close of proceedings Wednesday afternoon, the state presented three rebuttal witnesses, but Henry Wilson was not among them. Wilson was in the state's witness room, but the state closed its case without this much-anticipated witness. The prosecution team may have gotten wind of the defense team's strategy. If the defense possessed sufficient evidence to prove that Nell Williams and her mother had paid both men to lie, this would be disastrous for Nell's already contested credibility.[15]

The prosecution's decision not to put Wilson on the stand meant that Roach and Johnson had to quickly develop a new strategy for exposing the bribery. On Thursday, December 10, Judge McElroy agreed to excuse the jury while Peterson's attorneys sought permission for the unusual act of placing the state's witness, Henry Wilson, on the stand. They wished to have Wilson confirm his signature on a document in their possession stating that he had been hired to testify against Willie Peterson. Defense Attorney Johnson insisted it was not their intent to prove that the state was complicit in the plot to find this witness, but they did seek to show he had been hired to testify. The judge ruled against the defense request and called the jury back into the courtroom for the closing arguments.[16]

In his instructions, Judge McElroy told the jury they had but two choices in a case of this magnitude: acquittal or finding the defendant guilty of murder in the first degree.

After forty-four hours of deliberation, the jury foreman indicated they were ready to return. The jury, he reported, was "hopelessly deadlocked."

Judge McElroy turned to the jury and asked everyone who believed agreement was impossible to please raise his hand. Every juror did so. Judge McElroy declared a mistrial and strictly forbid jurors to discuss the evidence in this case or their opinion as to the defendant's guilt or innocence, warning that to do either could be deleterious to any further proceedings.[17]

The outcome in this case was virtually without precedent. The stunning news swept across the nation. When had an all-white jury failed to convict a black defendant charged with murdering a white woman? For a jury to be "hopelessly deadlocked," at least one of its members had to break rank with a cardinal tenet of Jim Crow white supremacy: if a white woman said, "a negro did it," you must not doubt her word. The inference that Nell Williams was lying, added to the indisputable suffering she had undergone, outraged many in Birmingham's white community.

"The Mystery Will Be Solved"

The black press interpreted a hung jury as an incontestable declaration of innocence. The *Atlanta World* declared, "History was written at the new Jefferson county courthouse."[18] An editorial in the *New York Amsterdam News* announced that even though Willie Peterson was by no means a free man, he had been "vindicated of any complicity in the murder of the two white society girls.... WILLIE PETERSON IS INNOCENT! There would have been no mistrial in his case if there had been the least scintilla of evidence against him."[19]

Standing outside the courthouse at the close of the trial, Attorney Johnson stepped into the limelight and assumed the role of spokesperson with the press. He could not contain his jubilation, and his remarks provoked much speculation in the weeks that followed. Hinting that explosive new evidence would be introduced at the next trial, he declared, "There will no longer be any argument or any doubts as to whether or not my client is innocent. No longer will there be any mystery as to how or why the girls met their death. The mystery will be solved."[20]

It is impossible to know for sure what Attorney Johnson was suggesting when he promised that, next time around, there would be no mystery as to how or why the women met their death. Would Johnson and Roach call Henry Wilson and his accomplice as defense witnesses in the second trial? Or did they have other evidence they planned to introduce to substantiate their unequivocal conviction that the shooter was white? Did they have white witnesses who would be willing to step forward and openly contradict Nell Williams's story about what transpired on the mountain?

The Atlanta-based *Afro-American* conjectured that the shooter was white, not black, and that the defense team, in the next trial, would reveal a cover-up: "It has been suggested that Peterson's lawyers had hoped to free their client without taking the lid off, but that now, with their backs to the wall, they are ready to shoot the works rather than see an innocent man deprived of his life."[21]

The NAACP continued to provide support for the defense team as they prepared their case for the second trial. They did not, however, possess the financial resources to undertake another thorough investigation comparable to the one that exposed Henry Wilson's ersatz identity. The ILD waged an independent campaign to free Willie Peterson, charging that the NAACP and its lawyers were doing an inadequate job. Communist Party workers and volunteers regularly blanketed black neighborhoods with flyers updating the community about the latest developments and setbacks in the Peterson case. Literature from the ILD and word-of-mouth announcements were a primary source of information about the case in poor black communities.[22]

The Second Trial

When Willie Peterson's second trial commenced on January 18, 1932, he had several strikes against him. Charles McPherson and Walter White had hoped to recruit Birmingham attorney Roderick Beddow to join the defense team. Only seven years out of law school, Beddow was already considered one of the foremost criminal lawyers in Alabama.[23] McPherson and White were deeply disappointed to learn that Beddow had agreed to serve as the lead prosecutor in Peterson's second trial and as defense attorney for Dent Williams. The Beddow and Williams families were friends, and Roderick Beddow took both cases as an act of kindness to his friends.

With Roderick Beddow on the prosecution team, the inexperience and ineptitude of Peterson's defense team proved even more glaring. Tensions and disagreements between Johnson and Roach had surfaced during the first trial, and they were accentuated as Johnson seized the lead and faced a formidable team of legal opponents. As Roach would later reveal, Johnson's ineptitude and failure to consult with Roach caused great friction between them. Roach was at times so agitated and embarrassed by Johnson's behavior in the courtroom that he became physically ill. Suffering from severe back pain and mental distress, Roach once again contemplated withdrawing from the case. At one point during the trial, he left the courtroom. At the urging of a friend, he returned for the sake of his client and resolved to do what he could for Willie Peterson.[24]

Beddow and Long employed a good cop/bad cop strategy in cross-examining defense witnesses. Assistant Solicitor Long sought to discredit and intimidate witnesses. He took those tactics as far as he could, and then Beddow stepped in to finish off the assault with a more measured but no less devastating line of questioning.

The selection of Judge H. P. Heflin was also a blow to the defense. Judge Heflin's brother, J. Thomas "Cotton Tom" Heflin, was a notorious former U.S. senator from Alabama, infamous as a vehement proponent of the convict lease system and white supremacy. Cotton Tom Heflin was one of the chief architects of the 1901 Alabama Constitution that barred black Alabamians from voting.[25] When speaking of the Scottsboro case, Cotton Tom made it plain that he hoped all nine defendants would be sentenced to death: "This dallying about with the Scottsboro rapists is a humiliating insult to the white race in Alabama. . . . It was putting wicked thoughts in the minds of lawless negro men and greatly increasing the danger to the white women of Alabama."[26]

The first indication that Judge Heflin might exhibit bias against the defense was his refusal to give a copy of the transcript from the previous trial to Johnson and Roach. He demanded they pay sizeable copying costs that the defense team could not afford. This alone put Johnson and Roach at a great disadvantage. Without a record of testimonies from the first trial, they could not impeach witnesses in the second trial by pointing to discrepancies between their testimonies in the two trials.

Often during the second trial, Judge Heflin seemed to be working in tandem with the state. With one or two exceptions, the court overruled every objection entered by the defense attorneys and sustained every objection made by prosecutors. One of the more egregious examples occurred during opening remarks, when Assistant Solicitor Long declared that the evidence showed "this defendant to be a gorilla in human form." Mr. Johnson objected to this vile language, stating it was the second time prosecutors had referred to the defendant as a "gorilla." The court overruled the objection.[27] Judge Heflin not only refused to sustain defense objections, he frequently failed to rule on them. This meant they were not entered into the court record, which would make an appeal process far more difficult for the defense.[28]

Inadequate funding was another disadvantage for the defense. Much of the money raised prior to the first trial went toward paying the private investigator that unearthed the information about Henry Wilson's false identity and testimony. None of that research ever came to light. Johnson and Roach could have used another investigative team to produce solid evidence backing their theory that the Shades Mountain assailant was white, but they had no pool of funds to draw from.

Furthermore, efforts to raise money in the black community were used by the prosecutors to discredit witnesses for the defense. All black defense witnesses were asked whether they had known about, or contributed to, fund-raising appeals to support Willie Peterson's defense. If they answered positively to one or both questions, Assistant Solicitor Long suggested this proved they were biased witnesses or unwitting tools for communist campaigns.

As the trial progressed, it became apparent that Peterson's lawyers either failed to prepare new elements in their defense or were prevented from introducing them by the prosecution and judge. Their case rested once again on three main legs: (1) Willie Peterson was nowhere near Shades Mountain on August 4; (2) he was too ill to have perpetrated the crimes described by Nell Williams; and (3) Peterson did not resemble the man whom Nell had described to authorities shortly after the attack. Because the prosecution was familiar with this three-pronged alibi, they came to the second trial better prepared to discredit and undermine each of those arguments. For example, during the first trial, the defense had asked Peterson to pull up his pant legs so the jury could see how emaciated he was. In the second trial, when the defense attempted to admit the same exhibit, Assistant Solicitor Long objected, "This is not a bawdy show," and the court upheld his objection.[29]

The prosecution, on the other hand, introduced a significant new element in their case: rape (or "ravishment"). In the first trial, Nell Williams made no mention of sexual assault, although she had named it in her grand jury testimony. Having failed to convict Peterson the first time, the prosecution team decided to bring the sexual assault to light in this trial. Nell Williams testified that the assailant had "ravished" Jennie Wood. The state did not have to prove rape because Peterson was charged with murdering Augusta Williams, but the prosecuting attorneys knew that the mere mention of rape would enrage an all-white male jury.

Dr. Adrian Taylor, Jennie Wood's attending physician, stated in court, "I examined to see if this negro had had sexual intercourse with Miss Wood." He confirmed that sexual intercourse had indeed taken place shortly before she was admitted to the hospital. Having found viable sperm in bloody fluid, he concluded that "there was no question about penetration and the actual ravishing of this young lady."[30]

The defense raised no objection to this testimony. They did not point out that evidence of sexual intercourse did not prove rape. Nor did they object to Dr. Taylor's use of the term "*this* negro"—a direct reference to the black defendant seated in the courtroom. The defense also failed to ask whether the assailant had attempted to assault the other two women. Dr. Taylor testified that he had not examined Nell or Augusta Williams, and no other physicians were called to testify about their examinations.

When Attorney Johnson cross-examined Nell Williams, he noted that the wooded area where the shootings occurred was known to be a place where picnics were held. The state objected to his description as immaterial, and the judge sustained the objection. One other time the defense tried to suggest the area was known to be a gathering place for campfires and parties. The state objected again, and the court sustained the objection. No further mention of picnics, parties, or campfires was ever introduced. The defense may have hoped to suggest that the women were on Shades Mountain that day for reasons other than Nell had stated. If that was their intention, the theory was never fully introduced or developed as plausible.

At the start of the second day of the trial, Attorney Johnson made a motion. It had come to his attention that one of the jurors, H. S. Duggar, was biased against the defendant. He asked permission to subpoena a witness who would testify that Duggar had told him, just days after the first trial, that if he were chosen as a juror in the second trial, he planned to "stick it to" the defendant.[31]

State Prosecutor Beddow reminded the court that on the previous day, when potential jurors were being interviewed, Mr. Duggar admitted that he had expressed previous opinions about the Peterson case. The defense had the option at that time to bar Mr. Duggar from serving on the jury, but they failed to do so. Judge Heflin agreed, and the trial resumed.[32]

As in the first trial, the state asked that the twenty-two-page transcript taken at Kilby Prison be entered as evidence into the trial records. This transcript recorded the interrogation of Peterson by Assistant Solicitor Long, shortly after his arrest, with no defense attorney present. It contained many questions that, unchallenged, could prejudice the jury against the defendant. Once again, the defense attorneys offered no objection to its inclusion in the trial record.

The defense introduced more than a dozen witnesses for the purpose of corroborating Peterson's testimony that he had been at home or in his neighborhood all day and evening on August 4. Assistant Solicitor Long cross-examined most of those witnesses with a belligerent, bullying demeanor. In a white supremacist culture where black people were expected to deferentially look down when responding to a white person, Long more than once shouted at black witnesses, "Look at me when you answer the question," "Look at me when I'm talking to you."[33] Long also sought to discredit the testimony of black witnesses as inherently biased if they had ever heard their pastor pray for Willie Peterson, been asked to donate money for his defense, or laid eyes on any of the ILD flyers distributed in their neighborhoods.

Assistant Solicitor Long did not reserve his intimidating and insulting manner for black witnesses only. When Officer Nollner took the stand, the officer offered testimony about the description Nell Williams gave him the night of August 4. That description differed significantly from the one given earlier in the trial by Nell Williams. The following interchange, initiated by Long, then took place:

LONG: So, you weren't trying to tell the truth were you?
NOLLNER: Do you mean I'm telling a lie?
LONG: That's my judgment.
JOHNSON (attorney for the defendant): We are going to object to
    Mr. Long arguing with the witness, and telling the witness he thinks
    he is lying.
NOLLNER: I don't think I should be insulted on the stand.
LONG: If they don't want it in I am willing for it to go out.

Judge Heflin said he would tell the jury not to pay any attention to this encounter between the witness and Mr. Long, but he never ruled on the objection, and it remained in the record.[34]

The Testimony of Annie Mae Davis

Assistant Solicitor Long interjected prejudicial statements so often the defense attorneys had difficulty staying abreast of them. One of the defense witnesses subjected to the most intensive and sustained cross-examination was Annie Mae Davis.[35] She was a black woman who worked for a white couple, Mr. and Mrs. T. F. Moore, who lived in the Highland Park section of Birmingham. On the afternoon of August 4, she and her employer, Mrs. Moore, drove up Shades Mountain and stopped behind the rocks where Nell, Augusta, and Jennie sat later that day. Mrs. Moore's daughter, Katheryn Morton, was with them and also a black chauffeur named Walter. Annie Mae Davis and Katheryn Morton had gotten out of the car to stretch their legs when Ms. Davis saw "a colored man" standing on the rocks. She remarked to Mrs. Morton, "Miss Kathryn look at that man how he is looking at you." Mrs. Morton suggested they get back in the car and told the chauffeur to drive away.[36]

After learning that an attack had occurred near those rocks on the very same day, Katheryn Morton and Annie Mae Davis went to the police to report what they had seen. Weeks later, after Willie Peterson was arrested and then shot by Dent Williams, Officer Burge of the Birmingham Police Department asked Davis and Morton to meet him at Hillman Hospital to identify the patient. Ms. Davis accompanied Officer Burge to Peterson's room. Mrs. Morton chose to remain in the waiting room.

Shortly thereafter, Davis met with the state's attorneys. Their hopes that she would serve as a key prosecution witness were dashed when she could not confirm that the man she saw lying in the hospital bed was the same man she saw on the rocks. Because Willie Peterson was lying in bed, she could not verify that the two men were of comparable weight and height. One of the attorneys showed Davis a gray hat and asked if it was the same hat the man on the rocks was wearing. She told them she remembered the "colored man" wearing gray overalls and scratching his head while staring at them from the rocks, but she did not see a hat.[37]

Katheryn Morton tried to convince Annie Mae Davis to ignore her doubts and testify that the man on the rocks was Peterson. Davis said she could not with integrity do that. Therefore, when Davis testified at the second trial, she was a witness for the defense. During cross-examination, special prosecutor Roderick Beddow accused her of having been pressured to change her testimony by defense lawyers, members of the black community, and possibly white communists. Davis denied all of that, saying she had been clear with prosecutors and Mrs. Morton that she could not be sure if the man on the rocks was Willie Peterson. She would need to see Peterson standing up and clothed. That way she could judge whether the two black men were comparable in stature.

During redirect examination, the defense asked Peterson to stand for Davis. Looking straight at the defendant, Davis said, "No sir, that isn't the man I saw on the mountain that day." She went on to say that the man on the rocks was much larger and darker than Peterson.[38]

Again, State's Attorney Beddow suggested Davis had been pressured to change her testimony, but she remained firm, contradicting every insinuation that she was mistaken, had acted under pressure, or was lying. Unable to sway Davis, Beddow changed course and asked Davis to confirm that the chauffeur, Walter, had been banished from his church and lodge because he refused to testify for the defense. Defense Attorney Johnson objected. Beddow withdrew the question but asked it again with slight rephrasing: "I will ask you whether or not you were present in a gathering of people in a church that evicted that man [Walter] from his church because he wouldn't come up here and swear this wasn't the negro."

Attorney Johnson again objected with vehemence, saying there was no evidence of any man being thrown out of a church, and even if there were it would have no bearing on this trial. Beddow replied, "We withdraw the question, Judge, temporarily." The judge was silent throughout this interchange.[39]

When Annie Mae Davis described what she observed the afternoon of August 4 as she stood looking at the rocks on Shades Mountain, she testified she saw two other people nearby.

"I saw white people up there. We parked our car and turned around and they were parked off in the woods. To the best of my knowledge it was a blue car, a big one. I am positive it was a big blue car.... There was a man and a lady in that car I saw in the woods. I didn't see but two and they was the two in the car, a lady and a man."[40]

If ever there was an opening for the defense to raise a question about the assailant's racial identity, this was it. But neither Johnson nor Roach asked any follow-up questions to keep the jury's attention on the fact that a white man and woman were in the same vicinity. They did not introduce any questions about the couple, the car they sat in, or whether the black man might have been standing guard for the couple. They did not, for example, note that the car Nell Williams drove down Shades Mountain on the evening of August 4 was Jennie Wood's large blue LaSalle.

Everyone—the prosecution, the defense, the judge, and presumably the jury—was focused on the black man.

Willie Peterson Takes the Stand

On Thursday, the fourth day of the trial, Willie Peterson took the stand and remained there for most of the day. He wore a dark suit and tie, yellow shirt, and tan shoes.[41] He began his testimony by recounting what he could remember of his whereabouts on Tuesday, August 4, the day the three women were attacked on Shades Mountain.[42]

He said that he was home alone that day. His wife, Henrietta, was working a three-day stint at her white employer's home, four miles northeast of where she and Willie lived. Midafternoon on August 4, Willie took a half gallon bucket and headed to Mattie Suttle's home about three blocks away. The Petersons and Suttles were friends from church. When the Suttles had extra milk on hand, they shared it with Willie and Henrietta, knowing they were strapped for money because Willie was unable to work. On his way to fetch the milk, Willie stopped and visited on the porch at another friend's home.

Attorney Johnson reminded the jury that those friends, along with Mattie Suttles, had testified earlier in the trial that they had seen Willie in the mid-to-late afternoon on Tuesday, August 4—right around the time the three women were abducted on Shades Mountain.

Describing the afternoon of September 23, the day of his arrest, Willie said he had just left his mother-in-law's. He had stopped by her place to let her know that Henrietta was sick.

"When I was stopped and arrested I was on 14th Street and Avenue G," Willie testified. "I was going to Beaman's place, to his store. When I was across the street, 14th Street there, Miss Williams and a gentleman . . . they stopped the car a little ahead of me. . . . They beckoned me to come up to the car, and I went to the car. . . . There was a young man and a young lady and an old lady in the car."

Defense Attorney Johnson asked what the driver said to him.

"He didn't say anything right then. He looked at me a good while. He didn't say anything to me until he got out the car and . . . told me to get in and he commenced talking to me. He asked me if I knew anything about that killing on the mountain, and I told him, no sir, I didn't know anything about it. He asked me if I owned a car, and I told him I used to own one but didn't now. I was next taken to jail. . . . Then they carried me to Kilby in the nighttime."

In answer to when he had next seen Nell Williams, Peterson said it was in the Jefferson County Jail, the night he was shot.

"She asked me was I the nigger on the mountain; said I looked like that nigger. And I can't remember all she said. Said did I know a preacher Brown, I think. I said I didn't know him."

Attorney Johnson encouraged Willie to tell what else occurred during that meeting in the jail.

"I got shot that night. Was shot three times. . . . Miss Nell was sitting down and the man who did the shooting was standing leaning over Miss Nell, and I saw her open her purse, but I didn't see her get nothing out of it. When she started opening her purse Mr. Long started talking to me. . . . My attention was attracted away and I was shot three times."

Attorney Johnson encouraged Willie to tell "what was next done right then and there," but Special Prosecutor Beddow objected that Johnson's question was "vague, uncertain, and indefinite." After considerable wrangling between the defense and prosecution teams, Willie was allowed to finish his testimony.

"I never saw Miss Nell Williams in my life before I saw her on 14th Street after I was arrested. I don't know anything about, and didn't have anything to do with, the shooting of those young ladies on the mountain. I saw the gun the young man had in his hand on 14th Street, and I saw the gun I was shot with that night in the county jail, and in my judgment it was the same gun."

During cross-examination, Assistant Prosecutor Long asked Willie to describe the injuries he suffered in the jail cell.

"I was shot three times in the breast," Willie said. "I had my arms like that [indicating how his arms were folded]."

"So you took the bullets sitting there like a mad dog?" Long asked.

"I didn't sit there and take it like a mad dog being shot," Willie answered. "I hollered, 'Lord have mercy.'"

Defense Attorney Johnson rose to his feet and objected that Assistant Solicitor Long's questions were immaterial, illegal, and insulting. Judge Heflin agreed, one of the few times the court sustained a defense objection.

Long then shifted his line of cross-examination and sought to undermine the defendant's alibi by confronting Peterson with statements he allegedly made when Long and Bailes interrogated him six months earlier in Kilby Prison. In rapid-fire succession, Assistant Prosecutor Long delivered a series of questions, each beginning with the same refrain: "Didn't you tell me in Kilby Prison that . . . ?" Unable to remember exactly what he had said so many months before, Willie responded repeatedly, "I don't remember" or "I don't know." After Willie had stated several dozen times that he did not remember or did not know, Assistant Prosecutor Long insisted that the defendant's alibi was laced with contradictions and lies.[43]

"You've Got No Right to Be Chicken-Hearted"

After five days of testimony, the judge began his hour-long instructions to the jury at 5:00 p.m. on Friday, January 23, 1932. Judge Heflin told the jury, "This defendant is charged with the most atrocious and inhuman crime that probably ever has been committed in Jefferson County" and therefore "you, as sensible and as courageous men, must do your duty. If you fail to render a verdict in this case, you will not do your duty."

Judge Heflin also stated, "You've got no right to be chicken-hearted in a case of this kind. If you believe, under the evidence in this case, that the defendant is guilty, you should convict him and put the punishment upon him that you believe he deserves. On the other hand, if you believe that he is not guilty, you ought to acquit him."[44]

After thirty minutes of deliberation, the jury reached its verdict but decided to retire for dinner before returning to the courtroom at 8:00 p.m. to render the verdict to a hushed courtroom: "We find the defendant, Willie Peterson, guilty of murder in the first degree and sentence him to death in the electric chair."

Willie Peterson sat unmoved as the verdict was read. The Williams family members hugged each other, relieved that the ordeal was finally over. Henrietta Peterson was led weeping from the courtroom by friends.[45]

The Appeal

When Judge Heflin confirmed the jury's verdict one week later, he set March 4, 1932, as the date of execution. Defense Attorney Johnson immediately filed a request for appeal that automatically stayed execution. The defense had ninety days from the date of sentencing to submit the appeal.

Attorney Johnson set about visiting local black churches and writing letters to national officials of the NAACP requesting $1,000 in financial assistance to defray the cost of preparing the appeal.[46] In his request for donations, Johnson expressed his unequivocal conviction that Peterson was innocent, and that the vast majority of people in Birmingham—white and black—believed he had been wrongly convicted.

The local and national leadership of the NAACP had serious reservations about Johnson's ability to successfully appeal this case to the State Supreme Court. In confidence, Charles McPherson wrote NAACP national secretary Walter White expressing his candid opinion of the attorney.

"Johnson is a rather blatant indiscreet but sensational lawyer who has considerable ability as an orator without the cunning to put it over in the presence of a discreet interrupter or blocker like Beddow. He has also been visiting Negro churches all over town soliciting funds as well as patronage in a haphazard manner."[47]

Walter White took the matter to his legal committee, convinced they should find someone more experienced and stable than Attorney Johnson. He also asked the advice of white leaders in Birmingham. As it turned out, Roderick Beddow would have been the first choice of white leaders such as Henry Edmonds, but he was not a viable option. Their next best recommendation was John W. Altman. Charles McPherson concurred. In addition to his private practice, Altman served as general counsel for the Alabama State Federation of Labor (ASFL). Lauding his abilities, McPherson wrote to White, "Once he gets going he is hard to stop. He is in my opinion the best man available in Birmingham having the machine and legal force which he has. . . . He has the reputation of being honest, reasonable and capable as well as a pugnacious never die type of fighter."[48]

Altman worked for the ASFL on a pro bono basis, but he did not offer a similar service to the cash-strapped NAACP. He agreed to take the case for a fee of $2,500, but only if they accepted his choice of Walter S. Smith, a local white attorney, as an associate. Altman confided in McPherson that he would make use of Attorneys Johnson and Roach insofar as they had something to offer, but they would not be directly involved in moving the case forward.

John Altman was not known as a progressive or a "friend of Negroes." In fact, several years after representing Peterson, Altman tendered his resignation as general counsel for the Alabama State Federation of Labor when, in

1936, it accepted black workers into full membership and invited them to serve on committees.[49] Despite his allegiance to white supremacy and his opposition to "racial mixing," Altman believed that Willie Peterson was the victim of egregious injustice. He told McPherson that "large numbers of high class intelligent white people" had called him by phone or spoken with him in person to congratulate him on taking the case.[50]

As secretary of the Birmingham NAACP, Charles McPherson was very worried about how the local branch would be able to generate the financial support needed to carry the appeal to completion. He therefore challenged Walter White to bring the full weight and authority of the national NAACP to bear in the appeal process.[51] White promised to take the matter up with his legal committee and get back to McPherson.

While members of the NAACP legal committee debated whether to accept McPherson's challenge, black leaders in Birmingham decided to launch their own campaign in defense of Peterson. On February 4, a special meeting of black clergy and lay people was held at the Metropolitan AME Zion Church in Birmingham to launch a new organization, the Federation of Religious and Civic Organizations. Its purpose was "to secure relief, protection, and justice in the courts for Willie Peterson" and to raise funds to pay the lawyers, court fees, and other expenses related to the appeal. Charles McPherson was present as an invited guest at the February 4 meeting. The federation elected an executive committee composed of nine members including Oscar W. Adams, Rev. J. W. Goodgame, Bishop B. G. Shaw of the AME Zion Church, Walter T. Woods, Grand Master of the A. F. & A. M. Masonic Lodges of Alabama, and P. D. Davis, Most Worshipful Secretary of the A. F. & A. M. of Alabama.[52] Federation leaders agreed that Attorney Altman was the best man for the job. He had been approached, and they were awaiting his decision.

Oscar W. Adams proved to be one of McPherson's staunchest allies in working to secure Peterson's freedom. Adams was a college-educated black man who moved to Birmingham in 1906 to work for the Great Southern Insurance Company. While working for Great Southern, Adams launched a weekly newspaper for Birmingham's black community called the *Birmingham Reporter*. It featured articles addressing issues of local, state, and national significance. The *Reporter* also carried advertisements by black businesses and announcements of religious, cultural, and political events in the black community.[53] As editor of the *Birmingham Reporter*, Adams was able to earn enough money to purchase a home in Smithfield, the neighborhood just north of downtown where members of Birmingham's black middle class rented or owned homes. He and his wife, Ella, and their two children lived just a few blocks from Charles McPherson and his wife, Alma. Like McPherson, Adams was a longtime member of the Birmingham NAACP who refused to forsake the organization when the membership rolls declined during the 1920s. Both he and McPherson believed that the campaign to free Willie Peterson might provide an excellent way to resuscitate the Birmingham branch.[54]

Charles McPherson was extremely heartened by the community support being fostered by the Federation of Religious and Civic Organizations. He was delighted that black pastors were stepping up and speaking out publicly in support of Willie Peterson. He reported to Walter White that Rev. M. M. Thornton accepted the federation presidency and challenged his clergy colleagues to provide bold and uncompromising leadership in the fight for Peterson's freedom. At the end of his report to White, he remarked that several elements of the case had never been brought to light in either trial. If the appeal could result in a rehearing of the case, he hoped that the defense would take a far more aggressive stance in the next trial: "For instance, the pistol with which the girls were shot, finger prints of the car cushion which they claimed he used. No pistol experts or police who investigated were called or put on the stand. I agree with you that a National detective should be employed to clear up the *mess* even if the report should result in *suicides*."[55]

After conferring with colleagues at the national level and local leaders in Birmingham such as Henry Edmonds, Walter White decided that the NAACP needed to throw its full weight behind the campaign to free Willie Peterson for four reasons: First and foremost, Peterson was clearly innocent of the charges. Second, a majority of "right-thinking" people in Birmingham believed he was innocent. Third, White did not want the Communist Party to take control of this case as they had with Scottsboro. And, fourth, he wanted to prove the communists wrong by demonstrating that it was indeed possible for black people to get justice in Alabama courts.[56]

In early March, Henrietta Peterson met with the executive committee of the federation and brought a message of "thanks and prayerful gratitude" from her husband. She was pleased that the community was coming together to raise funds on Willie's behalf, and she expressed that it was heartening to both of them to experience this tangible support.

The Klan regularly paraded their automobiles in the streets of Woodlawn near the Petersons' residence, hoping to intimidate and silence those who were working to reverse Willie's conviction, but their threats did not deter the black pastors and other community leaders who had joined forces to raise money for the appeal and to work to secure Peterson's freedom.[57]

Three Victims Of Escaped Slayer

Augusta Williams (*left*), Nell Williams, and Jennie Wood. *Birmingham Post*, August 5, 1931.

According to the testimony of Nell Williams, these are the boulders on Shades Mountain where she, Augusta Williams, and Jennie Wood sat just moments before they were abducted on August 4, 1931. This photograph was entered by the state into evidence marked "Exhibit A" in Trial Transcript, *State of Alabama v. Willie Peterson*, no. 65583 (Circuit Court of Jefferson County, Birmingham, Alabama, January 18, 1932). PHOTO COURTESY OF ALABAMA DEPARTMENT OF ARCHIVES AND HISTORY.

The woods on Shades Mountain where Nell Williams said that she, Augusta Williams, and Jennie Wood were held captive for four hours on the evening of August 4, 1931. This photograph was entered by the state into evidence marked "Exhibit C" in Trial Transcript, *State of Alabama v. Willie Peterson*, no. 65583 (Circuit Court of Jefferson County, Birmingham, Alabama, January 18, 1932). PHOTO COURTESY OF ALABAMA DEPARTMENT OF ARCHIVES AND HISTORY.

U.S. Steel's blast furnaces, photographed by the Farm Security Administration in 1937.
PHOTO COURTESY OF THE LIBRARY OF CONGRESS.

Black neighborhood, 1525 Seventh Alley S. in Birmingham, ca. 1953. PHOTO COURTESY OF BIRMINGHAM, ALABAMA, PUBLIC LIBRARY ARCHIVES.

Intersection of Eighth Ave S. and S. Fourteenth Street in Birmingham where Willie Peterson was arrested on September 23, 1931. Photo ca. 1949. PHOTO COURTESY OF BIRMINGHAM, ALABAMA, PUBLIC LIBRARY ARCHIVES.

Photos of Willie Peterson taken in Hillman Hospital in fall 1931. These photographs were entered by the state into evidence marked "Exhibit F" in Trial Transcript, *State of Alabama v. Willie Peterson*, no. 65583 (Circuit Court of Jefferson County, Birmingham, Alabama, January 18, 1932). PHOTO COURTESY OF ALABAMA DEPARTMENT OF ARCHIVES AND HISTORY.

Old Jefferson County Jail in Birmingham, where crowds gathered on the night of September 23, 1931, after Willie Peterson was arrested. PHOTO COURTESY OF BIRMINGHAM, ALABAMA, PUBLIC LIBRARY ARCHIVES.

'GIRL'S BROTHER WHO
SHOT NEGRO AT JAIL
AT LIBERTY ON BOND

Dent Williams. *Birmingham News*, October 3, 1931.

Home of the Williams family, 2504 Aberdeen Road, in Redmont, ca. 1968.

Dr. Charles A. J. McPherson, secretary of the Birmingham branch, NAACP, in his office. PHOTO COURTESY OF CAROLYN W. MCPHERSON.

Dr. Charles A. J. McPherson, secretary of the Birmingham branch, NAACP, holding his son, ca. 1942. PHOTO COURTESY OF CAROLYN W. MCPHERSON.

Walter White (*left*), executive secretary of the NAACP, with Charles Hamilton Houston, dean of Howard Law School and NAACP chief legal counsel, ca. 1935. PHOTO COURTESY OF THE LIBRARY OF CONGRESS, PRINT AND PHOTOGRAPHS DIVISION, VISUAL MATERIALS FROM THE NAACP RECORDS.

Oscar W. Adams, publisher of the *Birmingham Record*. PHOTO COURTESY OF THE
LIBRARY OF CONGRESS, PRINT AND PHOTOGRAPHS DIVISION, VISUAL MATERIALS
FROM THE NAACP RECORDS.

Hosea Hudson, Communist Party organizer, photographed in 1968.

Birmingham's chief of police, Fred H. McDuff. PHOTO COURTESY OF
BIRMINGHAM, ALABAMA, PUBLIC LIBRARY ARCHIVES.

Jefferson County sheriff James Hawkins. PHOTO COURTESY OF
BIRMINGHAM, ALABAMA, PUBLIC LIBRARY ARCHIVES.

Rev. Henry M. Edmonds, senior pastor of Independent Presbyterian Church in Birmingham and Alabama chair of the Commission on Interracial Cooperation. PHOTO COURTESY OF BIRMINGHAM, ALABAMA, PUBLIC LIBRARY ARCHIVES.

Birmingham attorney Roderick Beddow, who served on the
prosecution team during Willie Peterson's second trial in January 1932.
Beddow was also lead defense attorney for Dent Williams for his
March 1932 trial. PHOTO COURTESY OF BIRMINGHAM, ALABAMA,
PUBLIC LIBRARY ARCHIVES.

Solicitor George Lewis Bailes, who served on the prosecution team during both of Willie Peterson's trials. Bailes was lead prosecutor for Dent Williams's March 1932 trial. PHOTO COURTESY OF BIRMINGHAM, ALABAMA, PUBLIC LIBRARY ARCHIVES.

HOUSE OF PAIN

While his conviction was being appealed, Willie Peterson continued to serve time in the Jefferson County Jail. Should his conviction be upheld, he faced the dreaded prospect of being transferred to Kilby Prison's death row. Kilby was known among prisoners by many names. Some called it "the death house." Clarence Norris, one of the Scottsboro defendants, called it "a house of pain."[1]

Located on 2,250 acres just four miles to the north of Montgomery, Kilby was built as Alabama's largest maximum-security prison for men in 1923. Intended to house a thousand prisoners, Kilby was often overcrowded, with many more prisoners confined to each cell than originally designed. Officials considered it a state-of-the-art facility with a hundred-bed infirmary, dairy farm, cotton mill, and shirt factory. For most prisoners, especially those who were black, it was a place devoid of hope.

There were thirteen cells on death row; six on each side of a hallway with a green door leading to the thirteenth room at the end. Behind that door stood the dreaded and infamous "Yellow Mama." Alabama's electric chair was nicknamed for the bright highway-line paint that covered it. When

Yellow Mama was in use, death row prisoners up and down the hall were visited by screams and the smell of burning flesh.[2]

Death row prisoners were seldom allowed outside their ten-by-twelve-foot cells, which contained a cot, small sink, and toilet stool. They were denied access to the prison yard for exercise. They did not eat with other prisoners in the massive dining hall. Food on a tray was slid through an opening at the bottom of the cell door. Once a week they were ushered from their cells, handcuffed and naked, with armed guards on both sides who led them down the hall for a brief shower. Six of the cells had small windows that looked out onto the prison yard. From those cells, prisoners could vicariously enjoy the glimpse of a prison-yard ball game. On the other side of the hall, no fragment of the sky, moon, or sun was visible, only the brick wall of an adjoining cell block. Lights stayed on day and night, so sleep was hard to come by.[3]

The food at Kilby Prison was notoriously tasteless and lacking in protein. Breakfast consisted of a roll, grits, and a piece of pale meat. Lunch and dinner were always some combination of beans and greens. If a prisoner was able to save up money from family or friends, he could ask the guard to bring him special foods from the commissary like sardines, potted meat, cakes, or pies. He had to slip the guard some extra money for the effort.[4]

The only ward at Kilby where white and black prisoners were housed on the same cell block was death row, but there were always far more black prisoners than white. And white prisoners were more likely to have their death sentence commuted to life imprisonment than black prisoners. Of the sixty-two men executed at Kilby Prison during the 1930s, only seven were white.[5]

Death row was often so crowded that two men had to be placed in one cell. A bunk bed was brought in to replace the cot. But the cell was not big enough for two men to move around at the same time, so one had to lie in the bunk while the other paced to exercise or walk off boredom. When a white prisoner was assigned to death row and there was not a single cell available, he was housed in a detention cell near death row rather than have him share a room with a black prisoner.[6]

Indignity and brutality were the steady diet for black prisoners on death row. Clarence Norris said the single hardest thing to endure on a daily basis at Kilby was the abuse suffered, physically and mentally, at the hands of sadistic guards. They hurled curses and insults, routinely calling men "nigger" or "boy"—seldom addressing black prisoners by name unless a lawyer or someone else from the outside paid a visit. The guards delighted in taunting prisoners about their dreaded execution, warning them that they were going "to fry tonight." The slightest infraction could occasion a beating, but often assaults were unprovoked. A guard might simply be showing off, reminding the prisoner just who was in charge, or he might lash out in white-hot hatred.

The warden ordered flogging as a special punishment for problematic inmates. The inmate was forced to lie face down on a blanket. One guard held the prisoner's shoulders while two other guards sat on his legs. A fourth guard administered the number of lashings the warden prescribed. Clarence Norris described the flogging as a sadistic ritual: "The very first lash would cut right through your skin, I mean it would tear your flesh to pieces. From then on the succeeding lashes would be tearing up numb flesh. By the time they finished with you, you'd be almost dead. They had a habit of beating you on one of your buttocks so that you wouldn't be able to sit on that side for at least a month. Some men were beaten so badly they had to be admitted to a hospital for two or three days."[7]

"Walk-by" was the term prisoners used when a man was led, shackled, down the hall to the execution room. Some condemned men nodded or said a parting word to the prisoners who stood watching behind the bars of their cells. Some cried out and were dragged through the green door screaming. Others looked straight ahead, expressionless.

Clarence Norris and Haywood Patterson described the first time they heard a man being executed behind the green door. His name was Willie Stokes, and he had been convicted of murder. Taken from his cell at midnight, "he went around and shook hands with all the prisoners and wished them luck," Clarence Norris reported. "He walked through the green door and they killed him. I couldn't see into the room where they had the electric chair, but I could hear every word and sound just like I was in there with them. . . . I was sick in mind and body after Will Stokes was killed. I didn't sleep or eat for days."[8]

"If I live to be a hundred I'll never forget that day," Patterson remembered. "When they turned on the juice for Stokes we could hear the z-z-z-z-z-z of the electric current outside in the death row. The buzz went several times. After the juice was squeezed into him a guard came out and gave us a report. 'Stokes died hard. They stuck a needle through his head to make sure.' I sweated my clothes wet."[9]

eleven

"A TEMPORARILY DETHRONED MIND"

Dent Williams had been free on $1,000 bail since October 2, 1931, when he shot Willie Peterson in the Jefferson County Jail. Although charged with assault with the intent to murder, Williams had not spent one night in jail. When his trial got underway Monday, March 8, 1932, he pled not guilty by reason of temporary insanity.

There was no disputing the fact that Dent Williams was the shooter. Therefore, the state's case was cut and dried. In opening remarks, assistant solicitor Greye Tate referred to Williams as someone "who had invaded and violated the precincts of justice." Sheriff Hawkins and Chief McDuff both testified that Williams had fired the nearly fatal bullets during an interrogation of Willie Peterson. Dr. D. J. Coyle, the physician who treated Peterson at Hillman Hospital after the shooting, testified that he had removed two bullets from Peterson's chest.[1]

Dent Williams's team of attorneys, led by Roderick Beddow, based their defense on twenty character witnesses who described that Dent had not been himself since the day his sister Augusta was murdered. Nell Williams and her mother testified that Dent had grown very depressed and exhibited strange behaviors after the attack on Shades Mountain. Nell told the jury that her brother reached a breaking point when she told him how she and Augusta had pleaded with "the Negro" not to attack them: "As I went deeper into the story Dent whitened and then flushed; his eyes took on a crazed look. He would clench his fist and gnash his teeth."[2]

Nell testified that her brother shot Willie Peterson in the jail after she pointed at Peterson and shouted, "You're the negro who killed my sister and little Jennie Wood and shot me—you know you're the negro, and you didn't think you'd ever see me again!" Nell added that it was only after discharging the gun that Dent "seemed to ease down from high nervous tension."[3]

Lawyers from the firm where Dent worked said their colleague became far more preoccupied with finding his sister's slayer than practicing law. Attorney Everett Parker said he grew very concerned about Dent's mental health when Dent revealed that a portrait of his grandfather had instructed him to find his sister's killer. Dent's friend, Sam Houston, told the jury that Dent had "acted strangely" and vowed to "get that negro" if it was the last thing he ever did. According to Mrs. B. B. Burton, a family friend and confidante, Dent had also promised Jennie Wood that he would "get the Negro that attacked her."[4]

Dent's close friend, F. C. Ausbon, testified that he had frequently accompanied Dent on late-night searches for "the Negro." According to Ausbon, Dent "fearlessly" entered black homes and stopped black men on the street. To prove Dent had become a man obsessed who lacked all common sense, Ausbon described how Dent once entered a building where several armed black men were gathered. Undeterred, Dent walked past an armed black guard and struck one of the other men when he reached for his gun.[5]

Ausbon grew so concerned about his friend's state of mind while they were searching for "the Negro" in Montgomery that he attempted to dissuade Dent from going out on another raid.

"I tried to get Dent to remain in our hotel room instead of going out into the dead of night. He socked me on the jaw and knocked me unconscious. When I came to myself, he was kneeling beside me and crying."[6]

In closing arguments for the prosecution, solicitor George Lewis Bailes argued that Willie Peterson was shot while in the arms of the law, "a place where every person, regardless of color or creed has reason to demand and expect protection." Defense attorney Roderick Beddow beseeched the jury to have compassion for Dent Williams and to see his deed as a natural act brought on by a "temporarily dethroned mind."[7]

On Tuesday, March 9, after deliberating for forty minutes, the jury delivered a verdict of not guilty by reason of temporary insanity. When the verdict was announced, the large crowd gathered in the courtroom erupted in applause.[8]

In retrospect, attorneys such as J. T. Roach found the timing of Dent Williams's trial unusual. Had the court operated on a normal calendar, Dent Williams should have been tried after Willie Peterson's first trial because the two men were indicted on the same day, October 9, 1931. It may be that Dent's attorney, Roderick Beddow, possessed enough power and prestige to pressure the court to alter its calendar. In any case, the postponement favored Dent Williams. He would stand a much better chance of being exonerated if Peterson were found guilty of murder in the first degree. Furthermore, as attorney J. T. Roach would later argue in a letter to Governor Miller, the rush to convict Willie Peterson was predicated in part on an effort to save Dent Williams. From the moment Dent tried to kill Peterson, Nell Williams was no longer free to change her mind about Peterson. To protect Dent, Nell had to remain adamant that he was the assailant.[9]

twelve

"AN OUTRAGEOUS SPECTACLE OF INJUSTICE"

On May 27, 1932, attorney John Altman submitted to Alabama's Supreme Court a sixty-five-page supplemental brief and argument on behalf of his appellant, Willie Peterson. The brief began with an extensive review of Altman's lengthy legal career, followed by a summary of the case in which he declared that *"the so-called trial of appellant was the most outrageous and horrible spectacle of injustice and wrong that was ever perpetrated in a Criminal Court of the State of Alabama."*[1]

Two propositions formed the heart of Altman's argument that Willie Peterson should be granted a new trial. First, the conduct of the trial was deliberately and consistently prejudiced against the defendant. Second, the evidence submitted by the state relied on one witness, Nell Williams, whose testimony was "improbable and contradictory."

In seventeen pages of examples drawn from the trial transcript, Altman documented how Assistant Solicitor Long interjected prejudicial statements and exhibited insulting, intimidating behavior toward the defendant, defense witnesses, and defense lawyers. Deplorable as Long's prejudicial antics were, Altman found the unmitigated bias of Judge Heflin more egregious still because jurors looked to the judge for guidance throughout the trial. Ten pages of the brief were devoted to cataloguing prejudicial quotes and rulings attributable to Judge Heflin.[2]

Altman sought to prove that the state's key witness, Nell Williams, was impeached because she delivered consistently contradictory testimony about the assailant's age, height, color, hair, and clothing. Furthermore, the material portions of Nell Williams's testimony were "grossly improbable and impossible."

"Miss Williams testified twice that the Negro took the keys of the automobile and that the ignition was cut off when he got the keys and put them in his pocket; that he leaned over where she and Miss Augusta were sitting to take the keys out; yet she testified that while Miss Augusta was lying on the ground, after the Negro had walked off through the woods with the keys in his pocket, Miss Augusta said: 'See if you can drive the car in and get help.'"[3] Nell Williams then testified that she got up and drove the car with one arm and a flat tire.

According to Altman, Nell Williams's testimony about the duration and location of the crime was also improbable and contradictory.

> The young lady testified that the guilty person was there from five-thirty o'clock until after dark; that he discharged his pistol a number of times; that none of the three ladies ever screamed; that Miss Wood was ravished without making resistance, etc.; that no efforts at escape were ever made, the only thing that was done by way of defense or offense was made when she and Miss Augusta Williams undertook to jump on the Negro and take his pistol away from him; that the automobile was parked with its front end in the edge of the public highway . . . [that] the time the Negro spent holding these three young ladies in subjection, according to the indications of the testimony of Miss Williams, was from five-thirty o'clock in the afternoon until at least eight o'clock, or after that night.[4]

Altman noted in Nell Williams's testimony that three or four cars passed on the road while she and the other women sat for ten minutes on the rocks atop Shades Mountain. Later, she testified that the assailant fired eight shots during the nearly three hours he held them captive. That those shots failed to attract attention from people in the vicinity seemed highly improbable to Altman.

Altman expressed compassion for what Nell Williams had endured in losing her sister and friend to such violence, but noted that she was under extraordinary pressure to identify an assailant. Having named Willie Peterson as the suspect, Nell Williams's unconscious mind naturally sought to vindicate itself upon the witness stand. Furthermore, she could not afford to entertain any doubts as to whether Peterson was indeed the assailant because her brother had attempted to murder him in the county jail. Altman therefore called upon the justices to consider and rule that Nell Williams's testimony was rife with partiality and improbability due to the ordeal she had suffered.

thirteen

A TUMULTUOUS YEAR

A full year would pass before the Alabama Supreme Court ruled on the appeal filed by John Altman in May 1932. That intervening year proved to be tumultuous on many fronts.

In November 1932, the U.S. Supreme Court issued a ruling that many white people in Alabama found disturbing and insulting. Overriding the Alabama Supreme Court, the justices declared that seven of the Scottsboro defendants must be granted new trials. The justification stated that the defendants had been denied adequate counsel in violation of the equal protection clause of the Fourteenth Amendment. The editors of the *Birmingham Post* declared, "No more stinging rebuke has been administered to a state court in years than the . . . decision . . . ordering the state of Alabama to retry the seven Negro boys."[1]

During the same year, many white business leaders in Alabama felt that the executive and legislative branches of the federal government were curtailing their rights to conduct business as they saw fit. Franklin Delano Roosevelt was elected president in November 1932. His new initiatives such as the National Industrial Recovery Act (NIRA), which protected collective bargaining rights for unions, were viewed as an attack on free enterprise at a time when companies were struggling to stay afloat.

The unprecedented growth that Birmingham had experienced for the past two decades had come to an abrupt and devastating halt. For the city of Birmingham, the Great Depression had created economic hardship of catastrophic proportions. Only half of Alabama's three thousand mines and mills that were in operation before the stock market crash were still operating in 1933. Employment in Birmingham's iron and steel industries declined from approximately 100,000 to 15,000 full-time workers. During the 1930s, a quarter of the city's population was unemployed, and 60 percent had only part-time work.[2]

The Growing Influence of the Communist Party

The hardest hit were members of Birmingham's black community. Before the onslaught of the Depression they had been relegated to the most menial, backbreaking, and poorly paid work in Birmingham's mines, mills, and factories. As production fell and workers were laid off, the programs and ideology espoused by the Communist Party were attracting an increasing number of underemployed and unemployed black workers. By the end of 1933, the party's dues-paying membership in Birmingham had risen to nearly five hundred, with many more participating in meetings, demonstrations, and rallies.[3]

In December 1932, communists organized a mass meeting of unemployed people on the old courthouse steps in north Birmingham, demanding more relief from the city for the thousands who were unemployed. Hosea Hudson, one of the organizers, estimated that an integrated crowd of at least seven thousand people turned out that day. A committee of nine was designated to talk with the mayor, Jimmie Jones. Mary Stevens, a white working-class woman, was appointed spokesperson. As she presented their demands, Jones interrupted and asked, "Do you believe in social equality for niggers?" Stevens responded, "Yes, why not? They are just as good as you and I are. Why not?"

Jones cut her off, saying, "That's enough from you," and then turned and ordered his police to go clear the crowd from the courthouse steps. In the melee that ensued, police kicked and clubbed people to the ground. According to Hudson, this police violence proved eye-opening for many of the whites in attendance "because this was the first time that many of them had ever been pushed around like that by the police."[4]

The frequency of these mass meetings and the numbers in attendance alarmed Birmingham officials. An officer of the U.S. Military Intelligence Division stationed in Birmingham admitted to his superiors in 1932 that the ILD had "created a favorable impression among Negroes and some reports intimated that Negroes were becoming bolder in aligning themselves openly with the Communists."[5]

Black communists such as Hosea Hudson, Angelo Herndon, and Al Murphy believed that a new and more just order was being birthed out of the collapse of Birmingham's oppressive economic system. Not only were workers showing enormous courage in voicing their demands and organizing work stoppages, they were evidencing a new willingness to break Birmingham's sacrosanct color line. As Nat Ross, a communist organizer in the Deep South, declared in *The Communist*, "A new day is dawning in the South as white and Negro union brothers stand shoulder to shoulder on the picket lines, facing the machine guns of the National Guards."[6]

The interracialism so feared by many in Birmingham's white community was a hallmark of this new order. Herndon and his comrade Al Murphy testified to a wholly new pattern of interaction between whites and blacks within the Communist Party. "We were called 'comrades,'" Herndon wrote, "without condescension or patronage. Better yet, we were treated like equals and brothers." Al Murphy was "confounded and elated" by the social equality practiced within party circles. Remembering his first Communist Party meeting, he wrote, "This was the first time I had ever sat in a gathering among Black and white persons in a Black man's home."[7]

An Uprising of Coal Miners in Birmingham

The election of President Franklin Delano Roosevelt and the reemergence of the United Mine Workers of America (UMWA) in the summer of 1933 had Birmingham's industrial bosses scrambling to consolidate their interests and protect their structural power. Throughout the 1920s, the Alabama Coal Owners Association waged an aggressive and successful campaign against the UMWA in Birmingham by conducting a virulent propaganda campaign denouncing the UMWA's promotion of "interracialism"—claiming that the UMWA sought to undermine long-held and cherished Southern traditions.

Before the convict lease system was outlawed in 1927, coal owners could utilize unpaid convicts supplied by the state as strikebreakers. When that was no longer possible, companies such as Tennessee Coal and Iron deputized employees to serve as armed patrols that threatened union organizers when they caught them on company property.

Those repressive policies were effective until the onset of the Great Depression and the election of Franklin Roosevelt in 1932. New Deal legislation such as the NIRA established the "right of labor to representatives of its own choosing" and provided industry-wide codes that governed conditions of employment. As soon as the U.S. House of Representatives passed the NIRA in May 1933, UMWA chief John Lewis dispatched William Mitch to Birmingham to resurrect the UMWA in Birmingham's coal mines. Mitch opened a UMWA headquarters in the Redmont Hotel and launched an aggressive recruitment campaign in early June. The effectiveness of his campaign testified to how desperate life had become for Birmingham's miners in the midst of the Great Depression and how eager they were to begin a collective fight for higher wages and better working conditions. Within two months, by July 1933, Mitch claimed to have recruited twenty thousand members or 100 percent of the miners.[8]

Frightened by these developments, industrialists launched a two-pronged attack: they hired men to physically intimidate union organizers, and they sought to convince white workers that the biracialism of the UMWA was a communist conspiracy led by "Reds" that had infiltrated union leadership. One of the most notorious opponents of the UMWA lived just a few doors down from the Williams family on Aberdeen Road in Redmont. Charles Fairchild DeBardeleben, owner of Alabama Fuel and Iron Company, vowed he would close his mines before allowing unionization. He displayed utter contempt for union organizers and considered them disposable waste. Employees were rewarded if they ratted on fellow workers or resorted to violence while seeking to stop union recruitment efforts.

When the UMWA began to gain adherents in the early 1930s, DeBardeleben went so far as to set out dynamite charges on the roads leading to his mines. Encouraging his employees to join him in these violent measures, he announced, "If you catch any of the organizers in the camp, you know what to do with them. Let the river be the deadline. . . . My office will back you up in anything you do to get rid of them."[9]

The ILD and NAACP Join Forces

On April 9, 1933, Scottsboro defendant Haywood Patterson was convicted and sentenced to death for a second time in Decatur, Alabama. His defense attorney, Samuel Leibowitz, made no effort to contain his bitterness. Returning to New York City after the second trial, Leibowitz told a *New York Herald Tribune* reporter that the two weeks he spent in Decatur left him feeling like he needed a "moral, mental and physical bath." He characterized the people who sat on the jury as "bigots whose mouths are slits in their faces, whose eyes pop out like a frog's, whose chins drip tobacco juice, bewhiskered and filthy."[10]

It could have been the unbridled anti-Semitism he faced during the trial or the barrage of taunts from townspeople who threatened to lynch him, along with the defendants, that led Leibowitz to abandon his professional decorum. Whatever the cause, his eruption of contempt set off a firestorm in Alabama. Even before the *Herald Tribune* story had been released, the *Montgomery Advertiser* declared that Leibowitz was "the voice of bigotry" and labeled him "arrogant, contemptuous and domineering." His ill-advised remarks confirmed for many white Alabamians that the charge of "bias" in this trial should be laid at the feet of ILD attorneys rather than Alabama's judicial system.[11]

The NAACP's national board of directors issued a public statement accusing the ILD of bungling the case and putting the defendants' lives in jeopardy. This was a position that Walter White would soon reverse after receiving a deluge of letters and telegrams protesting the NAACP finger pointing.[12] In correspondence with William L. Patterson, the ILD legal director, White proposed they put aside their differences for the sake of the Scottsboro defendants and offered to help pay the expenses of Haywood Patterson's appeal and future trials.[13] For ideological purists within the ILD it was anathema to work with the NAACP on any campaign, but William Patterson advised them that this was an offer they could not afford to spurn. Their coffers were nearly empty, and the new appeal phase was just getting started. He wrote a conciliatory reply to White that opened the door for collaboration in the Scottsboro case: "Our national committee welcomes the splendid offer of financial cooperation made by your organization. We believe that in this united front . . . tens of thousands more workers and their sympathizers can be drawn into a sincere, consistent and relentless struggle for the nine Scottsboro boys."[14]

Meanwhile, Willie Peterson languished in the Jefferson County Jail awaiting the decision of the Alabama Supreme Court. Like the defendants in the Scottsboro case, Peterson found himself in the center of this vortex buffeted by people, organizations, and forces that sought to claim him as a symbol of their longed-for liberation or condemn him as an embodiment of all that threatened the South.

PART III

NEVER TURNING
BACK

fourteen

STAYING ON THE FIRING LINE

On June 22, 1933, the justices of the Alabama Supreme Court ruled that they had carefully reviewed all the questions submitted by counsel for Willie Peterson and could find nothing that warranted a reversal of his conviction in Judge Heflin's court. In a unanimous decision, the seven justices found no violation of the defendant's constitutional rights—either state or federal. Neither did they discover any support in the record to uphold the defense suggestion that there had been discrimination based on race.[1]

The ruling of the Alabama Supreme Court was a severe blow to those in the black community who had rallied hard and raised an unprecedented amount of money to fund the appeal. Most of all, the news was heartbreaking to Willie Peterson, Henrietta, and their neighbors and friends who had courageously stepped forward to testify on his behalf.

The ILD issued press releases criticizing the NAACP for mismanaging the appeal and declared they were taking over the case. The *Southern Worker* announced that the ILD planned to hold a protest in Birmingham on August 13, demanding Peterson's release, and organizing to take their demands directly to Governor Miller.[2] Charles McPherson was keenly aware that the ILD was gaining support and favor among Alabama's black population, largely as a result of the ILD's brilliant organizing—both nationally and internationally—in support of the Scottsboro defendants. In a confidential letter to Dr. Robert R. Moton, president of Tuskegee Institute, McPherson acknowledged, "Every Negro, North and South, has been profoundly stirred by what the ILD has accomplished. It has their complete confidence for sincerity and courage, even where they do not endorse its policies. The ILD grip on the imagination of the Negro is a very real and potent thing."[3]

For Charles McPherson and other moderate black leaders in Birmingham, the Peterson case became a litmus test for the future. In his letter to Dr. Moton, McPherson described what he believed the stakes to be in this critical time: "If the NAACP loses out in the Peterson case, the leadership of Negroes in the South passes irretrievably to the ILD. The very best way that the State of Alabama can help the ILD take over the leadership of Negroes in the South is to further Willie Peterson's martyrdom."[4]

Charles McPherson, attorney Walter Smith, and Oscar Adams, editor of the *Birmingham Reporter*, met to develop a strategy to counter the ILD's accusations and make it clear to the black community that the NAACP was still in charge of this case. They also visited Willie Peterson in the Jefferson County Jail and reassured him that the NAACP was continuing to fight for his freedom. The Federation of Religious and Civic Organizations was raising funds for the new appeal. Should the Alabama Supreme Court refuse their request for a rehearing, they planned to take his case all the way to the U.S. Supreme Court. Every piece of this news was relief for Willie Peterson. McPherson, Adams, and Smith helped Peterson draft a public statement repudiating the ILD and letting people know that he was continuing to work with the NAACP's legal counsel. The next day, Adams ran a front-page article in the *Birmingham Reporter* announcing Peterson's repudiation and calling on members of the black community to donate money to the NAACP and federation's joint campaign for his release.[5]

In the wake of the Alabama Supreme Court ruling, Charles McPherson vowed to redouble his energy, time, and resources spent to secure justice for Willie Peterson. Three weeks after the court's ruling, he wrote an impassioned letter to Walter White arguing that the Peterson case was in many respects more important than the Scottsboro case: "It involves a poor defenseless Negro, victimized by white supremacy in its vilest form. Every issue involving the rights of the Negro is involved in this case right in the hot bed of discrimination, mob action and everything else."[6]

McPherson was proud that the local campaign had raised an unprecedented amount of money for the appeal—nearly $2,500. It was for him a visible sign of "outraged public sentiment" in Birmingham. Nevertheless, the Birmingham branch needed the resources and support of the national offices, and McPherson once again implored Walter White to enter this appeals phase no holds barred.

Charles McPherson may have felt emboldened to issue this passionate appeal because, just one month earlier, he had been awarded the prestigious Madam C. J. Walker Gold Medal at the NAACP's national annual conference in Chicago. The award committee was unanimous in its selection of Charles McPherson from a national pool of nominees, stating that he had performed outstanding service in "the face of the prejudices, handicaps and plain dangers of a southern city." In particular, the committee lauded McPherson's tireless work to free Willie Peterson, "who was framed as a scape-goat for the bitter feeling aroused in Alabama by the Scottsboro case and other alleged interracial crimes."[7]

Charles McPherson pledged to Walter White that his people in Birmingham would "support an aggressive militant fight if made by the NAACP."[8] Most of all, McPherson argued, Peterson needed a topflight team of attorneys that could take the case all the way to the U.S. Supreme Court. McPherson had no doubt that Smith and Altman possessed the skill and zeal to continue the legal battle, but Altman had just suffered a stroke that paralyzed his left side, and McPherson worried that he would not have the strength to do the job. There was so much at stake. A win could move the struggle for justice forward. A loss could cause black people in the South to lose hope.

"We must therefore fight and fight to win. We oppose mob action, conspiracy or any other form of color discrimination and feel called upon to combat it. . . . Our Birmingham branch must keep on the firing line right in the heart of the south without retrenchment. . . . The public demands it. Justice is crying for it. Willie Peterson is hanging on as it were to see justice done."[9]

fifteen

CHARLES HAMILTON HOUSTON

In July 1933, Walter White delivered two pieces of good news to Charles McPherson. A wealthy friend offered to contribute fifty cents on every dollar the Commission on Interracial Cooperation (CIC) raised in support of the Willie Peterson campaign. And Charles Hamilton Houston, esteemed vice dean of Howard Law School, would soon be coming to Birmingham to investigate the case and help the local branch develop a comprehensive and vigorous campaign to free Willie Peterson.[1]

During the previous two years, Walter White had actively courted Houston, hoping Houston would lead the NAACP's legal office and develop a comprehensive plan for legally dismantling segregation and racial discrimination. The invitation was tempting for Houston—and he would ultimately accept—but he could not yet imagine how he would combine the monumental task of shaping NAACP legal strategy with his demanding work at Howard.

When the Alabama Supreme Court upheld Peterson's death sentence, White consulted Houston about the case and asked him to take an active role in supporting the Birmingham branch. Houston agreed to do so because the Scottsboro and Peterson cases represented "a social crisis which may determine future leadership in the South," Houston wrote.[2] These cases also provided an opportunity for young black lawyers to gain hands-on experience with the guidance and support of Houston's continuing mentorship. Whenever Houston traveled to the South to investigate a case, he took Howard law students or former students with him.

Walter White was ecstatic when Charles Houston accepted the case. Few legal scholars possessed the brilliance, scrupulosity, and passionate commitment that Houston brought to his work. From a very early age, Houston seemed destined to play a seminal role in challenging the concept of "separate but equal" and dismantling the legal fortress of Jim Crow.

Houston was born in 1895 in Washington, DC, a year before the U.S. Supreme Court issued its historic ruling in the *Plessy v. Ferguson* case sanctioning segregation and enshrining the "separate but equal" principle that would define race relations in the United States for the next half century. As the only black student in the class of 1915 at Amherst College, Houston graduated Phi Beta Kappa and was one of the commencement speakers for his class. He taught English and Negro literature at Howard University before entering the army in World War I. The experience of serving in the segregated army was a defining moment in Houston's life, one he looked back on as he challenged the foundations of segregation. His daily experience of racism in the armed services was the impetus for studying law: "I made up my mind that I would never get caught again without knowing my rights; that if luck was with me, and I got through this war, I would study law and use my time fighting for men who could not strike back."[3]

After leaving the army, Houston entered Harvard Law School in 1919 and achieved the same academic success he earned at Amherst, becoming the first African American to serve on the editorial board of the *Harvard Law Review*. Upon graduating, Houston began teaching at Howard Law School with a burning desire to train a new generation of black lawyers to serve in cities and towns throughout the country. Houston's commanding presence as a professor and vice dean in the early 1930s attracted many students to Howard's law school. One of the students Houston mentored was future Supreme Court justice Thurgood Marshall, the first African American to serve on that highest judicial bench.[4]

Charles Hamilton Houston did not share the antipathy toward the ILD that White, McPherson, and Edmonds had in common. He admired the Communist Party's campaign to free the Scottsboro defendants and was not shy about saying so.[5] He believed the Scottsboro case was a critical turning point in the movement for racial justice because it "caught the imagination of Negroes as nothing else within a decade." Houston publicly congratulated the Communist Party on its intrepid and uncompromising efforts to save the lives of the black defendants: "The communists have been the first to fire 'the masses' with a sense of their raw, potential power, and the first to preach openly the doctrine of mass resistance and mass struggle."[6]

Frequently, Houston sent donations to the ILD and kept close contact with his friend and colleague William Patterson, who served as director of the ILD.[7] Throughout his tenure with the NAACP legal team, Houston urged the two organizations to work for common goals rather than focus on what divided them.

The generous pledge of matching gifts by an anonymous donor signified growing involvement of the CIC in the Peterson case. Walter White often turned to his friend Will Alexander for advice and counsel. It may have been Alexander's gift for mollifying white conservatives while encouraging white progressives that Walter White respected and utilized. As executive director of the national CIC, Alexander had years of experience bringing together white and black Southerners opposed to racial violence. Alexander believed that segregation was morally indefensible, but he had learned early on that he might not keep his job as CIC director or make inroads into white enclaves of power if he expressed those convictions publicly. He therefore settled for an organizational stance that worked to decrease the most flagrant abuses of Jim Crow without advocating that it be abolished.[8]

As Houston prepared to make his investigative trip to Birmingham, Walter White invited Will Alexander to Birmingham to brief Houston on the Peterson case and the current mood in Birmingham.[9] Alexander felt he had insufficient knowledge about the case to properly advise Houston, so he contacted Episcopal bishop William G. McDowell in Birmingham, who sent a summary of the Peterson case, acknowledging that the little he knew of it came from "common report." McDowell doubted there was much that could be done to reverse Peterson's conviction.[10] The white bishop revealed that he was prone to believe Nell Williams's testimony because she was "of the best class" and "a well balanced person of intelligence and belongs to a quiet and highly respected family."[11]

By McDowell's own admission, he did not possess firsthand knowledge of the case and therefore relied on the opinions of his white colleagues. This paucity of in-depth acquaintance was revealed when he asserted that there had been "no hysteria" associated with the case. McDowell diminished the incident, saying Nell's brother shot Peterson "but wounded him only slightly."[12]

After meeting with Bishop McDowell, Alexander sent his white associate Robert Eleazer on two fact-finding missions to Birmingham, meeting with civic leaders to assess public opinion with regard to the Peterson case. Alexander also made another trip to Birmingham in August and spoke with Sheriff Hawkins, Chief McDuff, editors of the white Birmingham papers, and the president of the Birmingham Bar Association, attorney William Wayne McMillan Rogers Jr. Alexander reported that all the people he and Eleazer had interviewed felt strongly that Peterson was not guilty of the murders.

Attorney Rogers confided in Alexander that there was considerable evidence in the case that had never seen the light of day during either trial. Alexander did not reveal the specific nature of that evidence in his letter to White. He did, however, convey Rogers's suggestion that the NAACP and CIC hire someone to assemble all those varied pieces of evidence into a coherent format so that they might be taken to Governor Miller.[13]

Alexander and Eleazer went about their investigations in a confidential manner, wanting neither to interfere in the work being done by Peterson's lawyers nor to arouse the attention of Roderick Beddow and his associates, who continued to be vehement in their insistence that Peterson was guilty. For those reasons, Alexander also chose not to share with Charles McPherson the information he and Eleazer had gathered.[14]

Houston's Confidential Memorandum

August 1933 proved to be a pivotal month with regard to investigations into the Peterson case. Charles Hamilton Houston made an investigative trip to Birmingham with another black attorney, Edward P. Lovett. During their four-day stay, August 7–10, they conducted extensive interviews with a significant number of "diverse citizens," including Willie Peterson, Peterson's defense attorneys J. R. Johnson and Walter Smith, Bishop McDowell, Birmingham police chief Fred McDuff, Jefferson County sheriff

James Hawkins, James E. Chappell, editor of the *Birmingham News*, and Roderick Beddow.[15]

With the exception of Roderick Beddow, none of the people Houston interviewed believed Peterson was guilty. Bishop McDowell and Mr. Chappell were ambivalent. They agreed that Peterson did not seem capable of the attacks, and yet they could not believe Nell Williams would lie or be mistaken about his identity. Chief McDuff, Sheriff Hawkins, and both of Peterson's attorneys were positive Peterson was innocent, and Houston found their arguments "unassailable."[16]

In a confidential memorandum that he wrote following his visit, Houston revealed that NAACP investigators had heard numerous unconfirmed reports that pointed to "a collateral motive for Miss Williams' testimony." Due to inconclusive proof, investigators abandoned those reports as unconfirmed rumors.[17]

To convict a man of murder in the first degree on the basis of one person's testimony was, according to Houston, a highly dubious affair. That Nell Williams's description of the assailant bore so little resemblance to the man she identified made the case more tenuous still. The fact that Jennie Wood's eyewitness description was at variance with Nell's cast even more suspicion on her testimony.[18] Houston was in complete agreement with John Altman's assessment that the material portions of Nell Williams's testimony were either "grossly improbable or impossible." In support of this contention, Houston revealed that there was some evidence—not introduced in court—that all three women may have been raped. As he stated in his memorandum:

> If this be true, the person who committed the crime must have been a sexual athlete to have ravished three different women in the space of two and a half hours, especially when the terrible nervous strain under which he must have been is considered. It is absolutely impossible to have even a suspicion that Willie Peterson would have been capable of this act on three women, each of whom was physically more robust than he. Miss Nell Williams testified that she and her sister, Augusta Williams, both jumped on the Negro at the same time and he casually shook them off. If both of them had jumped on Peterson they would have crushed him to the ground by their weight alone.[19]

Having personally interviewed Peterson, Houston contended that Peterson would not, and could not, lecture the women about racial oppression:

"A few minutes contact with Willie Peterson would convince anyone that he would not dream of lecturing white people on the race problem, and that he never has known or discussed anything about Communism."[20]

The interrogation on October 2, 1931, was for Houston another defining moment that argued for Peterson's innocence. After Dent Williams shot Peterson three times, Assistant Solicitor Long pressed him to confess so that he could meet his maker in peace. Peterson had impressed Houston as a deeply religious man. The fact that he adamantly stated his innocence in the face of imminent death was one more indicator that he was telling the truth: "Anyone who knew Peterson, his religious background and overpowering belief in an afterlife and Hell would realize that he would not go down to the brink of death, shot three times through the chest, with a lie on his lips. Under the circumstances, he had the prospect of everlasting peace to gain, and nothing to lose since he and everyone around him believed him as good as dead."[21]

Houston believed that the circumstances surrounding Peterson's arrest pointed incontrovertibly to his innocence. There was nothing stealthy about Peterson's demeanor that day. He was walking peacefully and unarmed. He had not fled the city. He did not run away or offer any resistance when called to the car. He was not nervous when he beheld the passengers in the car, including Nell Williams. He simply asked what they wanted. From the moment of his arrest to the day Houston filed his confidential memorandum, Willie Peterson insisted that he was nowhere near Shades Mountain that day and that authorities had "the wrong Negro."[22]

Nell Williams's Engagement Announced

While Charles Hamilton Houston was investigating the murders on Shades Mountain, Clark and Helen Williams were preparing to announce their daughter's engagement to Louie Reese Jr. A large photograph of Nell and the accompanying announcement were given a prominent place in the *Birmingham Age-Herald*'s Society News on Sunday, August 13, 1933. The wedding was heralded as "one of a number of events which will hold the attention of society during the early Fall."[23]

Nell was described as "an admired member of the younger set," who had recently graduated from Birmingham-Southern, where she was a "popular representative of Kappa Delta Sorority." Louie, the only son of a prominent real estate developer, was in business with his father, who had recently served as president of Birmingham's Real Estate Board.

At some length, the announcement explained that both Nell and Louie were descendants of "noteworthy" families with deep roots in Alabama. It was noted that Nell's paternal ancestors were among "the original settlers in North Alabama" that played a "notable part in the state's civic history." Like his fiancée, Louie was lauded as a member of "pioneer Alabama families," whose paternal ancestors had contributed "100 years of distinguished achievement" to civic and commercial affairs.

Working behind the Scenes

While awaiting the second ruling from the Alabama Supreme Court, the Alabama CIC and the CIC national headquarters worked behind the scenes collecting data, interviewing community leaders, and preparing a letter to Governor Miller asking him to institute a clemency hearing. They were less sanguine about a positive ruling from the courts and wanted to make a strong case for clemency. Will Alexander made weekly visits to Birmingham in August and September 1933, and his associate Robert Eleazer joined that effort in October.

In a phone conversation with Walter White on September 28, Alexander revealed that a group of "lawyers and influential citizens" had been meeting regularly in Birmingham to prepare an exhaustive brief on the Peterson case. This brief provided information about "a great deal of evidence" that was never mentioned or entered in either of Peterson's trials. Alexander did not enumerate the content of that evidence, but he stressed that this group was working independently of Peterson's lawyers. As soon as they finished the brief, they planned to notify Frank Dominick, who would, in turn, go to see Governor Miller and lay the groundwork for a delegation that intended to take the brief to the governor and have a private session with him about its contents. Alexander assured White that this could be a breakthrough for Peterson because Dominick was a trusted advisor to Governor Miller, having served as his campaign manager in 1931. Not only did Dominick promise to help secure an appointment with the governor, he said he would urge Governor Miller to take this committee's findings and recommendations very seriously.[24]

When Will Alexander received his copy of Charles Hamilton Houston's confidential memorandum, he found a personal letter attached. Houston had learned that Alexander was in Birmingham collecting data in the event that they had to file for clemency. This deeply concerned Houston. He felt strongly that neither the CIC nor the NAACP ought to approach the governor about executive clemency until every other avenue of redress was exhausted. Otherwise officials might get the wrong impression: "It should be made plain to the authorities that we do not feel executive clemency is adequate. In our opinion there is a gross miscarriage of justice, and a miscarriage of justice should be corrected by the Court rehearing the case."[25]

Houston ended his letter to Alexander with a critique and warning for the CIC: "May I report to you as a friend that young Negroes throughout the country are of the opinion that the Interracial Commission is losing its drive. They say it is slowing down, and that in a time when leadership should be more vigorous than ever it is not to be found out in front."

Within a few weeks, Alexander received a confidential interoffice letter from Robert Eleazer reporting on his conversation with Oscar Adams of the *Birmingham Reporter*. In line with Houston's September 4 letter to Alexander, Adams warned Eleazer not to initiate negotiations with the governor until all state and federal judicial avenues had been exhausted. Adams said that black people in Birmingham had no sympathy whatsoever with a clemency movement at this juncture; they hoped to see Willie Peterson exonerated and freed.[26]

sixteen

A LYNCHING IN TUSCALOOSA

Within days of Charles Houston's investigative trip to Birmingham, a lynching took place near Tuscaloosa, sixty miles southwest of Birmingham. The victims were two black men, Dan Pippen, age eighteen, and A. T. Harden, age fifteen. Two months earlier, on June 14, they and their friend Elmore Clarke had been arrested for the murder of an eighteen-year-old white woman. There was no credible evidence linking these three men to the crime, but authorities were intent on charging them.

The families of the young men retained the services of three ILD lawyers. Under pressure from authorities, Harden and Clarke backed out of their arrangement with the ILD, but Pippen refused to do so. When the three ILD lawyers arrived in town for Pippen's August 2 trial, word spread quickly that "Communist Jew lawyers" had come to stir things up, and thousands of people gathered at the courthouse. Presiding judge Henry B. Foster asked Governor Miller to send in the National Guard, and he appointed local attorneys for all three defendants, including Pippen. As the trial commenced, Judge Foster refused to recognize the ILD attorneys, disqualified the jury, adjourned the court, and ordered the National Guard to escort the lawyers out of town. The three defendants were remanded to the Tuscaloosa County Jail while awaiting a new trial.[1]

In an editorial titled "The Good in a Mob," the *Tuscaloosa News* declared that sometimes the positive aspects of a mob outweigh its inherent dangers. The thousands gathered at the courthouse had, according to the editors, sent a clear and definitive message that "the people of Tuscaloosa County are not to be bull-dozed and insulted by the International Labor Defense, as have other Southern people in recent months."[2]

On the evening of August 13, 1933, Tuscaloosa County sheriff R. L. Shamblin ordered two of his deputies and a private detective to take Pippen, Harden, and Clarke to Birmingham. Shamblin later explained that he had removed the men for safekeeping because the threats of violence and lynching in Tuscaloosa were unremitting. En route to Birmingham, two cars of armed men stopped the deputies and apprehended Pippen, Harden, and Clarke. The deputies offered no resistance. The kidnappers drove the three men to Bibb County, where they were shot and left for dead. Clarke survived and made his way to the home of a black woman who lived in the area. He was later turned over to authorities. The deputies claimed they did not know the identities of the vigilantes who stopped their car and seized the three men.[3]

Once again, the *Tuscaloosa News* blamed the lynching on the ILD. Comparing communists to carpetbaggers who had flooded into the South after the Civil War, the editors declared that both groups endorsed social equality and gave rise to lynch law: "May God forgive the carpet baggers of today who returned this foul thing to our midst.... Dan Pippen and A. T. Harden, two young Negroes accused of the murder of a white girl, lie dead. They died at the hands of an unidentified mob, but they were 'LYNCHED' by the communistic organization known as the International Labor Defense whose promoters may now enjoy to the fullest the havoc they have wrought."[4]

Sheriff Shamblin made no effort to arrest the lynchers. He, too, laid blame at the feet of the ILD lawyers who he claimed came to Tuscaloosa with the intention of stirring up violence. Governor Miller expressed outrage at the killings and instructed Attorney General Knight to conduct a thorough investigation and convene a grand jury.

Ten days after the lynching of Pippen and Harden, eleven civic and religious leaders in Birmingham's white community published a declaration in the press condemning this latest example of "lynch law":

> As citizens who love the good name of the state of Alabama, we deplore the injury done to the cause of law and order by the shooting of three Negroes taken Sunday, Aug. 13, from Tuscaloosa deputies by a small group of armed men.
>
> Whatever the crimes of the prisoners, they were awaiting trial under the laws of the state, and all outside interference had been carefully excluded by the court. The majesty of the state cannot yield to lynch law.
>
> We commend the governor, the attorney general and Judge Foster for their prompt action; and we call on all good citizens to rally public opinion to their support, that the persons guilty or responsible may be found and punished, whether they be in official or private life, and the laws of the state vindicated in the eyes of all men.
>
> (Signed)

DONALD COMER	ED S. MOORE
R. H. CROSSFIELD	A. LEO OBERDORFER
JAMES E. DILLARD	W. S. PRITCHARD
ROBERT JEMISON, JR.	HENRY UPSON SIMS
WILLIAM G. MCDOWELL	GUY E. SNAVELY
M. H. STERNE[5]	

The *Birmingham News* followed up with a lengthy editorial praising the courage and clarity of these leaders for placing "in full view the attitude of right-minded citizens in Alabama." The editors painted a sharp contrast between the enlightened, sane citizens of Alabama, represented by these eleven men, and those who embraced anarchy and the "wild medicine of 'white supremacy.'" The editorial blamed "loud political leaders" who had fanned the flames of hatred and "antagonism toward the Negro" during every election over the previous twenty years. Those who advocate racial violence would not be dissuaded by a simple condemnation of lynching, the editors declared, because "they thrive on condemnation." Required is a leadership of integrity "which will teach them that the Negro is not really their enemy, and that they may attain self-respect in better ways than a querulous insistence upon 'white control.'"[6]

The *Birmingham News* had earlier published a scathing indictment of the Tuscaloosa lynching. Titled "Alabama Is Disgraced by a Heinous Crime," the editorial declared that shame "of the blackest dye" had been brought upon the whole state. The rest of the world could be expected to react with justifiable reproach. The editors praised Governor Miller and Judge Foster for calling a special session of the grand jury and cast aspersions on those who so ruthlessly took the law into their own hands. But they blamed the "unwarranted interference" of the ILD for inflaming the lynchers: "To that extent, the blood of the victims be on the hands of the I. L. D."[7]

In response to the Tuscaloosa murders, the ILD organized a statewide conference in Birmingham that focused on the crime of lynching and filed formal charges against Sheriff Shamblin, his deputies, Judge Foster, and the private detective for their role in the murders of Pippen and Harden. This enraged many white citizens of Tuscaloosa. A local anticommunist organization, the Tuscaloosa Citizens' Protective League, terrorized Tuscaloosa's black community, raiding black homes in the name of rooting out communists.[8]

Just weeks after Pippen and Harden were lynched, rage boiled over into another lynching in Tuscaloosa. An eighty-four-year-old black man, Dennis Cross, had been held on suspicion of rape. After police dismissed as groundless all charges, a white mob ignored their findings, dragged Cross out of his bed, and killed him.[9]

Under the leadership of Rev. Edmonds and Bishop McDowell, the CIC made investigative trips to Tuscaloosa and became convinced that the lynching of Harden and Pippen was an "inside job" orchestrated by Sheriff Shamblin and his staff.[10] At the encouragement of Edmonds, the CIC's Southern Commission for the Study of Lynching undertook an exhaustive investigation of the case and published a special report titled *The Plight of Tuscaloosa: A Case Study of Conditions in Tuscaloosa County, Alabama, 1933.*

On October 2, the Tuscaloosa grand jury ruled that there was insufficient evidence to indict anyone for the murders of Pippen and Harden. Despite strenuous efforts to secure an indictment, a thorough investigation was hindered by the noncooperation of the sheriff's department and the recalcitrance of local residents.[11] One week later, the proceedings of a new grand jury produced no indictment in the lynching of Dennis Cross.

When Charles Hamilton Houston returned to Washington in August 1933, he organized a delegation of representatives from the NAACP, the ILD, and the American Civil Liberties Union to meet with President Roosevelt and brief him on the Tuscaloosa lynchings. After waiting several hours at the White House, the delegation was informed that the president was too busy organizing his new administration to meet with them. Houston was incensed by both the president's evasiveness and the rude way they were treated at the White House.[12] Nevertheless, Houston refused to be deterred and continued his efforts to bring the Tuscaloosa lynchings to the president's attention.

On August 24, Houston was granted a meeting with the attorney general, Homer S. Cummings. This time Houston's delegation was even larger and included the three ILD lawyers who had attempted to represent Pippen, Harden, and Clarke in Tuscaloosa. The group sought federal intervention in the case, arguing that Sheriff Shamblin had violated the law by allowing the young men to be seized. Cummings invited the delegation to submit a brief substantiating their claims that Shamblin had violated a federal code dating back to Reconstruction and should be federally indicted.[13]

On October 13, 1933, Houston and his two colleagues, Leon Ransom and Edward Lovett, submitted to the Justice Department a brief stating that if the federal government failed to intervene in this case, the United States would be guilty of egregious hypocrisy: "A Nation which can raise its hands at the atrocities perpetrated . . . under the Nazi government in Germany cannot, if it be honest and honorable, remain quiescent in the face of barbarities practiced daily within its own boundaries." Attorney General Cummings would eventually decline to prosecute Sheriff Shamblin, but not before Houston and the NAACP created a sensation by publishing the brief in pamphlet form and distributing two thousand copies to newspapers and periodicals, members of Congress, and every governor.[14]

The Cost of the Mob

Henry Edmonds's name was conspicuously absent from the list of civic leaders who signed the Tuscaloosa declaration that appeared in the *Birmingham Age-Herald* on September 25, 1933. Why Edmonds declined to be the twelfth signatory on that statement is puzzling, especially considering the sermon he preached six weeks later at Independent Presbyterian Church titled "The Cost of the Mob."[15] Drawing heavily on a recently published book, *The Tragedy of Lynching*, Edmonds delivered a blistering condemnation of lynching.[16]

With uncompromising bluntness, Edmonds enumerated the manifold costs of racial violence: the unspeakable suffering experienced by the black victim and his surviving community of family and friends; the irreparable damage to local jurisdictions when the rule of law was abandoned and the mob gained ascendency; the loss of human decency, integrity, and civilized behaviors through the monstrous display of cruelty, abuse, and violence; the trauma suffered by white children brought to lynchings and hoisted on the shoulders of their parents so they might get a better view of the brutality; and the material cost of the jails, homes, businesses, and schoolhouses that the mob burned to the ground or otherwise destroyed.[17]

Citing research compiled in *The Tragedy of Lynching*, Edmonds declared that, as a rule, lynch mobs consisted of poor, young, and uneducated white men. These rabble-rousing vagrants often traveled from a distance to the towns where lynchings took place. Edmonds's portrait of the typical lyncher may have allowed his congregants to breathe a sigh of relief because Independent Presbyterian Church did not have members who fit that demographic description. But Edmonds failed to cite two other findings of *The Tragedy of Lynching* that might have struck closer to home: the silent acquiescence of local citizens who did nothing to interrupt or protest the lynching, and the all too prevalent indifference of local law enforcement officers.[18] These omissions were surprising because, just weeks before he wrote this sermon, Edmonds spent several days in Tuscaloosa investigating the lynching of Dan Pippen and A. T. Harden. Edmonds knew how probable it was that Sheriff Shamblin or his deputies had notified the lynchers that Pippen, Harden, and Clarke were being transported to Birmingham. Edmonds also knew that the lynchers were most likely not outsiders to Tuscaloosa. He may not have felt prepared to reveal all this on that Sunday morning, but, in retrospect, it is noteworthy that he failed to name the fact that local citizens and law enforcement were all too often complicit despite the usual claim that lynchings were "at the hands of persons unknown."

Nevertheless, elements of Rev. Edmonds's sermon were bound to make some members of Independent Presbyterian Church uncomfortable. He boldly stated that many black people who escaped a near lynching were later found to be innocent. White accusers frequently framed innocent black men to cover up their own derelictions or divert attention from the real criminal who was white. Edmonds cited a case in Virginia where a white woman had accused a black man of rape. The alleged assailant was convicted and sentenced to death. A new trial was granted and the defendant acquitted when newly acquired evidence showed that the woman had falsely charged the black man in an effort to conceal her affair with a married white man. Edmonds described the case of eighty-four-year-old Dennis Cross in Tuscaloosa, who was framed and lynched before a trial could be held: "The evidence against him was that he was seen running away from the scene of the crime. Since his death it is brought out that he was paralyzed and could not have run a step." And then, revealing his outrage at this wanton violence, Edmonds named another recent killing in nearby Decatur, Alabama, the town where the Scottsboro defendants were being retried: "And nobody has remotely claimed that the Negro recently shot in Decatur was guilty of anything. He was shot simply because the mob spirit was about, he was near and was black."[19]

"The Cost of the Mob" was an uncommonly strong condemnation of lynching from a prominent white preacher in Jim Crow Birmingham.[20] Edmonds ended the lengthy polemic by stating that lynchings could not be blamed on communist agitation, the slowness of Southern courts, or the hideousness of the original crime. The primary cause of lynching, Edmonds said, was the belief that black people were second-class citizens and their treatment as such. Speaking directly to the people of wealth and influence sitting before him in the pews, Edmonds declared, "If the dominant people of Alabama should say this morning and mean it, 'The Negro being a person shall not be misused,' mob rule would stop in an hour."[21]

A Different View of the "Lynching Situation"

On November 9, 1933, less than one month after marrying Nell Williams, Louie Reese Jr. wrote Governor Miller praising his decision to send the National Guard to usher the ILD lawyers out of Tuscaloosa. Reese felt it was "high time" that Alabama authorities confronted the influx of "damned" Yankees from the North and East, and prevent them from dictating how things should be run in Alabama.

According to Reese, the editors of the *Birmingham News* made a grave mistake when they condemned the Tuscaloosa lynching "in such a drastic and public way." He felt the editors had unfairly characterized the whole state as "criminal." Reese insisted that lynchings would not take place if Alabama courts did what they were supposed to do: convict the accused. And the reason the courts were failing to follow through with the appropriate judgments could be laid at the feet of those "foreign elements." People resort to lynching, Reese wrote, when they cannot get justice in the courts.

Toward the close of his letter, Reese voiced his "sentiment" about the case of Willie Peterson—convicted of "the murder of two and the wounding of one of Birmingham's finest young women." The fact that Peterson's execution had been stayed was, according to Reese, directly attributable to the influence of outside agitators. Reese did not say that he and Nell Williams were married. Nor did he mention that his brother-in-law, Dent Williams, had taken the law into his own hands, perhaps fearing the court might not convict Willie Peterson. Reese simply ended the letter reiterating his "heartiest appreciation" for the way Governor Miller had dealt with those foreign elements in the Tuscaloosa case.[22]

seventeen

MOVING THE CASE FORWARD

In October 1933, the Alabama Supreme Court refused the request for a re-hearing in the Willie Peterson case. Will Alexander, national director of the CIC, reached out to Walter White, expressing his disappointment in this latest setback and pledging the CIC's support should the NAACP decide to take the case to the U.S. Supreme Court. That was indeed the intention of Walter White and the NAACP's National Legal Committee. White wasted no time contacting Charles McPherson, reiterating his commitment to move ahead with an appeal to the nation's highest court. There was, how-ever, one important proviso: Charles Hamilton Houston must be involved in every phase of the appeal. White had no intention of supplanting John Altman as lead counsel for this new appeal, but Altman would need to work with Houston in preparing it. The National Legal Committee was prepared to throw its full weight behind this final appeal on the condition that Houston sign off on "any and all documents before they were filed."[1]

Charles McPherson did not relish the thought of initiating that con-versation with John Altman, who had returned to his legal practice after recuperating from his stroke. McPherson knew that Altman prided himself on being one of the best attorneys in Alabama. Altman might resent the suggestion that he should be accountable to another lawyer, let alone a black attorney. Furthermore, McPherson would need to remind Altman that the NAACP could not pay him top dollar. Their national legal funds were stretched to the limit with a number of vitally important cases, and they had to raise funds from a black constituency that was in dire straits due to the Depression.[2]

For moral support, McPherson asked Oscar Adams to accompany him on his visit to Altman. They discovered that Altman had already prepared paperwork for an appeal to the U.S. Supreme Court. After expressing delight that Altman was still on board, McPherson handed him Walter White's letter. Altman read the letter in its entirety and asked but one question: "Who is Mr. Houston?" McPherson explained that Houston, a Harvard Law School graduate and vice dean of Howard University Law School, was deeply involved in the NAACP's litigation campaigns. Stressing that Altman would continue as lead attorney, McPherson said that final terms and arrangements could best be worked out when Charles Houston returned to Birmingham in the near future. If John Altman was perturbed by this new arrangement, he did not express it. He agreed to proceed as planned, saying he expected to be paid $1,500 for his services plus stenographic expenses.[3]

In anticipation of welcoming Charles Houston back to the city, McPherson planned a conference for the wider community to become acquainted with the eminent vice dean of Howard Law School, hoping to enlist key leaders from the white and black communities to speak. Their presence and support would issue a strong and unified message that the NAACP was still very much in charge of the Peterson case. On October 30, 1933, three hundred people—white and black—attended the conference. People had to be turned away, and one of the speakers, Rabbi Newfield, was unable to deliver his address because the large crowd prevented his entering the hall. Oscar Adams gave a stirring introduction of the evening's main attraction, Charles Hamilton Houston, who spoke about the continuing scourge of lynching.[4]

Charles McPherson was elated by every aspect of the evening: the overflow crowd, the outpouring of support for the Peterson case, and the enthusiastic response to Houston's address. After so many setbacks and disappointments in recent months, McPherson drew heart and hope from this gathering. His only regret was that Henry Edmonds declined the invitation to speak that evening and did not attend. McPherson hoped that Edmonds would bring a message of support and partnership as chair of the Alabama CIC. He may have also hoped for Edmonds's presence that night, knowing that Rev. Edmonds just two weeks earlier had condemned lynching from the pulpit of Independent Presbyterian Church.

During a private meeting with McPherson, Edmonds declined the invitation because of "intimate and delicate relations with Williams and Wood families." Before making a definitive decision on the matter, Edmonds said he would seek the advice and counsel of Bishop McDowell. He called the next day and suggested that McPherson invite attorneys Altman and Smith to speak in his stead.[5]

An Uneasy Partnership

The collaboration between attorney John Altman and the NAACP grew stressful and tension filled during the appeal process, often related to finances. In mid-November Altman sent Walter White an invoice reminding the NAACP secretary that he was due a total of $1,438. Altman reminded White that he had reduced his fee for the U.S. Supreme Court work to a level "some attorneys would consider a ridiculous amount" because he was aware that the Depression had weighed very heavily on "our colored people," and he marveled at "their ability to get along as well as they do."[6]

The working relationship between John Altman and Charles Hamilton Houston was also strained. Altman's letter to Walter White ended with a side comment betraying Altman's annoyance that his work was being held up to scrutiny by a black man. In a previous letter, White conveyed complimentary remarks about Altman that Houston had made. White passed these statements along as a gesture of collegiality and appreciation, but it may have angered John Altman that a black man felt free to pass judgment on him even when positive. Altman offered a brief acknowledgment of the compliment and then added, unnecessarily, "[Houston] is certainly a very clean cut, high classed, intelligent man."[7]

Having been advised of Altman's impatience to be paid, Houston sent Altman a letter assuring him that a check would be sent as soon as possible. As a cost-cutting measure, Houston volunteered to do routine work that might be required in Washington such as filing documents with the clerk of the Supreme Court.[8]

When Oscar Adams got wind of Charles Houston having volunteered to contact the clerk at the Supreme Court, he sent Altman a confidential letter, encouraging Altman to use his own connections at the Supreme Court rather than going through Houston: "While I appreciate Mr. Houston's ability and interest in the case, I am just of the opinion that some white attorney in Washington . . . should make this presentation. This is not to question Mr. Houston's ability, but in making our last step for the life and liberty where we believe the person absolutely innocent, every precaution, in my judgment, should be taken."[9]

Altman was pleased with Adams's encouragement and decided to act accordingly. He wrote Houston, reiterating that he knew an attorney in Washington who was on a most friendly basis with the clerk of the Supreme Court. That attorney would do this favor for only $50, and therefore Houston need not bother himself with the task. Without waiting for Houston's response, Altman enclosed a copy of his letter to that attorney asking him to perform the service.[10] Being granted no real choice in the matter, Houston graciously bowed out, stating that he wanted Altman to do whatever was necessary to save Willie Peterson.[11]

In early January 1934, Altman telegraphed Walter White and Charles Houston asking for $115 in printing costs for the U.S. Supreme Court briefs. White failed to respond in a timely fashion, so Altman decided to send a typewritten copy to the court instead. When McPherson learned of this, he was concerned that this violation of Supreme Court protocol might jeopardize the case. Had they fought this hard for so long only to have the case go belly up because of $115 in printing costs? McPherson contacted Altman immediately and promised they would reimburse him for the printing costs. Altman informed him that time had run out, and the typewritten copy would have to do. If the court failed to review the case because of improper forms, Altman said he would hold Walter White and Charles Houston responsible. McPherson was deeply distressed and thought it morally indefensible that Willie Peterson's fate might come down to $115 in printing costs. Altman assured McPherson that meeting the deadline was paramount, and the typewritten copy would in all likelihood be acceptable to the court.[12]

Sheriff Hawkins's Intervention

On Friday, January 5, 1934, Sheriff James Hawkins walked out of the Jefferson County Jail with Willie Peterson. Together they rode to Montgomery, where Sheriff Hawkins delivered Peterson to authorities at Kilby Prison.

After the Alabama Supreme Court refused to hear his case for the second time, Peterson was forced to take up residence on Kilby's death row. A ruling from the U.S. Supreme Court might alter this fate, but for now Peterson was dreading what awaited him at Alabama's House of Pain.

This anticipated trip to Kilby Prison may have caused Sheriff Hawkins to write the letter that he hand-delivered to Governor Miller that day. From the outset, Hawkins found it difficult to believe that Willie Peterson was capable of committing the reprehensible crimes on Shades Mountain. After two years of observing Peterson at the Jefferson County Jail, he was more convinced than ever that they had the wrong man in custody. With a new execution date only ten days away, Hawkins knew he had to come clean with the governor.

"I don't believe Willie Peterson is the Negro who committed this offense," Hawkins wrote, "and this belief is shared by Chief Fred H. McDuff, who is even more familiar with the facts than I am. When I attempt to analyze and assign reasons for my belief there is very little to base it on, yet I have the feeling in my heart that convinces me that it is my duty to appear before you and make a full and frank statement of all matters pertaining to this case, which have come under my observation. . . . The young women who suffered outrages at the hands of some Negro are members of our best families and my closest friends. It is embarrassing to me to do or say anything that would displease them, but I am not willing to go through life feeling that my silence might have allowed an innocent person, although a Negro, to die."[13]

On January 8, 1934, one week before Willie Peterson was scheduled to die in the electric chair, Governor Miller announced he was delaying the execution. The reason given was Sheriff Hawkins's letter. Hawkins was by no means the first white person to voice reservations about Peterson's guilt to the governor, but his protracted involvement in the murder investigations made his letter especially compelling.[14]

The Williams family, as well as the prosecution team, let no time elapse before issuing rebuttals to the sheriff's letter. Attorney Roderick Beddow dismissed Hawkins's reservations as "maudlin sentiment" and reiterated what he had declared in court: Peterson's guilt was incontrovertible because Nell Williams had three hours of daylight to study the perpetrator's face, stature, and mannerisms.

"If Miss Nell Williams does not know who committed the offense for which Peterson was convicted, who does? She is a young woman of poise, high intellect, absolutely devoid of malice and surely she of all people would not want to offer an innocent victim upon the callous altar of revenge, for this would mean that the guilty participant would go free."[15]

Clark Williams and Wade Wood Jr., brother of Jennie Wood, issued equally emphatic statements condemning Sheriff Hawkins's "vague, indefinite and uncertain feelings" as completely contrary to the facts in the case. Noting that officers had brought nearly a hundred black men before his daughter, Clark Williams declared that she scrupulously refused to identify an innocent man. Yet from the moment she laid eyes on Willie Peterson, she had never doubted he was the guilty party.[16]

Clark Williams reiterated that the assailant had vowed to get even for the mistreatment of black people and had lectured the women about the "Scottsboro Boys" as a case in point. He doubted that Birmingham's former police chief Fred McDuff would back Hawkins in his outrageous claims. Williams also insisted that the sheriff's "vague feelings of the Negro's innocence would vanish" if it were his daughter who had sustained such a vicious attack.[17]

The next day, editors at the *Birmingham News* lauded Sheriff Hawkins for his "very deep earnestness and fine courage." They urged Governor Miller to conduct a thorough investigation before making a decision.[18]

"The Social Implications of This Case"

While awaiting word from the U.S. Supreme Court, the NAACP leadership sought assistance from religious and civic leaders, who were encouraged to write Governor Miller imploring him to grant commutation of Peterson's sentence to life imprisonment. At the root of their appeals were three core arguments. First, this was a critical time in the history of race relations in the South. Second, all the evidence in this case pointed to Peterson being "the wrong Negro." And third, the execution of Peterson could have "profound social implications."[19]

The national NAACP staff contacted the *New York Times*, the Associated Press, and other publications stressing the critical importance of this case. In Birmingham, Charles McPherson wrote J. E. Chappell, editor of the *Birmingham News*, thanking him for his fair and consistent editorial support of their efforts to secure justice for Willie Peterson. McPherson then asked Chappell to go a step further and write an editorial about the "deeper social implications of this case."[20] Chappell responded with a wary tone, saying he was not convinced that an editorial about the deeper social implications would be wise at this particular time. Nevertheless, he asked McPherson to send a memorandum explaining exactly what social implications he had in mind. McPherson immediately forwarded this request to the national staff of the NAACP. Walter Harris, national vice president of the NAACP, sent Chappell a two-page memorandum stating what was at stake in this case:

> The great test is presenting itself to Alabama, and the South, to decide between two procedures, two methods, two types of organizations available to the Negro as a whole, as a mass unit. . . . If you electrocute this apparently innocent man, you will hasten the death of that *last* hope that the Negro has for fair treatment in your courts, he shall be forced to lose faith in our orderly procedure and in you, and shall be forced to resort to such salvation as shall spring from that latent resentment that is constantly, slowly, but we fear surely, being stimulated by multiplied injustices, into violence, a latent violence born of the hatreds of years of oppression and suppression which shall, if continued burst forth into an expression unparalleled by the recorded events of history. The greater social implications have been divulged, not to incite or to excite, but to inform for the greatest good for the greatest number.[21]

James Chappell may not have known that his associate editor, Charles Feidelson, made an appointment to see Governor Miller on Saturday, January 6, as soon as he learned about Sheriff Hawkins's letter. Feidelson had practiced law and served as a juvenile judge in Savannah, Georgia, before coming to Birmingham in 1925. It may have been the respect he had earned as a columnist and associate editor that gave him an entrée to the governor, who was eager to hear his perspective on the Peterson case. Governor Miller listened as Feidelson explained how the Peterson case could either strengthen or weaken conservative black leadership in Alabama. As Feidelson later reported to Will Alexander, "I took up the fight between the N. A. A. C. P. and the I. L. D. and argued that Peterson's execution would be likely to make a majority of Alabama Negroes turn to 'mass pressure' as their only hope. The governor was most appreciative."[22]

On January 22, 1934, Peterson's attorneys received word that the U.S. Supreme Court refused to grant a new trial. Their last resort was to bring pressure on Governor Miller to grant clemency to Willie Peterson. The governor agreed to convene a pardon board hearing in Montgomery on February 6, 1934.

Conflict of Interest

The pardon board consisted of four members: governor Benjamin Meek Miller, attorney general Thomas Knight, secretary of state Pete Jarman, and state auditor John Brandon. Defense attorney John Altman was determined to do everything in his power to prevent Attorney General Knight from serving on the pardon board for Willie Peterson's clemency hearing. In his opinion, that would be an undeniable conflict of interest. Knight had chaired the grand jury that indicted Peterson and was also present in Washington, DC, when the Supreme Court refused to hear the Peterson appeal. On January 31, Altman wrote Attorney General Knight demanding that he recuse himself from the pardon board hearing.

Altman addressed the letter "Dear Tom," but the substance of his message was anything but warm and friendly. Altman accused Knight of conspiring to prevent the U.S. Supreme Court from considering Peterson's case. In Altman's view, Knight continued to function as a prosecutor long after the grand jury had finished its work. Therefore, Altman demanded that Knight recuse himself and issue a public statement clarifying that he was doing so without prejudice to the petitioner. In case Knight was not persuaded by legal arguments, Altman suggested that he consider the moral implications: "If you should act as prosecutor and Judge on that hearing and should condemn the Negro to death it is my idea and my opinion that you will never get that thought out of your mind as long as you live."[23]

Altman described how Willie Peterson (whom he consistently referred to as "the Negro") had been subjected to a "vicious trial" during which he was "substantially murdered in the name of the law," providing specific examples of underhanded behavior on the part of Assistant Solicitor Long. Altman found Long's "cruel and relentless effort to obtain a conviction" particularly deplorable because Long had declared after the grand jury hearing that Peterson was not any more guilty than he was.

Altman said he was writing Knight personally because he did not want to have to make a public protest. Nevertheless, he made it clear he would do just that if Knight did not recuse himself. He warned Knight that using "the Negro" for political gain would be foolish and self-destructive because his office was flooded daily by letters and calls from white people saying they believed Peterson was innocent.

By letter, Knight acknowledged his participation in the case before the Supreme Court, but he did not believe he was instrumental in having the hearing denied. He vehemently objected to Altman's insinuation that he used his official duties for political purposes. Knight stated that he had not yet decided whether he would serve on the pardon board or recuse himself, but whichever choice he made, it would not be to curry political favor or friendships. Noting that this was the first time "that an Attorney for a condemned person has suggested that the prosecutor should not sit as a Member of the Pardon Board," he assured Altman that whatever he decided, his action would be taken "without prejudice to Peterson."[24]

Fred McDuff's Repudiation

Three days before the pardon board hearing, Birmingham residents awoke to another surprise in the Peterson case. In a letter to the governor, released to the press on February 3, 1934, Birmingham's former police chief Fred McDuff repudiated Sheriff Hawkins's contention that he was in full agreement about Peterson being "the wrong Negro." McDuff declared that Willie Peterson had been fairly tried and convicted, and he saw no good reason to intervene: "It would be presumptuous on my part to question the correctness of the verdict and judgment of conviction as being right and just when I know of no competent evidence that would warrant me to do so."[25]

Why former Police Chief McDuff publicly distanced himself from Sheriff Hawkins was open to debate. Some speculated that he chose to align himself with the circuit court's decision because he was running for sheriff. Others suspected that the Williams family and their attorney, Roderick Beddow, prevailed upon him. In either case, the stance McDuff took in his letter to Governor Miller was totally at odds with statements he had previously made on many different occasions to Peterson's defense attorneys and community leaders.

Fred McDuff's repudiation shocked and enraged John Altman. Only four days previously, McDuff had spoken at length with Altman and provided ample evidence for why he firmly believed Willie Peterson was not the guilty party. On the eve of the pardon board hearing, the *Birming-*

ham News featured a lengthy letter from Altman to McDuff, charging that McDuff had "about faced" and demanding that McDuff disclose the real author of his letter. Altman then listed nine pointed questions addressed to McDuff, all beginning with the phrase "Did you not tell me . . . ?" and each referring back to the reasons McDuff had articulated why he believed Peterson was innocent.[26]

McDuff's reply was curt. In a two-sentence statement given to the press, McDuff denied having given Altman or anyone else prior information that could be construed as inconsistent with his letter to the governor.[27]

John Altman was not the only person surprised and infuriated by Fred McDuff's turnaround. Charles Hamilton Houston sent a blistering telegram to McDuff on the eve of the pardon board hearing: "Birmingham News quotes you as repudiating stand taken by you last summer. . . . Unwilling to believe political candidacy influenced your decision. No profit riding into office over innocent man's body."[28] Charles Feidelson also took action when hearing of McDuff's repudiation. He wrote Will Alexander, saying that McDuff's behavior was a "shameless about-face" and urging Alexander to send Houston's report of his investigative findings to the governor.[29]

In response to this controversy, Governor Miller postponed the pardon board hearing until March 5 and extended the date of execution to March 30. That postponement provided needed time for Peterson's lawyers to recruit more witnesses and secure additional documents. Altman urged Charles Houston to draw up affidavits for everyone who was present at the interview with Chief McDuff the previous summer, including Robert Eleazer, Walter Smith, Charles McPherson, and Edward Lovett. Altman believed those documents would provide a strong antidote to McDuff's repudiation. In the presence of a notary public, those affidavits were signed and sent to Governor Miller.

"Swing Low, Sweet Chariot"

On Friday evening, February 9, 1934, the men on Kilby Prison's death row experienced five walk-bys. Willie Peterson saw five black men pass by his cell, one after the other, headed for the green door. That night the state of Alabama put to death Ernest Waller, Solomon Roper, Harie White, Bennie Foster, and John Thompson. As Clarence Norris later told it, "I'm not sure why all of them was put to death, but I do know you could actually smell burning flesh all up and down death row after they was executed."[30]

Had Governor Miller not received the flood of letters calling for clemency, Willie Peterson might have been the sixth black man to die that night.

Since being convicted of murder and sentenced to death in January 1931, Willie's date of execution had been set and then postponed five different times. Each time an appeal was rejected or the lower court's decision upheld, fear must have shot through Willie's veins as he waited to hear the new date of his execution.

Before each walk-by on death row, a black chaplain employed by the state paid a visit to the condemned man, peppering him with questions to elicit a last-minute confession of guilt. It looked better for the governor and Alabama's judicial system if prisoners confirmed the truth of their death sentence. The chaplain couched his questions in religious language, arguing that the prisoner would not want to meet his maker with a lie on his lips. He also hammered home that the condemned prisoner had nothing to lose at this point; he might as well confess. Without the condemned man's consent, the black chaplain always accompanied black prisoners into the execution room, singing, "Swing low, sweet chariot, coming for to carry me home." As the prisoner was being strapped into the chair, he would sing, "Two white horses, coming in line, coming in line, coming to carry me home."[31]

The next morning, guards brought two prisoners to the dead man's cell and ordered them to clean the room from top to bottom. When that guard was L. J. Burrs, he always sat and sang while the men scrubbed the floors and walls:

> She'll be comin' round the mountain when she comes,
> She'll be bringing two white horses,
> She'll be bringing two white horses,
> She'll be bringing two white horses when she comes.[32]

The efforts to coerce confessions from the five black men who died on February 9 may have triggered flashbacks for Willie Peterson. There's a good chance he had a restless night, remembering how Assistant Solicitor Long towered over him shouting while he lay bleeding on the jailhouse cot:
"You are dying, Willie. You can't die with a lie on your lips."

Willie may have also remembered the moment he opened his eyes two days later and saw Solicitor Bailes standing by his hospital bed, feigning concern about Willie's critical condition. Within minutes the state's attorney revealed the true nature of his visit.

"If you thought you were going to die, Willie, would you want to say anything?"

Barely conscious, Willie had summoned the strength to proclaim his innocence one more time. The dejected prosecutor shook his head, turned, and left the room.

Two and a half years later, with the smell of burning flesh permeating his cell, Willie may have wondered when that preacher would appear at his cell door, demanding a confession and singing, "Two white horses, coming in line, coming in line, coming to carry me home."

eighteen

NO NEGROES ALLOWED

Walter White, national secretary of the NAACP, stepped up his involvement in the Peterson case by contacting key leaders in the Birmingham community, asking them to appear at the pardon board hearing. Henry Edmonds was among the leaders who received this urgent appeal from White: "It is our firm conviction that should Peterson be executed it will be the gravest blow to interracial relations struck for many years. . . . [It] would give Communists the most powerful argument they have ever had for propaganda among Negroes. They would contend throughout America and the world that this is a clear-cut example that there is no hope whatsoever of orderly appeals to justice. We must not—we cannot—permit the hardboiled and ruthless attitude of the prosecution to destroy much of what it has taken years to create."[1]

Edmonds assured Walter White that he had written the governor conveying those very sentiments and that he planned to attend the hearing. White also asked Charles Houston and Robert Moton, president of Tuskegee Institute, to make the trip to Montgomery on February 6. As a courtesy,

Houston wrote attorney John Altman, saying he wished to be present as a spectator, but did not want his presence to interfere with Altman's handling of the case or provoke opposition against Peterson.[2]

Altman responded immediately, warning that Houston and "all members of Peterson's race" should refrain from attending the pardon board hearing: "It is inevitable that it will do harm for any Negro to be present. It is certain that it will benefit Peterson if we have no Negroes there and at least apparently trust his fortunes and his life to the judgment and hearts of white men."[3]

Altman did not in any way apologize for this demand or acknowledge that it might have been an affront to Houston and other black leaders. Nor did he concede that Willie Peterson would have good reason to be wary about trusting his life to the judgment and hearts of white men. Up to that point, virtually every white man who possessed the structural power to decide Peterson's fate had worked for his conviction or remained silent while others were doing so. Sheriff Hawkins and Chief McDuff harbored suspicions that Peterson was the wrong man from the start, but it took Sheriff Hawkins two and a half years to step forward and publicly state those reservations. Furthermore, neither man had been willing to bar Dent Williams from the October 2, 1931, interrogation, despite the fact that their deputies had heard him threaten to murder Willie Peterson.

John Altman was a white man who had diligently worked to get a fair trial for Peterson, but he had failed in all three of his appeals. Nonetheless, he believed that this time Peterson's life would be spared, not on legal grounds but by stirring the consciences and "the heartstrings" of the white men on the pardon board. Altman was just as certain that this effort would be undermined by the presence of black people—especially those who possessed the erudition, reputation, and stature of Dean Houston and President Moton. Altman intended to implore the members of the pardon board to exhibit noblesse oblige to Willie Peterson, whom he described as a "poor helpless Negro," dependent on their mercy. Having black people present who were neither poor nor helpless would undermine his strategy.[4]

To add insult to injury, Altman requested that Charles McPherson and Oscar Adams send a delegation to Montgomery to ensure that "no Negro goes into the room." The black people in this delegation could be near the capitol, but Altman stipulated that they must keep enough distance so as not to be detected by any white people entering and exiting the hearing room.[5]

Houston responded to Altman by letter, stating that he did not agree that the presence of black people would be detrimental to Peterson's case. Nevertheless, he would respect Altman's wishes and abide by his decision.

Walter White was deeply ambivalent about Houston's decision to respect Altman's wishes. The NAACP had made a concerted effort to champion the case of Willie Peterson. It would be natural that black people would want to be present for the clemency hearings, which were open to the public. White did not want to go against the lead attorney's wishes, but he feared that the absence of black people at the hearing would give the governor the wrong impression. Willie Peterson's supporters had been flooding the governor's office with letters and telegrams saying that black people throughout the South were anxious to see the governor do the right thing and grant commutation. If no black people were present, would that give the impression that they lacked interest in the case?[6]

After conferring with trusted colleagues like Will Alexander, Walter White decided to accede to Altman's demand. He then telegraphed Governor Miller to inform him that the NAACP had consented to Altman's request, but the governor should not interpret the absence of black people as lack of interest in this case. White implored the governor to act with courage "to prevent gross miscarriage of justice" and to prevent the communists from using Peterson's execution "as basis for claim that orderly appeals to courts of law are futile."[7]

Charles Houston's Groundbreaking Appeals

John Altman may have had other reasons for fearing Charles Houston's presence at the hearing, reasons he did not name in his letters to NAACP officials. During the preceding year, Charles Houston had been intimately involved in another case that shook the South and made national news. It had striking parallels to the Peterson case. George Crawford, a twenty-eight-year-old black man who did odd jobs for a living, was arrested and charged with killing Agnes Ilsley, a wealthy white woman in Middleburg, Virginia, and her maid, Nina Buckner, also a white woman. Both were bludgeoned to death. Although many townspeople suspected that Agnes Ilsley's brother committed the murder, George Crawford was charged with the crime.[8]

Fearing for his life, George Crawford fled town and eluded authorities for months before being apprehended. In January 1933, one year after the Virginia murders, Crawford was arrested for minor larceny in Boston. The Loudon County, Virginia, grand jury that indicted Crawford sought his extradition to stand trial in Virginia for the murder of Agnes Ilsley. That's when Houston joined a team of Boston NAACP lawyers who were challenging the constitutionality of the extradition because the Virginia grand jury that indicted Crawford had no black jurors. Houston argued that the Virginia indictment of Crawford was illegal and violated due process guaranteed by the Fourteenth Amendment.

Houston hoped to set a precedent in the Crawford case that would have far-reaching consequences for indictments of black people. In future cases, if black people indicted in the South escaped to the North, Southern states would be prevented from gaining extradition so long as they barred black people from serving on juries. In April, federal district judge James Lowell granted a writ of habeas corpus in Massachusetts and freed Crawford. Lowell declared that he saw no reason to send Crawford back to Virginia to face trial when the U.S. Supreme Court would likely later declare the trial illegal. When they got wind of the decision, Southern members of Congress were incensed by what they considered a brazen violation of states' rights.[9]

On October 15, the U.S. Supreme Court upheld the Virginia court's right to try Crawford. Houston and the NAACP lost the battle to block extradition, but the ripples of Judge Lowell's ruling were already being felt in Virginia. For the first time in thirty years, several Virginia counties had selected black people to serve on grand juries.

Houston agreed to serve as lead counsel in the Crawford trial so long as he could select an all-black team of lawyers to assist him. As he wrote to Walter White, "The men here [at Howard Law School] feel if Crawford could be defended by an all-Negro counsel, it would mark a turning point in the legal history of the Negro in the country."[10] The presence of an all-black counsel was unprecedented in Virginia. All four lawyers had to commute each day from Washington, DC, to Leesburg because no one dared offer them lodging. The *Washington Post* described the trial as "perhaps the most remarkable in the history of southern jurisprudence."[11] After a weeklong trial and three hours of deliberation, the all-white jury convicted Crawford but sentenced him to life imprisonment. This sentence was unexpected because the state had pressed for the death penalty.

"The Greatest Traitor" in Alabama's Ruling Class

On February 10, 1934, Charles Houston wrote John Altman a frank and lengthy letter informing him that Henrietta Peterson had joined forces with the ILD. She was distraught to learn that black people were barred from the hearing and angry that the NAACP was willing to settle for clemency rather than pressing for her husband's release from prison. The ILD had distributed handbills throughout Birmingham criticizing the NAACP for selling out and announced that a delegation of black people, including Mrs. Peterson, were planning to seek entrance to the hearing in Montgomery. Failing that, they would stage a demonstration nearby.[12]

Charles Houston also expressed his belief that former chief McDuff's act of betrayal was more than shameful; it was a gross violation of the office to which voters in Alabama had elected him. If white leaders in Alabama refused to hold McDuff accountable, that failure could "mean the end of all hope in Alabama's political integrity." Houston put the question very directly to Altman: "Let us be perfectly frank with ourselves. If you were a black man and Willie Peterson were executed, and McDuff's repudiation were allowed to stand, how much faith would you have left in Alabama politics or Alabama officials?"[13]

Altman found Houston's letter deeply troubling. He feared that Houston might broadcast those sentiments more widely throughout the state of Alabama. Responding to Houston, he warned that the pardon board and governor would likely take great offense in hearing such opinions, and that could be disastrous for Peterson: "Please pay attention to this. . . . Don't take any chance whatever on letting it get out where it might reach or be reported to the Pardon Board and the Governor. . . . If it does so Peterson will be very greatly damaged."[14]

Charles Houston was willing to honor John Altman's plea not to attend the pardon board hearing, but he refused to be dissuaded from sending urgent appeals to numerous white leaders throughout Alabama in language similar to the one he sent attorney Walter S. Smith on February 13: "I am sure that you see that Chief McDuff is the greatest traitor that the ruling class in Alabama could possibly have, because as their chosen representative, as the man whom they set up as their exponent of public virtue, he demonstrates by his conduct that the ruling class is unfit for the position they occupy and cannot be trusted with the impartial and fearless enforcement of the law. The McDuff repudiation is just as dangerous to the public peace and welfare of Alabama as an open flame around a powder keg."[15]

nineteen

A FLOOD OF LETTERS

In the weeks leading up to the pardon board hearing, the governor's office received letters on both sides of the clemency question. Helen Williams, Nell Williams Reese's mother, implored the governor to let the death sentence stand. She described how her daughters and Jennie Wood "begged Willie Peterson for their lives, but he told them he would kill them if they were the Virgin Mary." She emphasized that Nell had never once doubted her identification of Peterson and that her daughter was a trustworthy witness: "Nell is positive Willie Peterson is the Negro, and she should know. If everyone knew Nell as I do, there would be no doubt."[1]

One of the strongest letters in support of clemency came from a close personal friend and legal colleague of Clark Williams, attorney John L. Sims. He wrote Governor Miller on January 7, 1934. Not hearing any response, he wrote a second and lengthier letter on February 5. He said it pained him to be at odds with the Williams family because he had such deep love and esteem for them. Not only had he known Clark Williams for years, he had roomed with Clark's brother, Charles, as an undergraduate at the University of Alabama. After enumerating different aspects of the case that pointed to Peterson's innocence, Sims said he believed "the heinous crime of criminal assault coupled with murder was tried and convicted rather than the defendant." He further asserted that the prosecution had encouraged the jurors to override any doubts they might have about the defendant's guilt so that they might teach "vicious members of the negro race a lesson" and convey to them "a stern warning" by finding Peterson guilty as charged.[2]

There was overwhelming support for Willie Peterson in Birmingham's black community. Rev. M. Taylor, a former pastor of New Morning Star Baptist Church, wrote the governor, bearing witness to Peterson's unassailable good character and attesting to Peterson's frailty. Bishop Benjamin Garland Shaw of the AME Zion Church in Birmingham showed no reticence about speaking in support of Willie Peterson. In an interview with a special feature writer from the *Pittsburgh Courier*, Bishop Shaw said he would leave Alabama forever if Willie Peterson was executed. When asked what he would like to say to the general public, Bishop Shaw replied, "If Willie Peterson dies in the electric chair I will stay in Alabama only long enough to pack up my belongings and get out of the state for good." He then added that he believed the governor would do the right thing and spare Peterson's life. Nevertheless, he felt it was imperative that black people convey their support: "Tell the colored people everywhere to write letters to the governor of Alabama imploring him not to send this man to his death."[3]

Letters and petitions also poured into the governor's office from black churches, clubs, and lodges in response to wide-scale organizing undertaken by the ILD. Armed with petitions, ILD representatives visited black leaders and spoke at specially called meetings in Birmingham's black neighborhoods. They urged people to sign petitions demanding freedom for Willie Peterson and the Scottsboro defendants, as well as calling upon the governor to halt the "mass execution" of Kilby prisoners scheduled for February 9, 1934.

Dozens of preprinted ILD petitions were sent to Governor Miller in January and February 1934, including a petition signed by the secretary of New Morning Star Baptist Church in Woodlawn, the church where Willie and Henrietta Peterson worshipped.

Date: 1-18-34

Governor,

Willie Peterson is innocent. Everybody knows he is innocent.

We, therefore, demand the immediate, unconditional and safe release of Willie Peterson and of all the framed-up prisoners you have in Kilby and other jails through the state.

Freedom for Willie Peterson, saved from the electric chair so far by the masses of the workers, Negro and white. Stop the Feb. 9 mass legal murder at Kilby! Freedom for the nine innocent Scottsboro boys.

We protest the denial of all workers' rights and particularly the rights of the Negro people.

Passed by "mass" workers and sympathizers
At New Morning Star Baptist

Secty Miss L. Starks[4]

It was former police chief Fred McDuff's repudiation that prompted Willie Peterson's attorney J. T. Roach to write a long, impassioned letter to Governor Miller informing him that he had consulted often with Chief McDuff in preparing for both trials. McDuff consistently expressed sympathy for Willie Peterson, saying he was convinced he had the wrong man in custody. For one thing, Peterson did not fit the description Jennie Wood had given McDuff before she died. Roach reiterated how tragic it was for Peterson that Jennie Wood's description of the assailant was ruled hearsay and thus never presented to the jury.

Because the Alabama Supreme Court had given so much weight to Nell Williams's positive identification of Peterson, Roach felt it imperative to explain why her identification was "one of the most unreliable and weakest points in the case." When asked during the first trial when she first spotted Peterson on September 23, 1931, Nell replied that he was "a little in advance" of her car. Roach pointed out that from that vantage point it would have been impossible for Nell to see "any more than a portion of the side of his face." When asked if Peterson was wearing the same clothes on September 23 as on the day of the attack, she replied, "No." When then asked if he was wearing the same hat, she said again, "No." When asked to tell the jury how she knew, at a distance, that he was the assailant, "she made no reply."[5]

Attorney Roach ended his letter saying he was no longer employed to defend Peterson and was therefore beholden to no one and nothing except his own conscience and his unwavering conviction that Willie Peterson was innocent.

twenty

A MULTITUDE OF REGRETS

The governor's office was packed with witnesses when the pardon board hearing was called to order at 10:05 a.m., Wednesday, March 6, 1934. Attorneys clashed and emotions erupted so often during the volatile twelve-hour session that the governor personally had to call periodic time-outs just to restore order. For both sides, the stakes could not have been higher. Time was running out for Willie Peterson. The governor had issued one last stay of execution until March 30. This hearing was Peterson's last court of appeals. For Nell Williams Reese and her family, their reputation, integrity, and community standing were on the line.

John Brandon, state auditor, was the only member of the pardon board able to be present. Secretary of State Jarman was ill and Attorney General Knight had recused himself in acknowledgment that his presence might constitute a conflict of interest. Nell Williams Reese, her parents, and her brother, Dent, were present, as were Jennie Wood's father and her brother, Wade Jr. Governor Miller inquired about Willie Peterson's absence. A physician from the Kilby Prison infirmary explained that Peterson was physically unable to testify. The severity of his tuberculosis made it impossible for him to sit upright.[1]

Attorneys Walter Smith and Robert Proctor represented Peterson. Due to health concerns, John Altman was unable to join them on the defense team. Attorneys Roderick Beddow, George Bailes, James Long, and Jack Stewart argued on behalf of the Williams family that the death sentence should be upheld.

This was an official gathering of the state pardon board, but full pardon was never really on the table. The NAACP, in consultation with the CIC, had decided to pursue a two-step process, believing that commutation of the death sentence was the most they could achieve at this stage. If the governor issued the commutation, NAACP officials were convinced his verdict would be met by widespread approval, thereby making the governor more amenable to issuing a full pardon at a later date.

The ILD considered this two-step strategy a cowardly compromise. Their press releases condemned the NAACP plea for clemency as a fraudulent ploy. The ILD also expressed outrage that no black people were allowed to testify at the hearing.

"Willie Peterson, framed-up Negro prisoner condemned to die in the electric chair, was not present at the 'open hearing' before Governor Miller on March 6. Neither were any other Negroes allowed into the Governor's office, where the hearing was being held. The white ruling class of the state of Alabama held an open Jim-Crow hearing, not to find out whether Willie Peterson was guilty or not, but to put an O. K. on the lynch sentence."[2]

Fearing that her husband's freedom would be bartered away at the hearing, Henrietta Peterson joined the ILD in issuing their denunciation of the pardon board hearing. In a flyer distributed in black neighborhoods weeks before the March 6 hearing, Henrietta was quoted as saying, "I want to appeal to the entire Negro people, to the workers, white and black, and to all sympathizers of right and justice to unite now to save my innocent husband, Willie Peterson."[3] A group of ILD supporters, including Henrietta Peterson, traveled to Montgomery in an effort to gain access to the hearing. Benjamin J. Davis, ILD attorney for Angelo Herndon in Atlanta, led the delegation. When police and the black chaplain from Kilby Prison blocked their entrance, the ILD delegation staged a demonstration across the street.[4]

Peterson's lawyers came to the hearing armed with a battery of sworn affidavits that were entered into evidence. In these affidavits and in the testimony of defense witnesses, a number of new facts about the case came to light. "Regret" was the sentiment consistently expressed by the defense witnesses as they confessed remorse for not stepping forward sooner to voice their conviction that Peterson was innocent. Sheriff Hawkins had started that train of regrets when he delivered his letter to the governor, stating, "I am not willing to go through life feeling that my silence might have allowed an innocent person, although a Negro, to die." Hawkins reiterated the letter's contents at the pardon board hearing when he stated, "I am convinced that Peterson was a sick negro, caused from mine dust or gas, and had been sick for a long period prior to the commission of this offense. Since his trial I have talked with responsible white people who know this to be a fact. The night of his arrest, when the handcuffs were removed from his wrist at Kilby Prison, Chief Austin called my attention to the fact that he was nothing but skin and bones and merely a skeleton."[5]

R. L. Moore expressed regret that he and other grand jury members had effectively passed the buck to the trial jury when they overrode their deep ambivalence about indicting Peterson. After hearing the testimonies of witnesses on October 7, 1931, the grand jury entered into secret deliberations. According to Moore, several jurors expressed doubts that Peterson was guilty, but they concluded that they had only two options: to indict Peterson for murder or "leave the impression that Nell Williams had lied." Many on the grand jury were hesitant about impeaching Nell Williams's reputation and integrity. Convinced that no trial jury would find Peterson guilty, they decided to return a true bill and let the trial jury issue the rightful acquittal rather than returning a no bill and branding Nell Williams a liar.[6]

The strongest expression of regret came from W. H. Tompart, deputy sheriff for Jefferson County. He told the pardon board that he felt compelled to appear at the hearing to clear his conscience. He had reliable knowledge that a group of white men had visited thirteen black people—all of whom could confirm Peterson's alibi—and threatened to burn their houses to the ground if they testified at the trial. Choked with tears, Tompart confessed that he had kept those threats to himself for far too long, and he pleaded with Governor Miller to spare Peterson's life. When Attorney Beddow sought to discredit Tompart's testimony by hammering him with rapid-fire questions and accusations, Governor Miller brought the proceedings to a halt. He reprimanded Beddow for his intemperate behavior, ordered the prosecutor to take several steps back from the witness, and demanded that he address Tompart in a proper and respectful manner.[7]

Another threat of violence came to light when Lewis G. Mullinicks testified for the defense. A railroad conductor by trade, Mullinicks had served on the jury during Peterson's first trial. He reported that after considerable discussion, the first ballot cast by jury members resulted in a seven-to-five vote for acquittal. In response, one of the jurors, James McKnight, became "very hot-headed" and began to raise "a lot of fuss," stating that he knew the father of one of the girls. McKnight then warned one of the other jurors, James Bradford, that if he voted for acquittal "he might not get back to his home at Warrior alive." According to Mullinicks, Bradford switched his vote and from that moment on, with each and every ballot, the vote was six for acquittal and six for conviction, resulting in a hung jury.[8]

Mullinicks stated further that he had consistently voted for acquittal in every ballot taken during the forty hours of jury deliberation. He remained adamant that the prosecution had failed to produce sufficient and convincing evidence to prove Peterson guilty. Among other things, Mullinicks found it strange and alarming that no fingerprints had ever been entered as evidence, noting that surely the assailant had his hands all over the automobile that night. Furthermore, seeing Peterson on the witness stand, he could not imagine how this "small, skinny, scrawny, sick-looking Negro" could be "physically able to commit the crimes he was charged with."[9]

Willie Peterson's attorneys consistently sought to prove that he was "the wrong Negro" because he did not fit the early description given by Nell Williams Reese. Due to his physical frailty, he could not have committed the crimes perpetrated on Shades Mountain. Furthermore, there was substantial evidence that other suspects more nearly matching the description on police circulars had been spotted by witnesses or detained by authorities before Peterson was arrested. Much attention was given to the fact that police circulars had described the murderer as having gold inlay in his lower teeth, something that Willie Peterson lacked.

Officer C. A. Nollner reiterated the testimony he had given during both trials, saying that Willie Peterson did not match the description given him by Nell Williams Reese on the night of August 4, 1931. "I don't think Willie Peterson is the guilty Negro," Nollner said. "I don't think he was given a square deal."[10] S. M. Arnett, deputy with the Sheriff's Department, testified that he and deputy Connie Austin had gone to the Peterson home shortly after Willie was arrested. They were searching for clothing and other items that might match Nell's description of the assailant. Arnett said that they were unable to retrieve anything but an old gray hat from Peterson's closet. It was clear to Arnett that it had not been worn for months, but Deputy Austin wiped the dust and cobwebs from it and "shaped it up" so that it would resemble the hat Nell had described to police.[11]

The only witness for the prosecution was Clark Williams. He testified that his family had been under assault for the past two years. They had received threatening letters and phone calls intended to intimidate Nell and get her to change her story. Williams was adamant that Nell's identification of Peterson as the killer had been unwavering since the day she identified him. When the governor asked Nell Williams Reese if she believed Peterson was guilty, she replied, "I certainly do. I could not possibly be mistaken. If I was not sure, I would never want to see him die."[12]

Assistant solicitor James Long testified that he was absolutely convinced of Peterson's guilt. When asked by defense lawyers why he had declared Peterson innocent after Peterson was shot in the Jefferson County Jail, Long did everything possible to deflect from this line of questioning before finally admitting he had uttered those words. But he quickly moved on, imploring the governor not to let Peterson die of natural causes. Putting Peterson to death would serve as a critically important deterrent, he argued. The execution would issue a strong and public warning to others that such crimes could not be committed with impunity.[13]

In his summary, attorney Roderick Beddow characterized Peterson as a consummate actor who had been able to sway some of Birmingham's most influential citizens, including Sheriff Hawkins. Beddow urged the governor not to fall for Peterson's act. Stressing the heinous nature of the crime, Beddow argued that the death penalty should be allowed to stand and warned that commutation could set two dangerous precedents. First, the governor might be perceived as bowing to the prejudicial opinions of people who were not present when the crime was committed. Second, commutation would repudiate the trustworthy testimony of the lone eyewitness and survivor, Nell Williams Reese.[14]

After eight solid hours of testimony with no appreciable break since 2:00 p.m., Governor Miller brought the meeting to a close at 10:10 p.m. He stated that he and Mr. Brandon needed sufficient time to review the written record from that day's hearing, as well as all the documents submitted. Before rendering a decision, they also needed to carefully read and analyze the large file of correspondence that had come to the governor's office before this hearing. The governor thanked everyone for the clear and efficient way that testimony and evidence were presented. He stated that this hearing had been the most interesting and compelling hearing he had ever convened.[15]

With that, the witnesses, attorneys, and family members filed out of the governor's office into the brisk March night, steeling themselves for the arduous task of waiting.

twenty-one

GRAVE DOUBTS AS TO HIS GUILT

On March 20, 1934, Governor Miller overrode state auditor John Brandon's recommendation that the sentence of Judge Heflin's court be upheld. Citing "grave doubts as to the Negro's guilt," Miller commuted Willie Peterson's death sentence to life imprisonment. In a three-page document that provided background for his ruling, Governor Miller indicated that Sheriff Hawkins's intervention had played a significant role. Most salient was Hawkins's contention that he had personally talked with every city and county officer involved in the case and every one of them, with one exception, believed they had "the wrong Negro."[1]

The tireless efforts of Charles Houston, Will Alexander, Charles McPherson, and Walter White paid off. They had urged clergy such as Henry Edmonds and William McDowell to write letters to Governor Miller expressing their doubts about Peterson's guilt. It was these "distinguished ministers of the gospel" that Governor Miller cited as presenting the most persuasive arguments for clemency.[2]

Governor Miller was probably also swayed by the argument that executing Willie Peterson could drive black Alabamians further into the arms of the ILD. At that historical juncture, Governor Miller may have feared making a martyr out of a former black miner. On March 9, just three days after the pardon board hearing, ten thousand miners had walked off the job in Jefferson and Walker counties.[3] This was the largest coal miners' strike to hit Alabama in decades. Governor Miller was under pressure from the operators to bring the miners to their knees. At the height of the standoff in 1934, one mine operator declared, "There has never been a time when a Governor of Alabama was faced with a greater crisis."[4]

Although Miller did not cite the miner's strike or the growing influence of the ILD as reasons for commuting Peterson's death sentence, both may have contributed to Miller's decision to grant a stay of execution. Peterson's allies had warned the governor that taking Peterson's life at this historic juncture would breed hopelessness in the black community and perhaps incite an uprising.

Reactions to the Governor's Decision

The headlines in Birmingham papers announcing the governor's commutation were as large and bold as the August 1931 headlines that reported the attack on Shades Mountain. Commutation for a black man convicted of killing a white woman was a rare and newsworthy event in Jim Crow Alabama. The Williams family and those who had worked with them to block clemency were outraged that the governor deigned to show this kind of leniency. In addition to believing his decision was a grave mistake, they considered it a slap in the face and an insult to Nell Williams Reese.

The editors of the *Birmingham Age-Herald* lauded Governor Miller for his wisdom and courage. They stressed that it was not his duty to pronounce Peterson innocent or guilty; he had only to decide if the facts warranted something "so irredeemable as electrocution." The editors were confident that many Alabamians would approve of the decision, considering the social forces at work in the state: "No one, who is aware of the way in which radicals have sought to capitalize on the Peterson case, can fail to count it fortunate that the governor of Alabama has seen fit to amend the decree of death."[5]

Responses in black communities and the black press ranged from celebration that Peterson's life was spared to outrage that full pardon was not granted. The *New York Amsterdam News* suggested that Peterson had been framed because the police "were either unable to solve the mystery or seeking to hide the identity of the real murderer."[6] The *Pittsburgh Courier* noted that in most states the defendant is innocent until proven guilty, but for black defendants in Alabama "reasonable doubt" is "elastically interpreted. So, guilty or not, Peterson will serve the same sentence a white man would if he were guilty."[7]

At the end of February, just days before the pardon board hearing, Willie Peterson had been admitted to the prison hospital, where he remained for weeks, suffering from an incapacitating flare-up of tuberculosis. The governor's recording secretary, Frank Covington, went to Kilby to tell Peterson in person about the commutation. Lying on his hospital cot, Peterson responded, "Tell the governor that I appreciate it." Covington told the *Birmingham News* that Peterson received the news "without a show of emotion."[8] Peterson's stoicism could be attributable to illness or to self-protection in the presence of a white messenger. It is also very possible that Willie Peterson was less than thrilled with Covington's message. He had just learned that the remainder of his days would be spent in an overcrowded, understaffed house of punishment and pain, cut off from Henrietta and others who cherished him.

Sentenced to Life in Kilby's General Population

When Willie Peterson's sentence was commuted to life imprisonment, he was transferred to the "colored section" of Kilby's general population. If he regained sufficient strength, Willie would be assigned work in one of the prison industries—the cotton mill, shirt factory, or auto-tag shop.[9]

For most inmates, the workday began well before dawn. The daily shift was twelve hours, and breaks were few and far between.[10] The same year Willie moved to the general population, Clarence Norris, one of the Scottsboro defendants, was transferred from death row to the general population. Norris worked in the shirt factory loading large spools of cotton string into weave shop machines that prisoners converted into fine cloth for shirts. Every time a string broke, he had only seconds to spare in rethreading the machine, or the entire weaving process throughout the factory would be disrupted. Looking back on that work, Norris said the pressure was unrelenting, and if "you were slower than they thought was necessary, you would be taken 'up-front' to the warden's office and whipped with a leather strap."[11]

In the early 1930s, Kilby's general prison population was dangerously overcrowded. Because of the disproportionate number of black prisoners, the overcrowding was especially dire in the black section. In an inspection summary dated January 24, 1933, Dr. G. M. Taylor, MD, reported that there were 852 black inmates in Kilby's general population but cots for only 732. Those without cots had to sleep on old mattresses strewn about on the floor of the prison chapel. Dr. Taylor's recommendation was to squeeze one more double bunk into the large "colored" cells to make room for ten men in each cell. The last line of his letter read, "The white men are being very well cared for."[12] When he returned six months later, Dr. Taylor was distressed to discover that sixty black men were sleeping each night in unsanitary conditions on the library floor. He also noted that at least eight hundred new mattresses were urgently needed throughout the prison.[13]

After Willie Peterson was sentenced to life imprisonment at Kilby, Henrietta moved from Birmingham to Montgomery so that she could be nearer to her husband, but visits were highly restricted. The move required leaving her church community and her job in the Miller household, where she had worked for several years. Her mother, Anna Hill, came to live with her in Montgomery, which lessened the emotional strain of starting over in a new city. But Henrietta carried daily anxiety about whether her husband was getting sufficient medical attention and whether anyone could assist her in helping him gain liberty.

There is no record that the Birmingham attorneys who defended Willie Peterson—Johnson, Roach, Altman, and Smith—continued to visit him or search for other ways to plead for his release from prison. They were most likely preoccupied with other cases, and may have felt that the governor's commutation was the best outcome they could achieve. The ILD was busy investing time, energy, and resources into the long series of appeals for the nine Scottsboro defendants, so Willie Peterson's case was put on their back burner.

A plethora of new cases had also landed on Dean Houston's desk as one of the chief litigators for the NAACP. Nevertheless, Houston was burdened by the thought that Willie Peterson still languished in Kilby Prison. The commutation may have been a partial victory for progressive forces in Alabama, but Peterson and his family still suffered the consequences of a thoroughly unjust system. On the last day of March 1934, Charles Houston sent a letter to Will Alexander, executive director of the Commission on Inter-racial Cooperation, expressing hope that Peterson's case not be abandoned:

My dear Dr. Alexander:

I have waited until now to express my appreciation to you, Mr. Eleazer and the Commission for your work and assistance in the Peterson case, so that you might recognize at once that what I say is the result of sober reflection.

I think the Peterson case is one of the finest victories for Southern inter-racial co-operation within a decade. Against considerable pressure we left all direct action in the Peterson case in the hands and under the control of the South. Southern liberal leadership responded in stout, courageous fashion. The result has given us all greater courage to carry through.

We do not want to think, however, that the Peterson case is closed. Our efforts to get the true facts should be vigorously continued from two aspects:

1. To find the real criminal and see that he is given his just punishment after due process of law;

2. To establish conclusively Peterson's innocence and restore to him his liberty.

Again we thank you,

Yours sincerely,

Charles H. Houston[14]

Alexander's response was brief. He agreed that the Peterson case should not be closed until innocence was established. He pledged that the CIC would do whatever they could "in that connection," but failed to offer next steps or a coherent plan of action.

The Birmingham branch and the national NAACP continued for the first few months of 1934 to raise funds for the fees due John Altman. In early May 1934, Charles McPherson wrote to Walter White reporting on the general mood in the city regarding the commutation of Peterson's execution. A large majority still rejoiced in what was accomplished, McPherson noted, but the "Communistically inclined" were bitterly disappointed that

Peterson had not been fully exonerated and released from prison. McPherson shared their disappointment but believed that the NAACP had chosen the "intelligent handling" of the case and accomplished all that was possible at that stage. The fight was not over, according to McPherson: "We are determined that we shall not stop until [Willie Peterson] is a free man."[15]

One year and seven months passed before Will Alexander took any action at all on Peterson's behalf. The delay was attributable in part to the fact that Alexander had taken a leave of absence from the CIC in April 1935 to work for Roosevelt's Resettlement Administration, a new agency created to provide aid to depressed rural communities. In November 1935, Alexander instructed his secretary, Emily Clay, to write James Saxon Childers, editor of the *Birmingham News*, to inquire whether the time was ripe for seeking a pardon for Willie Peterson from newly elected Governor Graves.[16]

Childers replied that he had conferred with two or three trusted leaders in Birmingham. He did not mention their names but went on to say that they, as well as he, believed "it would be a mistake to stir things up now. Particularly with the Scottsboro case looming up again." Furthermore, Graves was not a governor known for granting pardons. Therefore, Childers and his colleague Mr. Chappell felt it would be "a distinct mistake to start that ball rolling at present."[17]

Emily Clay responded with gratitude for Childers's reply and concurred that the attitude he expressed on behalf of "others in Alabama" seemed "very wise." She hoped that the people outside Alabama who seemed eager to get a pardon for Peterson would "take the advice of people within the State."[18]

Presumably at the request of Will Alexander, Emily Clay then wrote Walter White on December 2, 1935, informing him that a source for which Dr. Alexander had great respect felt that it would not be advisable at that time to stir things up and pursue a pardon for Willie Peterson. She quoted the salient paragraphs from Childers's letter without citing him by name and then concluded, "In view of this, Dr. Alexander believes that it would be much better to wait until the Scottsboro case is out of the way before beginning any effort to have Peterson pardoned."[19]

When Governor Miller announced the commutation, Willie and Henrietta Peterson may have felt a modicum of relief. For two years, they had lived with the unrelenting fear that Willie would draw his last breath strapped to the electric chair. His lawyers may have rejoiced with each new stay of execution, but those judicial rulings brought no real or lasting peace to Willie and Henrietta. Between Willie's conviction in January 1932 and the commutation in March 1934, Willie was forced to ready himself emotionally, physically, and spiritually for death by electrocution six different times. As each new date of execution drew near, his lawyers were able to secure a stay of execution by filing a new appeal or by asking the governor for clemency. But each stay was followed by a new date of execution. For two full years, the scourge of Yellow Mama was omnipresent, stifling every hope, dream, or longing Henrietta and Willie might have harbored.

That fear, that horror, was lifted on March 20, 1934. But the commutation also dissipated the urgent need for intervention and action to fully pardon Willie Peterson. As weeks stretched to months, the ILD petitions calling for Willie's release decreased in number. No rallies were organized by the NAACP to demand Willie's pardon. The presses, white and black, fell silent.

twenty-two

JIM CROW JUSTICE

The governor's commutation may have enraged the Williams family and friends, but it also accorded Nell and her husband, Louie Reese Jr., the freedom to pursue their lives as newlyweds in relative peace and quiet. Gone were the endless attorney appointments, police investigations, and newspaper interviews. Nell could let go at last of the dread that came with mounting the witness stand one more time.

In their first years of marriage, Nell and Louie lived with his parents in their two-story, four-bedroom home in Forest Park, a residential neighborhood southeast of downtown where Birmingham's wealthiest families had built homes before the Redmont District and Mountain Brook were developed. As Louie rose in the ranks of his father's profitable real estate and insurance company, Nell and Louie were able to purchase their own home in Mountain Brook. In 1938, at age twenty-five, Nell gave birth to their first child.[1]

After the governor's commutation in March 1934, neither Nell Williams Reese nor Willie Peterson remained the focus of Birmingham's journalists or law enforcement officials. The same cannot be said of Nell's brother, Dent Williams.

Accomplice in Strikebreaking Violence

In addition to his legal profession, Dent Williams served in the Alabama National Guard, having enlisted in February 1932. Within the year, he was promoted to second lieutenant of Company L in the 167th Infantry.[2] His captain, Walter "Crack" Hanna, recognized in Williams a man well suited for the coterie of guardsmen Hanna recruited as security for Tennessee Coal and Iron (TCI), then a subsidiary of U.S. Steel.

Walter Hanna worked for both the National Guard and TCI. The second employer was not openly acknowledged. Hanna had a secret TCI phone number by which the bosses could enlist his services as security to funnel corporation funds and coordinate strikebreaking activities carried out in partnership with the Birmingham Police Red Squad.[3]

During the 1934 miners' strike, a white union official and several black strikers signed sworn statements charging that Captain Walter Hanna and Lieutenant Dent Williams had beaten them, trying to coerce them to confess that they, the strikers, had committed acts of violence.[4] The fact that neither Hanna nor Williams were indicted suggests that the Birmingham Police saw no crime at work in TCI's violent tactics or in the National Guard's involvement.

Disorderly Conduct and Aggravated Assault

On the night of July 28, 1935, Dent Williams and Harry Willis were arrested at the corner of Tenth Avenue and Twenty-Fourth Street North in Birmingham. One of the arresting officers, H. B. George, said he and his partner, J. T. Howell, had received "complaints from a half dozen Negroes that Williams and Willis were riding around, calling Negroes to their car, forcing them to get in, driving them around and throwing them out after beating them."[5]

Officer George said he found an open pint of liquor in the car; the two men had clearly been drinking but were not drunk. Williams and Willis were jailed for disorderly conduct, aggravated assault, and violation of the liquor law. Williams put up $100 in bond for both himself and Willis. Williams was to be tried the following day in Recorder's Court, but his request for postponement until August 8 was granted.[6] No record of a subsequent trial has been found. Apparently, the charges were dropped.

The Kidnapping and Beating of Joseph Gelders

One year later, Dent Williams was once again in the news—this time as a suspect in the beating of a white radical organizer. On September 23, 1936, Joseph S. Gelders was kidnapped, severely flogged, and left unconscious in a field eighty miles from his hometown of Birmingham. One month later, on October 19, Gelders picked Dent Williams and Walter Hanna from a lineup as two of the three men who abducted him on a deserted street in Birmingham.[7]

Gelders was the son of a highly respected Jewish family in Birmingham. While teaching physics at the University of Alabama in the early 1930s, he became alarmed by the growing antiradical violence so endemic throughout Alabama at that time. The killing of black strikers in the 1934 ore miners' strike was particularly disturbing to Gelders. In August 1935, he joined the National Committee for the Defense of Political Prisoners (NCDPP) and soon thereafter resigned from teaching to accept a position in New York City as secretary of the NCDPP. A year later, he returned to Birmingham, where he founded and worked for the Southern headquarters of the NCDPP. During his first year in this new capacity, Gelders was warned that his pro-union activities had caught the eye of TCI officials and that he had better leave town to protect himself. Gelders ignored the warning and remained undeterred in his radical activities. Not long after, he was kidnapped and beaten severely.

Gelders would later describe in graphic detail the horror he endured that night in testimony before the La Follette Committee, a U.S. Senate subcommittee instituted to investigate violations of free speech and the rights of labor.[8] According to the committee's records, on the evening of September 23, 1936, Gelders took the bus home from a meeting of the NCDPP. Getting off the bus and walking toward his home, Gelders heard footsteps behind him. When he turned to see if he was being followed, an assailant whom he later identified as Walter Hanna came running toward him and hit him with a club. Still standing, Gelders turned to flee and ran right into another man, later identified as Dent Williams, who hit him so hard with his fist that he broke Gelders's nose. Another man, later identified as James

Leslie, appeared, and the three strong-armed Gelders into a waiting car, throwing him onto the floorboard between the front and back seats.

Gelders testified that Hanna drove and Williams sat in the left rear seat immediately above his head. Williams and Leslie continued to club, beat, and kick Gelders until they thought he was unconscious. Gelders did not lose consciousness, but he lay very still for the rest of the ride to make them think he had passed out. He estimated they drove more than two hours, stopping once to get gas and another time to pick up a fourth man. As they drove, Leslie and Williams joked about how they planned to dispose of Gelders.

"What are we going to do with him?" Leslie asked.

"Kill him, I reckon," Williams replied.

"Where are we going to throw him?" Leslie inquired.

"In the river."

When they finally came to a halt, Williams pulled out a long black leather strap with a carved handle that was folded in his clothing. Pulling Gelders from the car, Williams struck his head against the running board and left him lying on the ground. Then Hanna delivered a lecture: "You are down here meddling with our business. You were warned last April to get out of here and at that time did get out but you came back. We are telling you now that if you don't get out and stay out you will be loaded with lead. . . . If you tell anybody what happened tonight you will be loaded with lead."[9]

The three men stripped Gelders, cutting his tie, ripping his pants in two, until he was clothed only in his trunks and socks. Then Williams threw him on his face and started flogging him: "I counted about 15 licks. They struck one very severe blow across the small of the back. When I was in that position one hit me in the mouth with a blackjack and another kicked me in my stomach, rolled me over and started in again and in quite a few moments I became unconscious."[10]

When Gelders regained consciousness, he was alone. He could not find the strength to stand up for several hours but finally steadied himself as the day was breaking. He wrapped the remnants of his clothes around him and walked haltingly for a half mile or more until he saw a house. The man who lived there gave him clothes and drove him into a nearby town. It was only then that Gelders realized he had been flogged near Maplesville, Alabama, about eighty miles from Birmingham.

A week after the kidnapping, a witness stepped forward saying he had seen a man stop his car across the road from where he worked, throw some scraps of paper into a field, and a little later come back and throw something that looked like a bat into the field. Thinking this suspicious, the witness took down the license plate of the car and called the police. The pieces of paper were from Gelders's wallet, and the sawed-off baseball bat had human hair stuck to it. Investigators traced the car to Walter Hanna.

The flogging of Gelders produced a storm of outrage and protest throughout Alabama, but two successive grand juries failed to indict the men whom Gelders identified as his assailants. When Senator La Follette telegrammed Hanna and Williams inviting them to appear before the hearing in which Gelders testified, Hanna ignored the invitation, and Williams responded by saying that he had no knowledge of the flogging and could therefore be of no help to them.

Joseph Gelders was one of at least ten reported victims of violence allegedly committed by Dent Williams in the space of five years: Willie Peterson, a white union official, "several" black strikers, six black men accosted on the streets of Birmingham, and Joseph Gelders. This tally does not include the black men whom Williams reportedly accosted in the weeks between August 4 and September 23, 1931, as he searched for the Shades Mountain killer.

Willie Peterson's Death in Kilby Prison

On June 30, 1940, Henrietta Peterson received word that her husband had died earlier that day in the Kilby infirmary of complications related to pulmonary tuberculosis. Henrietta had lived in dread of the day this news would come. Willie had suffered from chronic tuberculosis long before he was imprisoned. In Birmingham, however, family and friends were near at hand to see him through the hardest days and nights. Henrietta and her mother had moved to Montgomery to be close by, but prison walls and bureaucratic restrictions made sustained caretaking impossible.

Nine years earlier, when Willie lay bleeding in the Jefferson County Jail, he pleaded with Assistant Solicitor Long to carry a message to Henrietta: "Tell her to meet me in heaven," he whispered. It is unknown whether Willie was able to speak final words aloud before he died in Kilby Prison or if that message was faithfully conveyed to Henrietta, giving her something to hold onto. Willie Peterson was forty-six years old when he died.

Dent Williams lived another twenty-six years. He served in World War II and the Korean War. He then remained on active duty in the National Guard, serving as Division Advisor for the Thirty-Third Division in Illinois before joining his wife in Seale, Alabama, and taking up his law practice there.[11]

When he died of a heart attack at the age of fifty-nine in 1966, Dent Williams was finishing out his first term as Russell County district attorney, an elected office. An obituary appeared in the *Birmingham News* under the title "G. Dent Williams, Russell DA, Dies." Adorned with a photo and two columns of text, Williams was hailed as a war hero who served his country and his region with distinction. There was no mention of his alleged criminal activities, and the article ended with the names of his surviving family members.[12]

When Willie Peterson died, the *Birmingham Age-Herald* ran an article titled "SLAYER OF TWO DIES IN PRISON, Willie Peterson, Figure in Jefferson Killing, Succumbs at Kilby." Surviving family members were not named. His military service was not mentioned. Not one word was spoken about Peterson apart from the role he was alleged to play in the murders of Augusta Williams and Jennie Wood. His life was reduced to that of a "slayer" who was convicted "late one Saturday night at his second trial [when] the jury brought in a verdict of death."[13]

The Legal Lynching of Willie Peterson

Black newspapers across the country reported Willie Peterson's death in a very different manner, reminding readers that Willie Peterson was innocent of the charges brought against him and that his case was destined to have lasting significance. The *Atlanta Daily World* declared that Peterson's death "had climaxed one of the most sensational cases ever to feature in the crime annals of Birmingham." The *Chicago Defender* pronounced Peterson's case the "second greatest criminal case" in recent Alabama history.[14]

For black Americans in 1940, Scottsboro was still considered Alabama's most famous criminal case. Because the original trials had been so grossly unfair, and the Communist Party so adept at broadcasting every new violation of the defendants' human rights, many white people understood for the first time what black people had always known, that "it was not simply lawlessness that jeopardized black safety but lawfulness as well."[15]

Coming on the heels of the Scottsboro trials, the Peterson case proved to be another striking example of how courtroom trials in Jim Crow Alabama could function like lynch mobs when the defendant was black. The notoriety of both cases gave credence to the term "legal lynching," first coined by the Communist Party in the 1920s when extrajudicial lynchings were on the decline, and the state was turning to capital punishment as the new lynching tree.[16] During the 1930s, Alabama executed sixty-one men; all but seven were black. Most of the sixty-one men were put to death for the crime of murder. Ten men were found guilty of rape, and every last one of them was black. One black woman was also executed for murder during that decade.[17]

In the 1930s, the NAACP continued to vigorously pursue its decades-long campaign to secure federal antilynching legislation, but their investment in the Peterson case signaled a growing commitment to defend the victims of "legal lynchings" who were "summarily tried and sentenced to death on flimsy evidence and trumped up charges, lacking adequate legal defense."[18] In the late summer and fall of 1933, while Charles Houston was working on the Peterson and Tuscaloosa cases, he concluded that there was very little difference between extrajudicial lynchings carried out by white mobs and the blatant injustice meted out in Alabama courts. Both were forms of racial terror designed to control black communities.[19]

When attorney John Sims implored Governor Miller to grant clemency to Willie Peterson, he did not use the term "legal lynching," but he described with incisive precision how Peterson's death sentence resembled mob violence. As his letter stated, "violent prejudices were purposely aroused" in Peterson's case to issue a "stern warning" to the black community that the white supremacist system—which proscribed social equality and miscegenation—must never be trespassed or violated.[20]

During his summary statement at the pardon board hearing, assistant solicitor James McKenzie Long implored the governor to carry through with Peterson's death sentence as a means of issuing just such a warning. After admitting that he himself had voiced great doubt as to Peterson's guilt, Long argued that his doubts were actually beside the point. A heinous crime had been committed. That fact was unassailable. If the governor should let Peterson escape the death penalty and die by natural causes, it would send a dangerous message of leniency to Alabama's black communities. Long insisted that killing Peterson in the electric chair would "teach others the penalty of like crimes."[21]

The campaign to free Willie Peterson achieved an incomplete victory. Willie was never fully exonerated or released from prison, but the struggle to save him produced a crack in the seemingly impenetrable fortress of white supremacy. When black newspapers reported Willie Peterson's death, they paid homage to a miner and veteran whose unjust conviction shone a bright light on Jim Crow justice, revealing how the trial of a black man could be "a lynching in disguise" and heralding a movement that would one day "reconstruct the entire Southern picture."[22]

EPILOGUE
The Community That Kept Faith

Eighty-five years have come and gone since Willie Peterson was arrested, tried, and unjustly convicted of murdering Augusta Williams on Shades Mountain in early August 1931. Today, few people in Birmingham or elsewhere in the country remember this case that rocked the city, unleashed a reign of terror, and ignited two national campaigns—one led by the NAACP and the other by the ILD.

When the struggle for justice in Jim Crow Birmingham is remembered today, events and images from the 1960s are what most often come to mind. The boycotts of segregated Birmingham businesses led by Dr. Martin Luther King Jr. and Rev. Fred Shuttlesworth. Black children and youth being toppled by high-pressure fire hoses and attacked by police dogs while marching peacefully through downtown Birmingham. Dr. King's "Letter from Birmingham City Jail."

Those events occupy center stage in our collective memory because they signified a crucial turning point in what became known as the civil rights movement and helped usher in the passage of the Civil Rights Act in 1964. But the civil rights movement was not born in the 1960s or in the preceding decade. It is centuries old, the work of many generations' labor; what historian Vincent Harding calls "the long black movement toward justice."[1] The 1930s are rife with historical antecedents to the uprisings, protests, and campaigns manifest in the 1950s and 1960s, which continue today. The presence of the communist Left in the 1930s helped hasten the end of Jim Crow by boldly claiming and enacting the vision of social equality.[2] The NAACP litigation campaigns led by Charles Hamilton Houston in the 1930s, including the Willie Peterson case, paved the way for the 1954 Supreme Court ruling in *Brown v. Board of Education*, which declared segregation in public schools to be unconstitutional. The ILD and the NAACP may have battled for control of legal cases in the 1930s, but together they forged an assault on white supremacy by seeking, each in its own way, "to eliminate the economic injustices wrought by slavery, debt peonage, and a wage labor system based on degraded black labor."[3]

The struggle for justice in Jim Crow Birmingham was led by black people such as Charles McPherson, Oscar Adams, and Hosea Hudson—with the assistance of white allies. That struggle was sustained and undergirded by countless others who defied white supremacy in daily acts of courageous resistance and insubordination—like the community of family and friends that stood with Willie Peterson, remaining steadfast in their love and support right to the end. In death, as in life, Henrietta Peterson was there for Willie. As soon as she learned of his death, Henrietta made arrangements to have Willie's body moved from Kilby Prison to the Lovelace Funeral Home in Montgomery for safekeeping until he could be brought home to Birmingham for final funeral arrangements and burial in Shadow Lawn Cemetery.[4] The *Atlanta Daily World* reported that "hundreds" came to view Willie Peterson's body and pay him homage in Birmingham.[5]

The hundreds who turned out to pay their respects at Willie's wake and memorial service may have included some of the people most prominently associated with the NAACP, ILD, and CIC efforts to secure his freedom. But the greatest number of those in attendance were most likely people whose names seldom if ever appeared in Birmingham's newspapers, black or white: Willie's immediate and extended family, members of New Morning Star Baptist Church, friends and neighbors in Woodlawn, miners who had worked with Willie, and others in Birmingham's poor and working-class black communities who came to honor his life and sacrifice. They knew all too well what it meant to be targeted and scapegoated with no way to prove their innocence and no structural power to protect themselves or their loved ones. They knew from personal experience what their ancestors meant when they sang, "I've been 'buked and I've been scorned, I've been talked about sure as you're born." They came to stand with their sister Henrietta and pay tribute to their brother Willie, who never ceased believing he was worth the justice and freedom so grievously denied him.

Many of those present for the memorial service on July 7, 1940, had kept faith with Willie and Henrietta Peterson from the moment of Willie's arrest to the day he died: Willie's uncle-in-law, Lee Beamon, who visited Willie in jail and desperately tried to find a lawyer courageous enough to defend him. Neighbors who dared to testify at Willie's trial, supporting his alibi, despite the bands of white men who roamed the streets of Woodlawn and threatened to burn their houses to the ground. Miners, friends, and church members who sat on the witness stand at both trials attesting to Willie's integrity and honesty, and enduring insults and indignities hurled at them by prosecution lawyers. Members of New Morning Star Baptist Church who risked becoming targets of antiradical violence by signing ILD petitions demanding that Governor Miller pardon Willie Peterson. Black men and women who helped pay for Willie Peterson's legal fees despite massive unemployment during the Depression. Family, friends, and neighbors who reached out to comfort and console Henrietta when it was clear Willie was never coming home again.

Long-metered hymns, moans of lament, and shouts of praise filled the sanctuary on Sunday afternoon, July 7, 1940. One by one, family and friends rose to testify that their brother Willie had crossed over and all the years of suffering, persecution, and injustice had now ceased. In his eulogy, Rev. Taylor surely witnessed to the faith that had sustained Willie Peterson in his darkest hours.

Jim Crow racism had the structural power to strip Willie Peterson of life, liberty, and the pursuit of happiness, but it could not break his spirit or coerce him into confession. Not at the corner of Fourteenth Street and Avenue G when police dragged him from the car and struck the first blow, doubling him over. Not on the jailhouse cot where he lay bleeding from gunshot wounds while Assistant Solicitor Long bent over him, inches from his face, bellowing, "You are dying, Willie. You can't die with a lie on your lips." Not on the witness stand when he was called a gorilla in human form, a consummate actor, and a mad dog. Not on death row when the chaplain walked by his cell singing, "Swing low, sweet chariot."

To the end, Willie Peterson continued to exercise the only instrument of resistance he still possessed: his voice.

"I am innocent. I haven't killed anybody."

August 1, 2017

Dear Dad,

During the past eight years, I have ached with the longing to talk with you face to face. Especially when I returned home from my trips to Birmingham. A torrent of new questions was unlocked during each of those trips, and I was frequently overcome with regret that I had not begun the research while you were still alive. To the very end of your life at age eighty-seven, you were lucid, showing no signs of dementia, and displaying a memory that put your children to shame. You would have been such a rich source of information and insight.

The desire to share my discoveries and ply you with questions was at times so intense I imagined knocking on your study door, peering in to find you at your desk, wearing that old blue cardigan streaked with ink stains. In my fantasy, I asked if I could interrupt and tell you what I discovered in Birmingham. You always responded with characteristic enthusiasm, "Yes, by all means, Melanie! Come in and tell me everything you learned. Don't leave out a single story."

If I could sit with you in the privacy of your study for uninterrupted blocks of time, I would read aloud every testimony from the grand jury transcripts that described the scene in the interrogation room where Dent Williams fired five shots point blank at Willie Peterson. I would quote Judge Heflin's instructions to the jury at the end of Willie Peterson's second trial, warning them "not to be chicken hearted" and "to do their duty." I would share the long list of unanswered questions about the murder scene on Shades Mountain that never came to light in either trial or during the appeals process. I would quote from articles and editorials published in black newspapers all around the country that questioned the veracity of Nell Williams's claim that a black man was the assailant. I would tell you about the drive-by shootings, arson fires, and mobs of white vigilantes that raged through Birmingham's black neighborhoods for weeks after the attack on Shades Mountain.

I would ply you with questions about Genevieve Williams: What did you love about her? Did she share your passion for reading? Could you reveal to her your unorthodox theological and political beliefs? Did she ever talk about that terrible night on Shades Mountain? Did you hold and comfort her when tears came? Or did she make it known that she never wanted to discuss the loss of her precious sister Augusta? How did you end the relationship? I would also share with you that I learned Genevieve died three years before I began my research.

I had always assumed, Dad, that you were involved with Genevieve when the murders happened. But early in my investigations, I realized that was unlikely because you and Genevieve were only thirteen years old in August 1931. It makes far more sense that you were dating three years later, after the pardon board hearing had taken place. It must have been the summer of 1934 when those confrontations on the Williamses' porch took place. Surely resentment toward your pastor and mentor, Henry Edmonds, still hung like a thick vapor in the Williamses' home. Only three or four months had passed since Edmonds had written Governor Miller, urging him to commute Willie Peterson's death sentence. According to Genevieve's family, Edmonds had committed a treacherous act of betrayal.

Those scenes on the Williamses' porch that you described are still so vivid to me after all these years. The more I learned about Dent Williams, the more I understood just how excruciating it must have been to sit on that porch, holding Genevieve's hand and hearing Dent rage about Willie Peterson. That is why, seventy-five years later, I went in search of the Williamses' house in Redmont. I had to stand on Aberdeen Road, look up the hill to see the house where Genevieve lived, and look down the hill to see the parsonage where Henry Edmonds wrote his sermons. I did not doubt the veracity of your story. I needed to bear witness to that place. Standing there, I wondered if the terror of becoming Dent Williams tipped the scales and caused you to radically change course.

I also searched the collected papers of Henry Edmonds in the Birmingham archives, hoping to find tangible evidence of his influence on your emerging critique of racism and segregation when you were in your early teens. When I came across an excerpt from his sermon, "The Cost of the Mob," I felt awe and deep respect that he dared preach such a bold and unflinching condemnation of lynching to his white congregation in 1933. Knowing you might have been in the congregation that day, I was anxious to read the whole text. But I could not locate it in Birmingham or online. When I discovered there was a copy on microfilm at the Woodruff Archives, I drove all the way to Atlanta to retrieve it.

Sitting in the archives, reading that sermon, I pictured you, fifteen years old, on the front pew of that enormous sanctuary, wide-eyed, hardly breathing, scribbling notes in your journal, trying to comprehend the horror and unspeakable suffering, asking God to show you what you could do to stop those terrible crimes perpetrated by people who looked like you.

"The Cost of the Mob" helped me understand why you spoke with such reverence about Henry Edmonds. But later in my investigations, I came across other writings by Henry Edmonds that I found deeply disturbing because they revealed his unwavering defense of segregation. He did not just espouse those beliefs in the 1930s. He died in 1960 still believing that an "intimate association" between the races was both dangerous and morally indefensible.[1]

I feel certain that you must have been aware of Edmonds's defense of segregation, but I never heard you speak of it or utter a critical word about him. I find this perplexing because I have good reason to believe that you began to outgrow your mentor before you left Birmingham at the age of twenty-one.[2] While a student at Birmingham-Southern College, you were devouring books by W. E. B. Du Bois, Langston Hughes, and Lillian Smith.

And you were involved in radical organizations like the League of Young Southerners and the Fellowship of Reconciliation that promoted social and economic equality between the races.[3]

Could it be that you unwittingly froze those early memories of Edmonds in time and resisted the urge to revisit his writings for fear that he might fall from grace? After all, you suffered repeated rejection at the hands of your father whenever you voiced your critiques of white supremacy. I wonder if you needed to cling uncritically to Henry Edmonds as a surrogate father because he helped plant in you the first seeds of a new consciousness.

I ask these questions, Dad, because I was also surprised to discover that Edmonds played a far more limited role in the Peterson case than you had described. In the story you told us, Henry Edmonds was "a voice crying in the wilderness," willing to risk disfavor and acrimony as an ardent and vocal advocate for Willie Peterson. But my research did not confirm that portrait. Yes, Edmonds harbored doubts about Peterson's guilt from the outset, but he was cautious about making those sentiments public. When solicited, Edmonds offered advice to those who were working on Peterson's behalf, and, at the encouragement of the NAACP, he urged Governor Miller to commute Peterson's death sentence. But Henry Edmonds was not the driving force in the years-long struggle to exonerate Willie Peterson and secure his freedom. That work was spearheaded and sustained by black leaders in Birmingham such as Charles McPherson and Oscar Adams working in concert with national NAACP leaders Walter White and Charles Hamilton Houston.

Reflecting on all of this, it's not surprising that I remember being intensely curious about the Shades Mountain story when I was in my early teens. I suspect I was thirteen at the time, because that's the year I read *To Kill a Mockingbird*. You and I must have talked about the striking similarities between your Shades Mountain story and *To Kill a Mockingbird*. It's no wonder that I later merged the two in my mind, interchanging Atticus Finch and Henry Edmonds. Both stories took place in Jim Crow Alabama in the 1930s. In both, an innocent black man was accused of assaulting a white woman. In both, a white man defied the racist norms of Jim Crow Alabama and sought to spare the life of the black defendant.

I remember, Dad, how captivated I was by the thought that you had lived through such a momentous time when you were a teenager not much older than me. Your story, intertwined with Harper Lee's, caused me to wonder what portentous events and decisions lay in store for me. If I were faced with a similar situation, could I find the courage and clarity to do the right thing?

The problem is, both were white savior narratives that portrayed black people as guileless victims without agency or a supportive black community. Neither story brought to light the social ferment, activism, and organized resistance occurring in Alabama's black communities in the 1930s.

Colin Dayan notes that *To Kill a Mockingbird* "buries the very real activism and resistance of black citizens in Alabama and throughout the South right at the time that Lee wrote her story. Its publication made invisible the very people it claimed to care about."[4] I came to see that a comparable paradox was embedded in your story, Dad. I know you intended it to be an indictment of white supremacy, but white supremacy was replicated in and through the Shades Mountain story you told us. With the exception of Willie Peterson, all the people in your story were white. Because, as a teenager, you knew only a sliver of the larger, far more complex history of the Willie Peterson case, your story mistakenly portrayed Henry Edmonds as the moral compass of the case, and it rendered invisible the black-led organizations, as well as the friends and neighbors of Willie Peterson, that tirelessly fought for his freedom.

Had we been able to talk face to face, I feel certain you would have welcomed these revelations and encouraged me to keep digging even when my discoveries contradicted pieces of your original story. That's the kind of critical thinking you embodied. I sensed your presence, urging me on, with each and every trip to Birmingham because I knew that you were committed, above all else, to the never-ending work of confronting racism and excavating the truths it has buried.

Researching and writing this book has taught me that we who are white must always critically interrogate the stories we have inherited from our forebears, even those that have inspired our passion for justice. Because white Americans remain largely ignorant about the manifold organizations, movements, and uprisings—led by people of color—that resisted racism in every region and every era of this country's history. Because *To Kill a Mockingbird* is still being taught as a core text about racism in three-quarters of America's public schools.[5] Because the white savior myth not only masks the rich history of resistance and reform, it diverts attention from the real work white people need to do in collaboration with people of color.

So much work remains to be done. The demonization and criminalization of black men remains a national disgrace. Eighty-five years after Willie Peterson was arrested on a Birmingham street corner, innocent black men throughout the nation continue to be racially profiled, stopped and frisked, thrown to the ground, choked, shot, torn from their families, locked behind bars, and sentenced to die. Eighty-five years after the legal lynching of Willie Peterson, the death penalty is still far more likely to be sought by prosecutors and imposed by juries if the defendant is black and the victim is white.[6]

So much work remains to be done.

Dad, I have always admired your capacity to engage in radical self-scrutiny. It is in that spirit that I have written this letter to you. I long for the humility and courage you displayed when it came to acknowledging what you had failed to see or understand. I hope that I might be as eager to learn from those who critically interrogate the stories I tell.

With fierce hope, gratitude, and love,

Melanie

ACKNOWLEDGMENTS

From start to finish, the research and writing of this book have been guided and sustained by an exceptionally generous and insightful circle of friends, colleagues, activists, family members, writers, and scholars. I am humbled and profoundly grateful for the steadfast companionship and unceasing encouragement that have graced every leg of this eight-year journey.

For the friends and mentors whom I call my "cloud of witnesses," my gratitude knows no bounds. You know who you are. Your photographs are arranged in a half circle in my study. I took your photos with me each time I left home to write or research this book and re-created that half circle in every place I stayed. When I hit a wall, I looked at your smiling faces and heard you cheering me on.

A special thanks to those who believed in this project when it was first taking flight and gave me the courage to press on: Monique Savage, Demetria Martinez, Jeanette Stokes, Joanne Abel, Laurel Schneider, Nan Jackson, Laura Apol, Julia Watts Belser, Patricia Shropshire, Gloria Nafziger, and April Allison.

Time and again, I benefited from the wisdom and expertise of readers whose thoughtful and meticulous feedback helped make this a far better book: Laurel Schneider, Robert Williams, Robert Corley, Demetria Martinez, Monique Savage, April Allison, Joanne Abel, Laura Apol, Naomi Ortiz, Nan Jackson, Marian Brooks Bryant, Emily Joye McGaughy, Lois McCullen Parr, and Pat Barnes-McConnell; with special thanks to Laurel Schneider, Robert Williams, Robert Corley, and Monique Savage, who not only read and edited multiple drafts but spent countless hours in conversation, helping me resolve the dilemmas I faced, clarify the questions I needed to ask, and protect the integrity of the narrative.

I am grateful to the people of St. Stephen's Community Church in Lansing, Michigan, whose prayers sustained me, and to the friends who consistently reached out to offer support and encouragement: Jeanette Stokes, Eugene and Maxine Cain, and Darlene and Glenda Franklin.

On trips to Birmingham, I was privileged to meet with scholars, writers, and community leaders who generously shared anecdotes, memories, and interpretations of their city's history. I am profoundly indebted to Robert Corley, in the history department, University of Alabama at Birmingham. There is no way to adequately express all that I learned from him about the history of Jim Crow Birmingham, the truth-telling task of historians, and the reparative work of engaged scholarship. The support and guidance that Robert Corley provided were essential touchstones in both my research and writing.

Special thanks also to James Baggett, whose knowledge of Birmingham history is inexhaustible; to Linda Nelson for imparting her extensive research about Henry Edmonds and the founding of Independent Presbyterian Church; to Houston Brown for providing valuable insights into the history of Birmingham's black community; and to Carolyn McPherson for sharing photographs and articles about her father, Dr. Charles A. J. McPherson.

In 2010, just weeks before his death, I had the honor of interviewing Marvin Yeomans Whiting, former director of the Department of Archives and Manuscripts at the Birmingham Public Library. The stories he shared about his own research into the Peterson case were invaluable.

I am grateful for the abundant hospitality of those who housed me, fed me, and provided crucial moral support during different stages of research and writing: Janet and Gene Griffin in Birmingham, Laurel Schneider and

Emilie Townes in Nashville, Laurie Fuchs and Lynette Hartsell in Durham, Eleanor Smith and Barbara Rose in Atlanta, and Laura Mol in Silver Spring. To those whose need for a house sitter matched my longing for solitude and the perfect place to write, thank you: Kathy and Rodney King in Durham; Carol Ingells and Robert Spitz in Santa Fe; and Spencer and Connie Shaw in Montevallo.

I would be remiss if I failed to express my debt to the historians whose books were foundational for my research and understanding about Jim Crow Birmingham, the Communist Party, and the NAACP in the 1930s: Nell Irvin Painter's *The Narrative of Hosea Hudson*, Robin D. G. Kelley's *Hammer and Hoe*, Patricia Sullivan's *Lift Every Voice*, Glenda Elizabeth Gilmore's *Defying Dixie*, Dan Carter's *Scottsboro*, and Charles E. Connerly's *The Most Segregated City in America*.

This book took root during three summer residencies at the Lillian E. Smith Center. To find a place of solitude and beauty in the mountains of north Georgia was itself a source of great joy; to be on the very mountain where Lillian Smith wrote *Strange Fruit* (1944) and *Killers of the Dream* (1949) was more than I could have imagined. I was ecstatic when I discovered the Lillian Smith Center in 2011. I had grown up hearing stories about Lillian Smith and her groundbreaking work as a Southern white writer and activist dedicated to dismantling segregation and white supremacy. In 1938, my mother was among a small group of students from Wesleyan College in Macon, Georgia, who spent a winter weekend with Lillian Smith and her partner, Paula Snelling, in north Georgia. Those two and a half days proved to be an unforgettable turning point in my mother's young life as she and the other students stayed up late listening to Lillian read from her manuscripts and talk about the horrific costs of white supremacy. Seventy-three years later, I was on that same mountain, writing the first drafts of this book and drawing inspiration from these two wise women: Eleanor S. Morrison and Lillian E. Smith. To make my joy complete, I had the privilege of spending many hours with Lillian's niece, Nancy Smith Fichter, and her husband, Robert Fichter, who came to north Georgia each summer from Tallahassee to oversee the residency program and lovingly care for the Lillian E. Smith Center.

The warmth, expertise, and generosity of archivists and reference librarians never ceased to amaze me. Thanks especially to James Baggett and Don Veasey at the Birmingham Public Library, Department of Archives and

Manuscripts; Laura Anderson and Wayne Coleman at the Birmingham Civil Rights Institute; Kayin Shabazz at the Division of Archives and Special Collections, Robert W. Woodruff Library in Atlanta; Norwood Kerr and Scotty Kirkland at the Alabama Department of Archives and History in Montgomery; Stephanie Perentesis, reference librarian at Michigan State University; and the staff who so patiently assisted me at the Library of Congress and the Moorland-Spingarn Research Center, Howard University, in Washington, DC, and the Microforms Department of the Birmingham Public Library Archives.

My family has been a constant source of strength. I am indebted to my siblings—Truman, Wendy, and Stephanie—for helping me remember our family stories more precisely and always encouraging me to carry on. This book is for the grandchildren and great-grandchildren of my parents, Truman and Eleanor Morrison: Anders, Jesse, Noah, Sarah, Seth, Tanya, Truman, Willie, Clara, Lydia, and Fiona—so that you may better understand the family history that is yours and pass it on to those who come after you.

It would please my father to know that his only sibling, my aunt, Harriet Poole, was an abundant source of ancestral documents, family letters, photographs, anecdotes about my grandparents, and memories of growing up in the Mountain Brook suburb of Birmingham during the 1920s and 1930s. I regret that Aunt Harriet is not alive to read this book, but she pronounced a blessing over it the last time we sat together and talked about the injustices that Willie Peterson endured.

It has been a joy to work with Duke University Press. I am especially indebted to my editor, Gisela Fosado, who recognized the possibilities of this book while it was still taking shape. Like a trusted midwife, she helped me birth its later incarnation through steady guidance, skillful critique, and unceasing encouragement. I also want to thank her editorial associate, Maryam Arain, who responded to every inquiry with patience and expertise. The critical feedback and insightful guidance I received from the peer reviewers helped me avoid pitfalls and gain clarity on several fronts.

To my beloved spouse, April Allison: you were there, from the moment this project first took hold of me to the day I released my grasp and let the manuscript go to press. As confidante, colleague, sounding board, editor, critic, and wise counselor, you journeyed with me—urging me on, keeping me grounded, loving me through hard times, and celebrating when discoveries brought joy.

Finally, I thank my father, Truman Aldrich Morrison Jr., for the stories he shared and the passion for justice he ignited in so many, including me.

INTRODUCTION

1 For a history of Independent Presbyterian Church in Birmingham, see Adams and Whiting, *Forward in Faith*.

2 For a description of Connor's order to use police dogs and fire hoses on demonstrators in May 1963, see McWhorter, *Carry Me Home*, 365–78.

3 Whiting with Nelson, *An Enduring Ministry*, 140.

4 To my knowledge, Dan Carter was the first historian to write about the Peterson case in the first edition of *Scottsboro: A Tragedy of the American South*, published in 1969. Carter's description of the Peterson case can be found in the revised edition, *Scottsboro: A Tragedy of the American South*, 129–35. Other historians who have written about the Peterson case include Kelley, *Hammer and Hoe*, 82–84, 87, 89–90, 109, 141; and Sullivan, *Lift Every Voice*, 170–72, 181–83, 187. Pam Jones, a writer in Birmingham with an interest in unsolved criminal cases, wrote an article titled "Alabama Mysteries," 4–6.

5 See Kelley, *Hammer and Hoe*, especially 82–90.

6 See Kelley, *Hammer and Hoe*, 82; Carter, *Scottsboro*, 132–35; Herndon, *Let Me Live*, 148–64.

1. AUGUST 4, 1931

1 "Three Held Captive in Woods Four Hours Are Robbed, Then Shot," *Birmingham Age-Herald*, August 5, 1931.

2 C. A. Nollner, testimony, Trial Transcript, *State of Alabama v. Willie Peterson*, January 18, 1932, no. 65583 (Circuit Court of Jefferson County, Birmingham, Alabama), 111–12, Alabama Department of Archives and History, Montgomery, Alabama.

3 Trial Transcript, *State of Alabama v. Willie Peterson*, January 18, 1932, 117.

4 "Negro Taken off Train in Anniston Possessed Pistol," *Birmingham News*, August 5, 1931.

5 "Three Held Captive in Woods Four Hours."

6 Fred McDuff, testimony, Trial Transcript, *State of Alabama v. Willie Peterson*, January 18, 1932, 187.

7 Marie Parks, "Wounded Girl Tells of Fatal Attack by Negro," *Birmingham Post*, August 5, 1931.

8 Parks, "Wounded Girl Tells."

9 "Negro Taken off Train."

10 "Negro Taken off Train"; Parks, "Wounded Girl Tells."

11 Parks, "Wounded Girl Tells."

12 "Kidnap Plot Led to Girl's Murder, Officers Believe," *Birmingham Post*, August 6, 1931, in "Murder and Murder Trials: A Scrapbook of Famous Jefferson County, Alabama Murders and Murder Trials, 1931–1940," microform, Birmingham Public Library, Department of Archives and Manuscripts; "Kidnap Plot Led to Girl's Death, Belief," *Birmingham News*, August 6, 1931.

13 Parks, "Wounded Girl Tells."

14 "Mountain Section Is Searched for Killer of Birmingham Girl," *Birmingham Post*, August 5, 1931, in "Murder and Murder Trials"; "Negro Taken off Train"; "Kidnap Plot Led to Girl's Murder."

15 "Kidnap Plot Led to Girl's Murder."

16 Adams, *Worthy of Remembrance*, 17.

17 Connerly, *"The Most Segregated City in America,"* 20.

18 Both the 1920 and 1930 U.S. Federal Census list Lucy Taylor as residing in the Williams home.

19 "Negro Taken off Train"; "Three Held Captive"; "Other Suspects Held in Attacks on Young Women," *Birmingham News*, August 6, 1931.

20 "Lonely Road Leads to Desolate Spot on Edge of Precipice Marked by Tragedy," *Birmingham News*, August 5, 1931.

21 "Negro Taken off Train."

22 "Other Suspects Held."

23 Fred McDuff, grand jury testimony, *State of Alabama v. Dent Williams*, October 7, 1931, no. 14402 (July Term, 1931), 3, Birmingham Public Library, Department of Archives and Manuscripts.

24 *State of Alabama v. Willie Peterson*, January 18, 1932, 59–60.

25 For literature on the fear of miscegenation in the Jim Crow era, see Feimster, *Southern Horrors*, esp. 158–85; Nell Irvin Painter, " 'Social Equality' and 'Rape' in the Fin-de-Siecle South," in *Southern History across the Color Line*, 112–33; Daily, "Is Marriage a Civil Right?," 186–87; Holden-Smith, "Lynching, Federalism, and the Intersection of Race and Gender," 37–39, 47–48.

26 "Alabama in Public Spotlight Again, Man Kills Citizens, Police Seek Slayer of Society Girl," *Pittsburgh Courier*, August 15, 1931.

27 "Second Victim of Birmingham Shooting Dies," *Norfolk New Journal and Guide*, August 22, 1931.

28 "Alabama's Fear of Reds Reaches Hysteria Stage," *Afro-American*, September 12, 1931.

29 For an analysis of the complex role white women played during the era of lynching, see Jordan, "Crossing the River of Blood between Us"; Painter, " 'Social Equality' and 'Rape,' " 112–33; Hall, "The Mind That Burns in Each Body," 334–37.

2. A CITY BESET BY FEAR

1 Connerly, *"The Most Segregated City in America,"* 14–15.

2 John W. DuBose, ed., *The Mineral Wealth of Alabama and Birmingham Illustrated* (Birmingham: N. T. Green and Co., 1886), 109, cited in Connerly, *"The Most Segregated City in America,"* 15.

3 Blackmon, *Slavery by Another Name*, 289.

4 Connerly, *"The Most Segregated City in America,"* 17.

5 Harris, "Reforms in Government Control of Negroes," 568.

6 Thornton, *Dividing Lines*, 146.

7 Thornton, *Dividing Lines*, 146–47.

8 Connerly, *"The Most Segregated City in America,"* 20.

9 Connerly, *"The Most Segregated City in America,"* 37.

10 See Kelley, *Hammer and Hoe*, 13–33.

11 Kelley, *Hammer and Hoe*, 14–15.

12 For information about Birmingham's ordinance outlawing criminal anarchy and assemblages of individuals deemed anarchists, see "City Moves against Criminal Anarchy," *Birmingham News*, June 17, 1930. The ordinance made it illegal to advocate criminal anarchy in print or by word of mouth. Membership in organizations that advocated criminal anarchy was also a criminal offense. In an effort to outlaw both private meetings and public demonstrations, the ordinance stipulated that it was unlawful for two or more people to "assemble for the purpose of advocating or teaching the doctrines of criminal anarchy." Conviction could result in fines up to $100 and 180 days in jail.

13 Kelley, *Hammer and Hoe*, 20.

14 Gilmore, *Defying Dixie*, 118–19.

15 See Carter, *Scottsboro*; Gilmore, *Defying Dixie*; Goodman, *Stories of Scottsboro*.

16 Gilmore, *Defying Dixie*, 126.

17 Gilmore, *Defying Dixie*, 126.

18 Kelley, *Hammer and Hoe*, 23.

19 Kelley, *Hammer and Hoe*, 40.

20 Kelley, *Hammer and Hoe*, 41–42.

21 "Negro Reds Reported Advancing," *Birmingham Age-Herald*, July 18, 1931.

22 "Kidnap Plot Led to Girl's Murder, Officers Believe," *Birmingham Post*, August 6, 1931, in "Murder and Murder Trials."

23 "On What Hateful Bread Does Communism Feed?," *Birmingham News*, August 6, 1931.

24 "Drive Launched to Halt Activity of Communists," *Birmingham News*, August 10, 1931.

25 Painter, *Southern History across the Color Line*, 112.

26 Quoted in Painter, *Southern History across the Color Line*, 119–20.

3. REIGN OF TERROR

1 "On What Hateful Bread Does Communism Feed?," *Birmingham News*, August 6, 1931.

2 "On What Hateful Bread."

3 "Reign of Terror Sweeping Birmingham," *Southern Worker*, August 29, 1931.

4 "Negro Taken off Train in Anniston Possessed Pistol," *Birmingham News*, August 5, 1931; "Mountain Section Is Searched for Killer of Birmingham Girl," *Birmingham Post*, August 5, 1931, in "Murder and Murder Trials"; "Three Held Captive in Woods Four Hours Are Robbed, Then Shot," *Birmingham Age-Herald*, August 5, 1931.

5 "Negro Taken off Train"; "Mountain Section Is Searched."

6 "Mountain Section Is Searched."

7 Kelley, *Hammer and Hoe*, 82; "Reign of Terror Sweeping Birmingham."

8 "Negro Store Here Wrecked by Blast," *Birmingham Age-Herald*, August 6, 1931.

9 "Shots Fired from Auto at Negroes," *Birmingham Age-Herald*, August 6, 1931.

10 "Other Suspects Held in Attacks on Young Women," *Birmingham News*, August 6, 1931.

11 "Kidnap Plot Led to Girl's Murder, Officers Believe," *Birmingham Post*, August 6, 1931, in "Murder and Murder Trials."

12 "Car Sought in Killing Probe," *Birmingham Post*, August 7, 1931.

13 "Terror Rages against B'ham Workers," *Southern Worker*, August 5, 1931; "One Negro Dead, Three Wounded in Shooting Affrays," *Birmingham Post*, August 7, 1931; "Two Negroes Are Shooting Victims," *Birmingham News*, August 7, 1931.

14 "Terror Rages"; "One Negro Dead"; "Two Negroes Are Shooting Victims."

15 "One Negro Dead"; "Terror Rages."

16 "Kidnap Plot"; "New Clues in Drive for Killer Spur On Armed Searchers," *Birmingham News*, August 8, 1931.

17 "Officers Turn to New Leads in Hunt of Girl's Slayer," *Birmingham News*, August 13, 1931.

18 "Other Suspects Held."

19 "No Need for Guerillas," *Birmingham Age-Herald*, August 7, 1931.

20 "The Moods for Revenge Must Be Jerked Up Sharply," *Birmingham News*, August 7, 1931.

21 "Two Negroes Are Shooting Victims"; "Negro Not Shot; Doctor Reports," *Birmingham Post*, August 8, 1931.

22 "11 Are Held as Murder Suspects," *Birmingham Age-Herald*, August 7, 1931.

23 "Articles Found in Cave May Lead to Negro Assailant," *Birmingham News*, August 9, 1931.

24 "Doctor Gives Newest Clue for Manhunt," *Birmingham Post*, August 11, 1931; "Officer to Return Negro Arrested Near Bluffton," *Birmingham Age-Herald*, August 14, 1931; "Girl in Failure to Identify Two," *Birmingham Post*, August 12, 1931; "Victim of Bullet Fails to Identify Negro Suspects," *Birmingham News*, August 12, 1931.

25 "Negro Beaten," *Birmingham Age-Herald*, August 11, 1931.

26 "Mountain Section Is Searched."

27 See Herndon, *Let Me Live*. The description of Herndon's arrest, interrogation, and beatings are taken from chapter 14 in *Let Me Live*, 148–64.

28 Herndon, *Let Me Live*, 148.

29 Herndon, *Let Me Live*, 149.

30 Herndon, *Let Me Live*, 150–51.

31 Herndon, *Let Me Live*, 154.

32 Herndon, *Let Me Live*, 154.

33 Herndon, *Let Me Live*, 155–56.

34 Herndon, *Let Me Live*, 161.

35 Herndon, *Let Me Live*, 158.

36 Herndon, *Let Me Live*, 159.

37 McGuire, *At the Dark End of the Street*, xviii.

38 Painter, *Southern History across the Color Line*, 121.

39 The fact that the rape of black women was not reported in Birmingham newspapers does not mean it did not occur. Black women in Birmingham were rarely successful in obtaining responses from law enforcement or community leaders, especially when they reported being raped by white men. The assault on twelve-year-old Murdis Dixon is a case in point. On April 26, 1932, Dixon was raped at knifepoint by a white man who had hired her to perform domestic chores. Witnesses came forward, but the Birmingham police failed to arrest the assailant. A group of black communists sought to enlist the help of clergy and other community leaders to bring pressure on the police, but they could not rouse sufficient support, and the police took no action. Only two black newspapers far removed from Birmingham made mention of the Dixon case: the New York–based *Negro World* and the *California Eagle*. For information on the Dixon case, see Painter, *The Narrative of Hosea Hudson*, 104–6; Kelley, *Hammer and Hoe*, 84–85; "Brute Attacks Little Girl," *California Eagle*, May 13, 1932; McGuire, *At the Dark End of the Street*, 10. For further information about the rape of black women in the Jim Crow era, see Hine, "Rape and the Inner Lives of Black Women in the Middle West," 912–20. Her research centers on black women who left the South and

came to settle in the Midwest. She posits that the "most common, and certainly the most compelling, motive for running, fleeing, migrating was a desire to retain or claim some control and ownership of their own sexual beings and the children they bore."

4. FEAR, LOATHING, AND OBLIVION

1 "New Clue in Murder Is Pushed," *Birmingham Age-Herald*, August 11, 1931.
2 "Miss Wood Succumbs to Wounds," *Birmingham Age-Herald*, August 14, 1931.
3 Clark Williams, grand jury testimony, *State of Alabama v. Willie Peterson*, October 7, 1931, no. 14401 (July Term, 1931), 7–11, Birmingham Public Library, Department of Archives and Manuscripts.
4 Williams, grand jury testimony, 11.
5 Williams, grand jury testimony, 11.
6 Williams, grand jury testimony, 10.
7 For information about the founding, mission, and accomplishments of the CIC, see Ellis, "The Commission on Interracial Cooperation"; and Sosna, *In Search of the Silent South*, 20–41.
8 For a summary of Edmonds's view of "separate but equal," see Edmonds, *A Parson's Notebook*, 282–83.
9 "Radical Activities in Alabama," Report of Sub-committee of State Interracial Commission, William George McDowell Papers, 1906–1938, AR1591, Birmingham Public Library, Department of Archives and Manuscripts.
10 "Radical Activities in Alabama."
11 Sworn affidavit of John W. Altman for the Peterson Clemency Hearing, February 5, 1934, Box D-66, NAACP Papers, Legal Files, 7. All citations to the NAACP Papers are from the microform edition *Papers of the NAACP: Part 6. The Scottsboro Case, 1931–1950* (Frederick, MD: University Publications of America, 1986). The original archives are housed at the Library of Congress, Washington, DC.
12 Sworn affidavit of John W. Altman, 7; Charles Hamilton Houston, Confidential Memorandum Re: State v. Peterson, September 2, 1933, Box D-66, NAACP Papers, Legal Files, 11.
13 Robert Proctor, Memorandum, March 6, 1934, Box L-40, NAACP Papers, Legal Files.
14 "Young Woman Dies as Police Search for Negro Killer," *Birmingham News*, August 14, 1931; "Officers Await Photographs of Chicago Negroes," *Birmingham Age-Herald*, August 15, 1931.
15 "Girl to See Suspect in Slayings," *Birmingham Age-Herald*, August 18, 1931.
16 "Proof Is Sought Negro Here Aug. 4," *Birmingham Age-Herald*, August 21, 1931.
17 "Resemblance to Slayer Is Noted in Photograph," *Birmingham Age-Herald*, August 17, 1931.
18 "Negro Is Held in West Virginia in Slayings Probe," *Birmingham Age-Herald*, August 26, 1931.

1 "Weather History for Birmingham, Alabama, Wednesday, September 23, 1931," Weather Underground, accessed August 30, 2016, https://www.wunderground .com/. The temperature on September 23, 1931, reached a record-breaking ninety-nine degrees Fahrenheit, sixteen degrees above the average temperature for that day. That record still stood in 2016.

2 For the description of the arrest, I have relied on the following sources: Willie Peterson, testimony, Trial Transcript, *State of Alabama v. Willie Peterson*, January 18, 1932, no. 65583 (Circuit Court of Jefferson County, Birmingham, Alabama), 167, 174, 179, Alabama Department of Archives and History, Montgomery, Alabama; Edward M. "Buck" Streit, grand jury testimony, *State of Alabama v. Willie Peterson*, October 7, 1931, no. 14401 (July Term, 1931), 11–12, Birmingham Public Library, Department of Archives and Manuscripts; Nell Williams, grand jury testimony, *State of Alabama v. Willie Peterson*, October 7, 1931, 5–6; interview of L. F. Beamon by Charles McPherson, October 23, 1931, Box D-65, NAACP Papers, Legal Files. Because there are no written records of what was going through Willie Peterson's mind on the day of his arrest, I have sought to describe what he may have been thinking and feeling in a manner consistent with the social context and the descriptions of Willie Peterson provided by family members, friends, neighbors, and employers in NAACP interviews and courtroom testimonies cited in this and other chapters.

3 Jacqueline Jones notes in *Labor of Love, Labor of Sorrow* that during the decade following the stock market crash, nine out of ten black women worked as agricultural laborers or domestic servants (199). New Deal programs such as the National Industrial Recovery Act and Social Security, instituted to provide protection for the most vulnerable workers, exempted those two categories of workers. White employers often expected black domestic servants to work longer hours at a faster pace for less money during the Depression (206–7). This means that most black women, perhaps Henrietta Peterson included, had to work harder, faster, and for longer hours, with none of the federal protections and benefits accorded other struggling workers. As Jones notes, "During the 1930s, eight or nine out of every ten black households lived on the thin edge between subsistence and complete economic disaster" (221).

4 "Negro Identified as Girls' Slayer Rushed to Kilby," *Birmingham News*, September 24, 1931.

5 W. M. Burge, grand jury testimony, *State of Alabama v. Dent Williams*, October 7, 1931, no. 14402 (July Term, 1931), 14, Birmingham Public Library, Department of Archives and Manuscripts; Sam Arnett, grand jury testimony, *State of Alabama v. Dent Williams*, 17.

6 "Victim Is Certain of Suspect's Guilt," *Birmingham News*, September 24, 1931.

7 "Victim Is Certain."

8 My description of the interrogation of Willie Peterson by solicitor George Lewis Bailes and assistant solicitor James McKenzie Long is drawn from the transcript recorded by J. W. Dickerson at Kilby Prison on September 25, 1931, and entered as evidence by the state in *State of Alabama v. Willie Peterson*, January 18, 1932, no. 65583, 221–43.

9 "Solicitors Gather Evidence in Slaying," *Birmingham News*, September 25, 1931.

10 "Negro to Face Court in Slaying of Girls," *Birmingham News*, September 26, 1931.

11 "Solicitors Gather Evidence."

12 "Negro to Face Court."

6. ATTEMPTED MURDER

1 Fred McDuff, grand jury testimony, *State of Alabama v. Willie Peterson*, October 7, 1931, no. 14401 (July Term, 1931), 3, Birmingham Public Library, Department of Archives and Manuscripts.

2 Clark Williams, grand jury testimony, *State of Alabama v. Willie Peterson*, October 7, 1931, 10.

3 I have re-created the scene of the interrogation in the Jefferson County Jail on October 2, 1931, from the testimonies of all those present at the interrogation that day. Those testimonies are recorded in the grand jury transcripts, *State of Alabama v. Dent Williams*, October 7–8, 1931, no. 14402 (July Term, 1931), 2–34, Birmingham Public Library, Department of Archives and Manuscripts.

4 "McDuff Has About Face in Stand on Case, Implication," *Birmingham News*, February 5, 1934.

5 "Grand Jury to Open Probe in Jail Shooting," *Birmingham Post*, October 3, 1931; Ralph Hurst, "Youth Declines to Discuss Attack on Prisoner in Cell," *Birmingham News*, October 3, 1931.

6 "State Probes Jail Shooting," *Birmingham Post*, October 7, 1931.

7 "Grand Jury to Open Probe."

8 "Father Says Shot Fired in Answer to a Prayer," *Birmingham Post*, October 3, 1931.

9 "Father Says Shot Fired."

10 "Father Says Shot Fired."

11 Hurst, "Youth Declines to Discuss Attack."

12 "Let Justice Be Done," *Birmingham Post*, October 8, 1931.

13 "Was Victim Shot to Seal His Lips?," *Pittsburgh Courier*, October 17, 1931.

14 "Lonely Road Leads to Desolate Spot on Edge of Precipice Marked by Tragedy," *Birmingham News*, August 5, 1931.

15 "Was Victim Shot to Seal His Lips?"

16 Hurst, "Youth Declines to Discuss Attack."

7. GRAND JURY TESTIMONIES

1 My description of Nell Williams's appearance before the grand jury is based on her testimony recorded in the grand jury transcript, *State of Alabama v. Willie Peterson*, October 7, 1931, no. 14401 (July Term, 1931), 1–7, Birmingham Public Library, Department of Archives and Manuscripts.

2 C. A. Nollner, testimony, Trial Transcript, *State of Alabama v. Willie Peterson*, January 1932, no. 65583 (Circuit Court of Jefferson County, Birmingham, Alabama), 113, Alabama Department of Archives and History, Montgomery, Alabama.

3 Nollner, Trial Transcript, *State of Alabama v. Willie Peterson*, 113.

4 "Exhibits," in J. T. Roach Papers, Birmingham Public Library, Department of Archives and Manuscripts; "Negro Taken off Train in Anniston Possessed Pistol," *Birmingham News*, August 5, 1931.

5 Fred McDuff, testimony, Trial Transcript, *State of Alabama v. Willie Peterson*, January 18, 1932, 187.

6 W. A. Disheroon, grand jury testimony, *State of Alabama v. Dent Williams*, October 7, 1931, no. 14402 (July Term, 1931), 15, Birmingham Public Library, Department of Archives and Manuscripts.

7 Fred McDuff, grand jury testimony, *State of Alabama v. Dent Williams*, October 7, 1931, 5–6.

8 E. L. Hollums, grand jury testimony, *State of Alabama v. Dent Williams*, October 7, 1931, 9.

9 Clark Williams, grand jury testimony, *State of Alabama v. Dent Williams*, October 7, 1931, 10.

10 R. E. Smith, grand jury testimony, *State of Alabama v. Dent Williams*, October 7, 1931, 19.

11 W. M. Burge, grand jury testimony, *State of Alabama v. Dent Williams*, October 7, 1931, 14.

12 Orville Haynes, grand jury testimony, *State of Alabama v. Dent Williams*, October 8, 1931, 31.

13 Haynes, grand jury testimony, *State of Alabama v. Dent Williams*, October 8, 1931, 31.

14 James F. Hawkins, grand jury testimony, *State of Alabama v. Dent Williams*, October 8, 1931, 34.

15 Charles McPherson, interview of Henrietta Peterson, October 24, 1931, Box D-65, NAACP Papers, Legal Files.

16 "I. L. D. Defends Victim of Ala. Lynch Justice," *Southern Worker*, October 31, 1931; "Move to Free Suspect in Ala. Girl's Slaying," *Norfolk New Journal and Guide*, October 31, 1931; "Move to Free Man Shot in Jail by Girl Victim's Brother," *Chicago Defender*, October 31, 1931.

17 Painter, *The Narrative of Hosea Hudson*, 87. For an extensive portrait of Hudson and his work in the Communist Party, see Painter, *The Narrative of Hosea Hudson*; and Kelley, *Hammer and Hoe*.

18 *Red Stockham Worker*, November 1931, James McDonald Comer, Avondale Mills Office Files, 1920–1958, AR7, Birmingham Public Library, Department of Archives and Manuscripts.

19 "Terror Rages against B'ham Workers," *Southern Worker*, August 5, 1931; "Reign of Terror Sweeping Birmingham," *Southern Worker*, August 29, 1931.

20 "Wounded Man to Face Lynch Court Nov. 9th," *Southern Worker*, October 24, 1931.

8. THE NAACP COMES TO LIFE

1 Kevern Verney, "To Hope Till Hope Creates: The NAACP in Alabama, 1913–1945," in Verney and Sartain, *Long Is the Way and Hard*, 109.

2 Verney, "To Hope Till Hope Creates," 109.

3 Sullivan, *Lift Every Voice*, 112.

4 Feldman, *A Sense of Place*, 266n103.

5 Feldman, *A Sense of Place*, 159.

6 Sullivan, *Lift Every Voice*, 112.

7 "Biographical Sketch, Chas. A. J. McPherson, Secretary of the Birmingham, Alabama Branch of the N.A.A.C.P.," Box G-2, NAACP Papers, Branch Files.

8 Charles McPherson to Walter White, October 4, 1931, Box D-65, NAACP Papers, Legal Files; McPherson to White, October 7, 1931, Box D-65, NAACP Papers, Legal Files.

9 Sullivan, *Lift Every Voice*, 73–74. Walter White's firsthand account of investigating lynchings for the NAACP can be found in his autobiography, *A Man Called White*, 39–43.

10 Sullivan, *Lift Every Voice*, 147–48.

11 Cited by Sullivan, *Lift Every Voice*, 150.

12 Sullivan, *Lift Every Voice*, 151.

13 Sullivan, *Lift Every Voice*, 178.

14 The conversation that follows between Charles McPherson and Henrietta Peterson is based on Charles McPherson's interview of Henrietta Peterson, October 24, 1931, Box D-65, NAACP Papers, Legal Files.

15 McPherson, interview of Henrietta Peterson.

16 McPherson, interview of Henrietta Peterson.

17 J. T. Roach to State Supreme Court, n.d., J. T. Roach Papers (1897.1.20), Birmingham Public Library, Department of Archives and Manuscripts.

18 Roach to State Supreme Court.

19 "Peterson's Counsel Issues Statement," *Birmingham Reporter*, November 7, 1931.

20 Charles McPherson, interview of L. F. Beamon, October 23, 1931, Box D-65, NAACP Papers, Legal Files.

21 "List of Character Witnesses," J. T. Roach Papers (1897.1.21), Birmingham Public Library, Department of Archives and Manuscripts.

22 McPherson, interview of L. F. Beamon; McPherson, interview of Henrietta Peterson.

23 McPherson, interview of Henrietta Peterson.

24 Wilson Fallin, author of *The African American Church in Birmingham, 1815–1963: A Shelter in the Storm*, writes, "In Birmingham the African American church boosted businesses, sponsored education, fostered moral disciplines, promoted values, dispensed benevolence, and led the civil rights movement in the city. Most of all, the church was a spiritual fortress and served as a shelter in the midst of the racist environment that sought to dehumanize blacks" (163).

25 Fallin, *The African American Church in Birmingham*, 49–50.

26 McPherson interview of Henrietta Peterson; Trial Transcript, *State of Alabama v. Willie Peterson*, no. 65583 (Circuit Court of Jefferson County, Birmingham, Alabama, January 18, 1932), 196–98, Alabama Department of Archives and History, Montgomery, Alabama.

27 Charles McPherson to Walter White, November 24, 1931, Box D-65, NAACP
Papers, Legal Files.
28 McPherson to White, November 24, 1931.
29 Charles McPherson to Walter White, December 9, 1931, Box D-65, NAACP Papers,
Legal Files.

9. MOUNTING THE DEFENSE

1 "Peterson to Plead Not Guilty," *Birmingham Reporter*, December 5, 1931.
2 Charles Hamilton Houston, Confidential Memorandum re: State v. Peterson,
September 23, 1933, Reel 7:178 in the Administrative Records of the Commission
on Interracial Cooperation, Atlanta University Center, Robert W. Woodruff
Library, 5.
3 There is no extant transcript of Willie Peterson's 1931 trial in the Circuit Court
of Jefferson County, Judge J. Russell McElroy presiding. Therefore, I have relied
on newspaper accounts of the trial, supplemented by correspondence between
Charles McPherson and Walter White of the NAACP.
4 "Court Taxed at Trial of Negro," *Birmingham Post*, December 7, 1931, in "Murder
and Murder Trials"; "Girl on Stand Identifies Negro," *Birmingham Age-Herald*,
December 8, 1931; Charles Edmundson, " 'That Is the Negro' Says Nell Williams
on Stand," *Birmingham Post*, December 8, 1931.
5 "Negro's Lawyers Call Witnesses as State Rests," *Birmingham News*, December 8,
1931.
6 "Willie Peterson Expected to Take Stand in Defense," *Birmingham News*, December 9, 1931; "Negro's Lawyers Call Witnesses."
7 "Willie Peterson Expected to Take Stand."
8 "Willie Peterson Expected to Take Stand."
9 Charles McPherson to Walter White, December 9, 1931, Box D-65, NAACP Papers,
Legal Files.
10 "Willie Peterson Expected to Take Stand."
11 McPherson to White, December 9, 1931.
12 Charles McPherson to Walter White, November 24, 1931, Box D-65, NAACP
Papers, Legal Files.
13 "Two Hours Left for Arguments in Peterson's Trial," *Birmingham News*, December 10,
1931; "Willie Peterson Presents Strong Alibi," *Birmingham Reporter*, December 12,
1931.
14 "Two Hours Left."
15 "Peterson's Fate in Hands of Birmingham Jury," *Atlanta Daily World*, December 11,
1931; "Two Hours Left."
16 "Peterson's Fate."
17 Ralph Hurst, "Peterson Case Declared a Mistrial," *Birmingham News*, December 12,
1931; "Peterson Case Mistrial after Jury Deliberates 44 Hours," *Birmingham
Reporter*, December 19, 1931.
18 "Jury Decides to Disagree about Peterson Fate," *Atlanta World*, December 16, 1931.

19 "An Innocent Man," *New York Amsterdam News*, December 16, 1931.

20 "Jury Decides to Disagree"; "Startling Testimony Expected at Second Trial of Accused Man," *Afro-American*, December 26, 1931.

21 "Startling Testimony Expected."

22 Kelley, *Hammer and Hoe*, 84; Charles McPherson to Walter White, November 7, 1931, Box D-65, NAACP Papers, Legal Files.

23 In June 1931, Walter White had asked Roderick Beddow to serve on the defense team he was seeking to recruit for the Scottsboro defendants. The other two lawyers were Clarence Darrow, famous for his role in the 1925 Scopes Trial, and Arthur Garfield Hays, a leading lawyer in the field of civil liberties. With this team of renowned lawyers, White hoped the NAACP would play a major role in appealing the Scottsboro convictions all the way to the Supreme Court. But he had to negotiate a working relationship with the ILD lawyers who had already been retained by the defendants' families. After lengthy negotiations, the ILD agreed to collaborate with Darrow, Hays, and Beddow but only if they renounced affiliation with the NAACP and took their marching orders from the ILD. This was unacceptable to White and his board of directors. For the second time, the NAACP team was forced to withdraw from the Scottsboro case and suffer another round of excoriating criticism in the black press.

24 J. T. Roach to State Supreme Court, n.d., J. T. Roach Papers (1897.1.20), Birmingham Public Library, Department of Archives and Manuscripts.

25 Watson, "J. Thomas Heflin."

26 Carter, *Scottsboro*, 271–72.

27 Trial Transcript, *State of Alabama v. Willie Peterson*, January 18, 1932, no. 65583 (Circuit Court of Jefferson County, Birmingham, Alabama), 248, lines 3–8, Alabama Department of Archives and History, Montgomery, Alabama.

28 Supplemental Brief, *Alabama v. Peterson*, Box D-65, NAACP Papers, Legal Files, 43.

29 Trial Transcript, 184, lines 16–17.

30 Trial Transcript, 72, lines 9–73, line 10.

31 Trial Transcript, 85, lines 19–31.

32 Trial Transcript, 91, lines 6–11.

33 Trial Transcript, 102.

34 Trial Transcript, 114, lines 11–20.

35 Annie Mae Davis's testimony and cross-examination are found in Trial Transcript, 155–61.

36 Trial Transcript, 156, lines 1–7.

37 Trial Transcript, 157, lines 32–37.

38 Trial Transcript, 158, lines 1, 18–19.

39 Trial Transcript, 156, lines 33–39, and 157, lines 1–7.

40 Trial Transcript, 155, lines 24–29.

41 "Only Short Time Needed to Settle Fate of Accused," *Birmingham News*, January 24, 1932.

42 The description of Willie Peterson's testimony and the direct quotes are taken from Trial Transcript, *State of Alabama v. Willie Peterson*, January 18, 1932, 166–69.

43 "Defendant on Stand for Hours," *Birmingham Age-Herald*, January 22, 1932.

44 The full text of Judge Heflin's oral charge can be found in Trial Transcript, *State of Alabama v. Willie Peterson*, January 15, 1932, 77–81.

45 "Peterson's Fate Will Be Up to State Supreme Court Following Conviction after Short Jury Deliberation," *Atlanta Daily World*, January 27, 1931.

46 J. R. Johnson to NAACP offices in New York City, February 2, 1932, Box D-65, NAACP Papers, Legal Files.

47 Charles McPherson to Walter White, February 3, 1932, Box D-65, NAACP Papers, Legal Files.

48 Charles McPherson to Walter White, February 7, 1932, Box D-65, NAACP Papers, Legal Files.

49 "No Color Line in State Federation of Labor So Alabama Lawyer Quits," *Crisis*, July 1936, 219.

50 Charles McPherson to Walter White, February 14, 1932, Box D-65, NAACP Papers, Legal Files.

51 McPherson to White, February 14, 1932.

52 Charles McPherson to Walter White, February 9, 1932, Box D-65, NAACP Papers, Legal Files.

53 Feldman, *A Sense of Place*, 109.

54 For a profile of Oscar W. Adams, see Feldman, *A Sense of Place*, 107–9.

55 McPherson to White, February 9, 1932, emphasis McPherson's. The reference to "suicides" concerns the rumor that Nell Williams had attempted suicide after the attack on Shades Mountain. McPherson had mentioned those rumors in a previous letter to Walter White, dated November 24, 1931. In that letter, McPherson stated, "It has also been reported that the Williams girl, the only survivor of the tragedy has made several attempts to commit suicide."

56 Walter White to Henry Edmonds, February 18, 1932, Box D-65, NAACP Papers, Legal Files.

57 Charles McPherson to Walter White, March 2, 1932, Box D-65, NAACP Papers, Legal Files.

10. HOUSE OF PAIN

1 Kinshasa, *The Man from Scottsboro*, 51.

2 Kinshasa, *The Man from Scottsboro*, 51

3 Kinshasa, *The Man from Scottsboro*, 56.

4 Kinshasa, *The Man from Scottsboro*, 56.

5 Norris and Washington, *The Last of the Scottsboro Boys*, 258–59.

6 Kinshasa, *The Man from Scottsboro*, 57.

7 Kinshasa, *The Man from Scottsboro*, 58–59.

8 Norris and Washington, *The Last of the Scottsboro Boys*, 50–51.

9 Patterson and Conrad, *Scottsboro Boy*, 25.

11. "A TEMPORARILY DETHRONED MIND"

1 "Lawyer Who Shot Willie Peterson in Jail Freed," *Atlanta World*, March 9, 1932; "Trial of Lawyer in Assault Case Near Jury Stage," *Birmingham News*, March 8, 1932.

2 "Dent Williams Case Near End," *Birmingham Post*, March 8, 1932.

3 "Dent Williams Case Near End."

4 "Lawyer Who Shot Willie Peterson"; "Dent Williams Case Near End."

5 "Lawyer Who Shot Willie Peterson."

6 "Lawyer Who Shot Willie Peterson"; "Dent Williams Case Near End."

7 "Williams Free by Jury Action," *Birmingham Post*, March 9, 1932, in "Murder and Murder Trials."

8 "Lawyer Who Shot Willie Peterson"; "Dent Williams Is Freed in Shooting," *Birmingham News*, March 9, 1932; "Attorney Freed Here in Shooting of Negro in Jail," *Birmingham Age-Herald*, March 9, 1932.

9 J. T. Roach to Governor Miller, February 5, 1934, J. T. Roach Papers, Birmingham Public Library, Department of Archives and Manuscripts. For this insight about the order of the trials, I am also indebted to Ray Huffstutler's unpublished paper for a University of Alabama at Birmingham graduate seminar.

12. "AN OUTRAGEOUS SPECTACLE OF INJUSTICE"

1 Supplemental Brief, *Alabama v. Peterson*, Box D-65, NAACP Papers, Legal Files, 19–20, italics mine.

2 Supplemental Brief, *Alabama v. Peterson*, 20.

3 Supplemental Brief, *Alabama v. Peterson*, 59–60.

4 Supplemental Brief, *Alabama v. Peterson*, 61–62.

13. A TUMULTUOUS YEAR

1 Cited by Carter, *Scottsboro*, 190.

2 Downs, "Great Depression in Alabama."

3 Kelley, *Hammer and Hoe*, 33.

4 Painter, *The Narrative of Hosea Hudson*, 137.

5 Quoted by Kelley, *Hammer and Hoe*, 86.

6 Nat Ross, "The Communist Party in the Birmingham Strikes," *The Communist*, July 1934, 690.

7 Quoted in Kelley, *Hammer and Hoe*, 112.

8 Alexander, "Rising from the Ashes," 70.

9 Norrell, "Labor at the Ballot Box," 215.

10 Carter, *Scottsboro*, 244.

11 "Justice Alone Matters," *Birmingham Post*, April 15, 1933.

12 Kelley, *Hammer and Hoe*, 86.

13 Carter, *Scottsboro*, 247.

14 William L. Patterson to Walter White, April 20, 1933, International Labor Defense Papers, cited in Carter, *Scottsboro*, 248.

14. STAYING ON THE FIRING LINE

1 Appeal from Jefferson Circuit Court, *Willie Peterson v. State of Alabama*, June 29, 1933 (October Term, 1932–33), Box D-65, NAACP Papers, Legal Files.

2 "ILD Calls Mass Conference August 13 in B'ham to Save Willie Peterson," *Southern Worker*, July 12, 1933.

3 Charles McPherson to Robert Moton, July 29, 1933, Box D-65, NAACP Papers, Legal Files.

4 McPherson to Moton, July 29, 1933.

5 "Condemned Man Still Hopeful—Attorneys Work for Re-Hearing—Money Needed," *Birmingham Reporter*, July 15, 1933.

6 Charles McPherson to Walter White, July 12, 1933, Box D-65, NAACP Papers, Legal Files.

7 Minutes of the January 5, 1933, meeting of the Madam C. J. Walker Awards Committee, held at the national office of the NAACP, 69 Fifth Street, New York City. A copy of the minutes was shared with the author by Carolyn McPherson, daughter of Charles A. J. McPherson.

8 McPherson to White, July 12, 1933.

9 McPherson to White, July 12, 1933.

15. CHARLES HAMILTON HOUSTON

1 Walter White to Charles McPherson, July 27, 1933, Reel 7:178 in the Administrative Records of the Commission on Interracial Cooperation, Atlanta University Center, Robert W. Woodruff Library.

2 Sullivan, *Lift Every Voice*, 171.

3 Charles Hamilton Houston, "Saving the World for Democracy," *Pittsburgh Courier*, August 24, 1940, cited in McNeil, *Groundwork*, 42.

4 For more on Charles Hamilton Houston and his legal work for the NAACP in the early 1930s, see McNeil, *Groundwork*; Sullivan, *Lift Every Voice*, esp. 157–89.

5 McNeil, *Groundwork*, 108ff.

6 Charles Hamilton Houston, "An Approach to Better Race Relations," address delivered to the thirteenth national YMCA convention, May 5, 1934, cited in Sullivan, *Lift Every Voice*, 162.

7 Sullivan, *Lift Every Voice*, 162.

8 Egerton, *Speak Now against the Day*, 48–49.

9 Walter White to Will Alexander, July 19, 1933, Reel 7:178 in the Administrative Records of the Commission on Interracial Cooperation.

10 Will Alexander to William McDowell, August 2, 1933, Reel 7:178 in the Administrative Records of the Commission on Interracial Cooperation.

11 William McDowell to Will Alexander, August 3, 1933, Reel 7:178 in the Administrative Records of the Commission on Interracial Cooperation.

12 McDowell to Alexander, August 3, 1933.

13 Will Alexander to Walter White, August 29, 1933, Reel 7:178 in the Administrative Records of the Commission on Interracial Cooperation.

14 Alexander to White, August 29, 1933.

15 Confidential Memorandum re: State v. Peterson, September 2, 1933, 1, Reel 7:178 in the Administrative Records of the Commission on Interracial Cooperation.

16 Confidential Memorandum, 2.

17 Confidential Memorandum, 2.

18 Confidential Memorandum, 5.

19 Confidential Memorandum, 10.

20 Confidential Memorandum, 8.

21 Confidential Memorandum, 8.

22 Confidential Memorandum, 16–17.

23 "Engagement of Miss Williams and Mr. Reese Is Announced: Wedding to Be in Fall," *Birmingham News-Age-Herald*, August 13, 1933.

24 Memorandum re: Long Distance Telephone Call to Dr. W. W. Alexander, September 28, 1933, Box 163–11, 19, Charles Hamilton Houston Papers, Moorland Spingarn Research Center, Howard University.

25 Charles Houston to Will Alexander, September 4, 1933, Reel 7:178 in the Administrative Records of the Commission on Interracial Cooperation.

26 Robert Eleazer to Will Alexander, Inter-office Correspondence, October 6, 1933, Reel 7:178 in the Administrative Records of the Commission on Interracial Cooperation.

16. A LYNCHING IN TUSCALOOSA

1 See Kelley, *Hammer and Hoe*, 88; Sullivan, *Lift Every Voice*, 172; Raper, *The Plight of Tuscaloosa*, 13–16.

2 Cited in Raper, *The Plight of Tuscaloosa*, 17.

3 Sullivan, *Lift Every Voice*, 172. See also Kelley, *Hammer and Hoe*, 88; Carter, *Scottsboro*, 276–77.

4 "Lynched—by the Carpet Baggers of 1933," *Tuscaloosa News*, August 14, 1933.

5 "A Statement," *Birmingham Age-Herald*, August 24, 1933.

6 "The Intimidation Theory in Our Racial Attitudes," *Birmingham News*, August 26, 1933.

7 "Alabama Is Disgraced by a Heinous Crime," *Birmingham News*, August 14, 1933.

8 Kelley, *Hammer and Hoe*, 88.

9 Raper, *The Plight of Tuscaloosa*, 27–28.

10 William McDowell to Charles Hamilton Houston, August 16, 1933, Box 163–11, 19, Charles Hamilton Houston Papers, Moorland Spingarn Research Center, Howard University.

11 Raper, *The Plight of Tuscaloosa*, 26.

12 Sullivan, *Lift Every Voice*, 172–73.

13 Sullivan, *Lift Every Voice*, 181–82.

14 Sullivan, *Lift Every Voice*, 182.

15 Henry Edmonds, "The Cost of the Mob," was reprinted as a CIC pamphlet from the *Birmingham Age-Herald*, October 8, 1933; a copy of the pamphlet can be found

on Reel 29:13 in the Administrative Records of the Commission on Interracial Cooperation, Atlanta University Center, Robert W. Woodruff Library.

16 Arthur F. Raper's *The Tragedy of Lynching* grew out of CIC alarm that lynchings in the South had doubled in number from 1929 to 1930. The CIC commissioned Dr. Arthur Raper, a white sociologist who served as the CIC's research director, and Dr. Walter Chivers, an African American professor of sociology at Morehouse College, to investigate and analyze the causes of those recent lynchings, and their findings resulted in the extensive treatise *The Tragedy of Lynching*.

17 Edmonds, "The Cost of the Mob," Reel 7:178 in the Administrative Records of the Commission on Interracial Cooperation.

18 Raper, *The Tragedy of Lynching*, 1–2.

19 Edmonds, "The Cost of the Mob."

20 Although "The Cost of the Mob" was an unusually strong condemnation of lynching for a white pastor to deliver in 1933 Jim Crow Birmingham, there were other white Southerners who publicly condemned lynching and worked for its abolition in the early 1930s. For example, Howard Kester, who identified as both Christian and socialist, worked with Walter White to investigate lynchings for the NAACP (Egerton, *Speak Now against the Day*, 78). Jessie Daniel Ames, a white Texan born in 1883, founded the Association of Southern Women for the Prevention of Lynching (ASWPL) in 1930. The ASWPL's Pledge against Lynching garnered the signatures of forty thousand white Southern women who declared lynching "an indefensible crime, destructive of all principles of government, hateful and hostile to every ideal of religion and humanity, debasing and degrading to every person involved." Ames worked to establish local ASWPL chapters throughout the South, but she refused to endorse the NAACP's efforts to obtain federal antilynching legislation, believing that antilynching laws should remain the prerogative of state governments. For information about Ames and the ASWPL, see Hall, *Revolt against Chivalry*. For a critique of Ames and her failure to work collaboratively with antilynching organizations led by black women, see Jordan, "Crossing the River of Blood between Us," 553–56.

21 Edmonds, "The Cost of the Mob."

22 Louie Reese Jr. to Governor Miller, November 9, 1934, Alabama Governor (1931–1935) Administrative Files, Alabama Department of Archives and History, Montgomery, Alabama.

17. MOVING THE CASE FORWARD

1 Will Alexander to Walter White, Western Union telegram, October 13, 1933, Reel 7:178 in the Administrative Records of the Commission on Interracial Cooperation, Atlanta University Center, Robert W. Woodruff Library; Walter White to Charles McPherson, October 17, 1933, Box D-66, NAACP Papers, Legal Files.

2 White to McPherson, October 17, 1933.

3 Charles McPherson to Walter White, November 3, 1933, Box D-66, NAACP Papers, Legal Files.

4 McPherson to White, November 3, 1933.

5 Charles McPherson to Walter White, October 22, 1933, Box D-66, NAACP Papers, Legal Files.

6 John Altman to Walter White, November 14, 1933, Box D-66, NAACP Papers, Legal Files.

7 Altman to White, November 14, 1933.

8 Charles Houston to John Altman, November 9, 1933, Reel 7:178 in the Administrative Records of the Commission on Interracial Cooperation.

9 Oscar Adams to John Altman, November 20, 1933, Box D-66, NAACP Papers, Legal Files.

10 John Altman to Charles Hamilton Houston, November 22, 1933, Box D-66, NAACP Papers, Legal Files.

11 Charles Hamilton Houston to John Altman, November 29, 1933, Box D-66, NAACP Papers, Legal Files.

12 Charles McPherson to Walter White, January 6, 1934. Copy of this letter found on Reel 7:178 in the Administrative Records of the Commission on Interracial Cooperation.

13 "Clemency Move for Peterson to Be Fought Here," *Birmingham News*, January 6, 1934.

14 "Doomed Negro Gets Hearing," *Birmingham Post*, January 8, 1934.

15 "Clemency Move for Peterson."

16 "Clemency Move for Peterson."

17 "More about Peterson," *Birmingham Post*, January 7, 1934, in "Murder and Murder Trials."

18 "Sheriff Hawkins' Letter on the Peterson Case," *Birmingham News*, January 7, 1934.

19 Charles McPherson to William McDowell, January 11, 1934, Box D-66, NAACP Papers, Legal Files; Charles McPherson to J. E. Chappell, January 12, 1934, Box D-66, NAACP Papers, Legal Files.

20 McPherson to Chappell, January 12, 1934.

21 Walter Harris to J. E. Chappell, January 27, 1934, Box D-66, NAACP Papers, Legal Files.

22 Charles Feidelson to Will Alexander, January 9, 1934, Reel 7:178 in the Administrative Records of the Commission on Interracial Cooperation.

23 John Altman to Thomas Knight, January 31, 1934, Box D-66, NAACP Papers, Legal Files.

24 Thomas Knight to John Altman, February 6, 1934, Box D-66, NAACP Papers, Legal Files.

25 "Evidence in Case of Negro Points to Guilt, Is View," *Birmingham News*, February 3, 1934.

26 "McDuff Has About Faced in Stand on Case, Implication," *Birmingham News*, February 5, 1934.

27 "McDuff Has About Faced."

28 Charles Hamilton Houston to Fred McDuff, Postal Telegram, February 5, 1934, Reel 7:178 in the Administrative Records of the Commission on Interracial Cooperation.

29 Charles Feidelson to Will Alexander, February 6, 1934, Reel 7:178 in the Administrative Records of the Commission on Interracial Cooperation.

30 Kinshasa, *The Man from Scottsboro*, 54.

31 Kinshasa, *The Man from Scottsboro*, 52–53.

32 Patterson and Conrad, *Scottsboro Boy*, 53.

18. NO NEGROES ALLOWED

1 Walter White to Henry Edmonds, January 25, 1934, Box D-66, NAACP Papers, Legal Files.

2 Charles Hamilton Houston to John Altman, January 25, 1934, Box D-66, NAACP Papers, Legal Files.

3 John Altman to Charles Hamilton Houston, January 29, 1934, Box D-66, NAACP Papers, Legal Files.

4 Altman to McPherson, January 29, 1934.

5 Altman to McPherson, January 29, 1934.

6 Walter White to Will Alexander, February 2, 1934, Box D-66, NAACP Papers, Legal Files.

7 Walter White to Governor B. M. Miller, Telegram, February 5, 1934, Box D-66, NAACP Papers, Legal Files.

8 Sullivan, *Lift Every Voice*, 164.

9 Sullivan, *Lift Every Voice*, 165–67.

10 Sullivan, *Lift Every Voice*, 183.

11 Sullivan, *Lift Every Voice*, 185.

12 Charles Hamilton Houston to John Altman, February 10, 1934, Reel 7:178 in the Administrative Records of the Commission on Interracial Cooperation, Atlanta University Center, Robert W. Woodruff Library.

13 Charles Hamilton Houston to John Altman, February 10, 1934, Box D-66, NAACP Papers, Legal Files.

14 John Altman to Charles Hamilton Houston, February 12, 1934, Box D-66, NAACP Papers, Legal Files.

15 Charles Hamilton Houston to Walter Smith, February 13, 1934, Box D-66, NAACP Papers, Legal Files.

19. A FLOOD OF LETTERS

1 "Peterson's Plea Is Opposed Here," *Birmingham News*, February 17, 1934.

2 John Sims to Governor B. M. Miller, February 5, 1934, Box D-66, NAACP Papers, Legal Files.

3 "Bishop Shaw Says He Will Leave Alabama 'Forever' if Willie Peterson Is Executed," *Pittsburgh Courier*, February 24, 1934.

4 L. Starks to Governor B. M. Miller, January 18, 1934, Alabama Governor (1931–1935), Administrative Files, Alabama Department of Archives and History, Montgomery, Alabama.

5 J. T. Roach to Governor B. M. Miller, February 5, 1934, J. T. Roach Papers, Birmingham Public Library, Department of Archives and Manuscripts.

20. A MULTITUDE OF REGRETS

1 "Peterson Case Is Given Board," *Birmingham Post*, March 7, 1934, in "Murder and Murder Trials"; "Peterson Negro on Hospital Bed as Hearing Nears," *Birmingham Age-Herald*, March 6, 1934; "Sister of Slain Girl Identifies Peterson Again," *Birmingham Age-Herald*, March 7, 1934; Robert Proctor, Memorandum, March 6, 1934, Box L-40, NAACP Papers, Legal Files.

2 "Governor Bars I. L. D. at Fake Hearing for Willie Peterson," *Southern Worker*, March 25, 1934.

3 ILD flyer, "Willie Peterson Saved," Box G-2, NAACP Papers, Branch Files.

4 "Governor Bars I.L.D. at Fake Hearing for Willie Peterson," *Southern Worker*, March 25, 1934; Kelley, *Hammer and Hoe*, 90.

5 James Hawkins, Affidavit, Pardon Board Hearing, March 6, 1934, Box D-66, NAACP Papers, Legal Files.

6 "Peterson Innocent, Governor Is Told," *Pittsburgh Courier*, March 17, 1934; Proctor, Memorandum, March 6, 1934.

7 "Peterson Case Is Given Board"; Proctor, Memorandum, March 6, 1934.

8 Lewis G. Mullinicks, Affidavit, Pardon Board Hearing, March 6, 1934; "Peterson Case Is Given Board."

9 Mullinicks, Affidavit, March 6, 1934.

10 "Peterson Is Not Slayer, Witness Says in Hearing," *Birmingham News*, March 6, 1934.

11 "Peterson Case Is Given Board."

12 "Peterson Case Is Given Board"; "Case of Peterson Is Up to Governor and Pardon Body," *Birmingham News*, March 7, 1934.

13 Proctor, Memorandum, March 6, 1934.

14 Proctor, Memorandum, March 6, 1934; "Peterson Case Is Given Board."

15 Proctor, Memorandum, March 6, 1934.

21. GRAVE DOUBTS AS TO HIS GUILT

1 "Peterson Is Spared from Death Chair," *Birmingham Post*, March 20, 1934; "Miller Spares Peterson from Death in Chair," *Birmingham Age-Herald*, March 21, 1934.

2 "Peterson Is Spared"; "Miller Spares Peterson." I searched extensively for the letters that Rev. Henry Edmonds and Bishop William McDowell wrote to Governor Miller urging him to commute Willie Peterson's death sentence. Unfortunately, I was unable to retrieve them. This was particularly disappointing given Governor Miller's statement that the arguments presented by Birmingham clergy had played a significant role in his decision to grant commutation.

3 Throughout the second half of 1933, William Mitch and his United Mine Workers associates fought to negotiate a contract with the coal owners that included an eight-hour workday, pay increases, and a "check-off" system that allowed the

UMWA to collect dues through automatic payroll reduction. When operators refused to sign a new contract at the beginning of 1934, strikes broke out at two Cahaba mines on February 19. Four days later, Governor Miller ordered the National Guard to the strike zone when a thousand strikers, black and white, disarmed fifteen deputy sheriffs and guarded the roads against strikebreakers. The governor's intervention failed to quell the strike. For more information about the strikes, see Alexander, "Rising from the Ashes."

4 Quoted in Alexander, "Rising from the Ashes," 75.

5 "The Peterson Case," *Birmingham Age-Herald*, March 21, 1934.

6 "Governor Commutes Peterson Sentence," *New York Amsterdam News*, March 24, 1934.

7 "Peterson Thanks Governor for Sparing Life," *Pittsburgh Courier*, March 31, 1934.

8 "Willie Peterson Reported Better," *Birmingham News*, March 21, 1934.

9 Garrett and MacCormick, *Handbook of American Prisons and Reformatories*, 115–16.

10 Goodman, *Stories of Scottsboro*, 346.

11 Kinshasa, *The Man from Scottsboro*, 69.

12 G. M. Taylor to W. F. Feagin, January 24, 1933, Alabama Governor (1931–1935) Administrative Files, Alabama Department of Archives and History, Montgomery, Alabama.

13 G. M. Taylor to W. F. Feagin, June 1, 1933, Alabama Governor (1931–1935) Administrative Files.

14 Charles Hamilton Houston to Will Alexander, March 31, 1935, Reel 7:178 in the Administrative Records of the Commission on Interracial Cooperation, Atlanta University Center, Robert W. Woodruff Library.

15 Charles McPherson to Walter White, May 9, 1934, Box G-2, NAACP Papers, Branch Files.

16 Egerton, *Speak Now against the Day*, 95; Emily Clay to James Childers, November 18, 1935, Reel 7:178 in the Administrative Records of the Commission on Interracial Cooperation.

17 James Childers to Emily Clay, November 22, 1935, Reel 7:178 in the Administrative Records of the Commission on Interracial Cooperation.

18 Emily Clay to James Childers, November 25, 1935, Reel 7:178 in the Administrative Records of the Commission on Interracial Cooperation.

19 Emily Clay to Walter White, December 2, 1935, Reel 7:178 in the Administrative Records of the Commission on Interracial Cooperation.

22. JIM CROW JUSTICE

1 Entry for Nell W. Reese, Jefferson County, Alabama, "1940 United States Federal Census" database, Ancestry.com, accessed June 25, 2017, http://ancestry.com.

2 "G. Dent Williams, Russell DA, Dies," *Birmingham News*, October 12, 1966.

3 McWhorter, *Carry Me Home*, 44.

4 Ingalls, "Antiradical Violence in Birmingham during the 1930s," 534.

5 "Brother of Murder Victim Is Arrested," *Birmingham Post*, July 29, 1935; Ingalls, "Antiradical Violence," 534, n. 71.

6 "Brother of Murder Victim."

7 See Ingalls, "Antiradical Violence," 526–38; McWhorter, *Carry Me Home*, 44–45; Kelley, *Hammer and Hoe*, 128–31.

8 For Gelders's full statement to the La Follette Committee, see Joseph S. Gelders testimony, U.S. Senate, Committee on Education and Labor, 75 Cong., 1 Sess., *Violation of Free Speech and Rights of Labor, Hearings before Subcommittee*, Pt. 3 (Washington, 1937), 772–88. Cited hereafter as La Follette Committee Hearings with applicable part and page numbers.

9 La Follette Committee Hearings, 3:782.

10 La Follette Committee Hearings, 3:782.

11 "G. Dent Williams, Russell DA, Dies."

12 "G. Dent Williams, Russell DA, Dies."

13 "Slayer of Two Dies in Prison," *Birmingham Age-Herald*, July 1, 1940.

14 "Famous Case Comes to Natural Climax," *Atlanta Daily World*, July 8, 1940; "Defendant in Peterson Case Dies," *Chicago Defender*, July 13, 1940.

15 Gilmore, *Defying Dixie*, 126.

16 Bright, "Discrimination, Death, and Denial," 215.

17 Norris and Washington, "Appendix," in *The Last of the Scottsboro Boys*, 258–59.

18 Sullivan, *Lift Every Voice*, 178.

19 Sullivan, *Lift Every Voice*, 181.

20 Sims to Miller, February 5, 1934, Box D-66, NAACP Papers, Legal Files.

21 Robert Proctor, Memorandum, March 6, 1934, Box L-40, NAACP Papers, Legal Files.

22 Gilmore, *Defying Dixie*, 126; Charles Hamilton Houston quoted by Sullivan, *Lift Every Voice*, 189.

EPILOGUE

1 Harding, *There Is a River*, xi.

2 Gilmore, *Defying Dixie*, 6.

3 Gilmore, *Defying Dixie*, 9.

4 Willie Peterson was buried in grave no. 1, lot 15, grave section 9, Shadow Lawn Memorial Gardens, Birmingham, Alabama. Shadow Lawn Memorial Gardens Cemetery Interments, Birmingham Public Library, Local Databases, http://bpldb.bplonline.org/db/shadowlawn.

5 "Peterson Dies in Alabama Cell," *Atlanta Daily World*, July 13, 1940.

AFTERWORD

1 Edmonds, *A Parson's Notebook*, 283.

2 After my father's death in 2006, I discovered a box of letters he had written my mother in 1940, two years before they married. My father was a student at Birmingham-Southern College in 1940 and my mother a student at Wesleyan

College in Macon, Georgia. In those letters, my father described his involvement in the League of Young Southerners, a Birmingham-based organization founded in 1938 by the Southern Conference for Human Welfare, the organization for which Joseph Gelders was an organizer. Although it was conceived as an interracial organization, the League of Young Southerners attracted mostly white young adults who identified as radicals, but not necessarily as communists. As president of the Birmingham-Southern YMCA, my father wrote editorials for the student newspaper *Hilltop News*, advocating economic and racial justice. With YMCA leaders at Miles College, a historically black college in Birmingham, my father organized interracial dialogue sessions that were most likely not sanctioned by Birmingham-Southern.

3 For background on the League of Young Southerners, see Kelley, *Hammer and Hoe*, 197–99; and Egerton, *Speak Now against the Day*, 158–59. For information about the Fellowship of Reconciliation's work for racial justice in the 1920s and 1930s, see Egerton, *Speak Now against the Day*, 125–26, 154; and Gilmore, *Defying Dixie*, 212.

4 Dayan, "Waiting for the New Atticus Finch."

5 Scott Martelle, "Educators Take a Hard Look at 'To Kill a Mockingbird,'" *Los Angeles Times*, June 21, 2000.

6 See Bright, "Discrimination, Death, and Denial," 211–59.

BIBLIOGRAPHY

Adams, Cathy Criss, and Marvin Yeomans Whiting. *Forward in Faith: The One-Hundredth Anniversary History of Independent Presbyterian Church, 1915–2015.* Birmingham, AL: Independent Presbyterian Church, 2015.

Adams, Cathy Criss. *Worthy of Remembrance: A History of Redmont.* Birmingham, AL: Redmont Park Historic District Foundation, 2002.

Adams, Charles Edward. *Blocton: The History of an American Coal Mining Town.* Briarfield, AL: Cahaba Tree Commission, 2001.

Adams, Jane, and Ida B. Wells. *Lynching and Rape: An Exchange of Views.* Edited and with an introduction by Bettina Aptheker. New York: American Institute for Marxist Studies, 1977.

Alexander, Peter. "Rising from the Ashes: Alabama Coal Miners, 1921–1941." In *It Is Union and Liberty: Alabama Coal Miners and the UMW,* edited by Edwin L. Brown and Colin J. Davis, 61–83. Tuscaloosa: University of Alabama Press, 1999.

Allen, James, Hilton Als, Leon F. Litwack, and John Lewis. *Without Sanctuary: Lynching Photography in America.* Santa Fe, NM: Twin Palms, 2000.

Ames, Jessie Daniel. *The Changing Character of Lynching: Review of Lynching, 1931–1941.* Atlanta: Commission on Interracial Cooperation, 1942.

Armes, Ethel. *The Story of Coal and Iron in Alabama.* Birmingham, AL: Chamber of Commerce, 1910.

Baldwin, James. *The Price of the Ticket: Collected Nonfiction, 1948–1985*. New York: St. Martin's, 1985.

Banner, Stuart. *The Death Penalty: An American History*. Cambridge, MA: Harvard University Press, 2002.

Banner, Stuart. "Traces of Slavery: Race and the Death Penalty in Historical Perspective." In Ogletree and Sarat, *From Lynch Mobs to the Killing State*, 96–113.

Blackmon, Douglas A. *Slavery by Another Name: The Re-enslavement of Black Americans from the Civil War to World War II*. New York: Doubleday, 2008.

Bright, Stephen B. "Discrimination, Death, and Denial: The Tolerance of Racial Discrimination in Infliction of the Death Penalty." In Ogletree and Sarat, *From Lynch Mobs to the Killing State*, 211–59.

Brownell, Blaine A. "Birmingham, Alabama: New South City in the 1920s." *Journal of Southern History* 38, no. 1 (1972): 21–48.

Brundage, W. Fitzhugh. *Lynching in the New South: Georgia and Virginia, 1880–1930*. Urbana: University of Illinois Press, 1993.

Camp, Jordan T. "Black Radicalism, Marxism, and Collective Memory: An Interview with Robin D. G. Kelley." *American Quarterly* 65, no. 1 (2013): 215–30.

Carr, Cynthia. *Our Town: A Heartland Lynching, a Haunted Town, and the Hidden History of White America*. New York: Crown, 2006.

Carter, Dan T. *Scottsboro: A Tragedy of the American South*. Rev. ed. Baton Rouge: Louisiana State University Press, 2007.

Clegg, Claude Andrew. *Troubled Ground: A Tale of Murder, Lynching, and Reckoning in the New South*. Urbana: University of Illinois Press, 2010.

Coates, Ta-Nehisi. *Between the World and Me*. New York: Spiegel and Grau, 2015.

Cole, Stephanie, and Natalie J. Ring, eds. *The Folly of Jim Crow: Rethinking the Segregated South*. Arlington: University of Texas Press, 2012.

Cone, James. "Legacies of the Cross and the Lynching Tree." *Tikkun*, October 26, 2012.

Connerly, Charles E. *"The Most Segregated City in America": City Planning and Civil Rights in Birmingham: 1920–1980*. Charlottesville: University of Virginia Press, 2005.

Corley, Robert Gaines. "The Quest for Racial Harmony: Race Relations in Birmingham, Alabama, 1947–1963." PhD diss., University of Virginia, 1979.

Cowett, Mark. *Birmingham's Rabbi: Morris Newfield and Alabama, 1895–1940*. Tuscaloosa: University of Alabama Press, 1986.

Curtin, Mary Ellen. *Black Prisoners and Their World, Alabama, 1865–1900*. Charlottesville: University Press of Virginia, 2000.

Daily, Jane. "At the Dark End of the Street: Black Women, Rape, and Resistance—a New History of the Civil Rights Movement from Rosa Parks to the Rise of Black Power." *Journal of American History* 98, no. 2 (2011): 490–91.

Daily, Jane. "Is Marriage a Civil Right? The Politics of Intimacy in the Jim Crow Era." In Cole and Ring, *The Folly of Jim Crow*, 176–208.

Davies, Sharon. *The Rising Road: A True Tale of Love, Race, and Religion in America*. Oxford: Oxford University Press, 2010.

Davis, Angela Y. *Women, Race, and Class*. New York: Vintage, 1981.

Dayan, Colin. "Waiting for the New Atticus Finch." *Al Jazeera America*, July 14, 2015. http://america.aljazeera.com/opinions/2015/7/waiting-for-the-new-atticus-finch.html.

Dorr, Lisa Lindquist. *White Women, Race, and the Power of Rape in Virginia, 1900–1960*. Chapel Hill: University of North Carolina Press, 2004.

Downs, Matthew L. "Great Depression in Alabama." In *Encyclopedia of Alabama*, April 21, 2015. http://www.encyclopediaofalabama.org/article/h-3608.

Dray, Philip. *At the Hands of Persons Unknown: The Lynching of Black America*. New York: Random House, 2002.

DuRocher, Kristina. *Raising Racists: The Socialization of White Children in the Jim Crow South*. Lexington: University Press of Kentucky, 2011.

Durr, Virginia Foster. *Outside the Magic Circle: The Autobiography of Virginia Foster Durr*. Tuscaloosa: University of Alabama Press, 1990.

Edmonds, Henry Morris. "The Cost of the Mob." Sermon reprinted from *Birmingham Age-Herald*, October 8, 1933. Atlanta: Commission for Interracial Cooperation, 1933.

Edmonds, Henry Morris. *A Parson's Notebook*. Birmingham, AL: Elizabeth Agee's Bookshelf, 1961.

Egerton, John. "Homegrown Progressives." *Southern Changes* 16, no. 3 (1994): 1, 4–17.

Egerton, John. *Speak Now against the Day: The Generation before the Civil Rights Movement in the South*. New York: Alfred A. Knopf, 1994.

Ellis, Ann Wells. "The Commission on Interracial Cooperation, 1919–1944: Its Activities and Results." PhD diss., Georgia State University, ProQuest, UMI Dissertations Publishing, 1975.

Equal Justice Initiative. *Lynching in America: Confronting the Legacy of Racial Terror*. Montgomery, AL: Equal Justice Initiative, 2015.

Fallin, Wilson, Jr. *The African American Church in Birmingham, Alabama, 1815–1963: A Shelter in the Storm*. New York: Garland, 1997.

Feimster, Crystal N. *Southern Horrors: Women and the Politics of Rape and Lynching*. Cambridge, MA: Harvard University Press, 2009.

Feldman, Glenn. *Politics, Society, and the Klan in Alabama, 1915–1949*. Tuscaloosa: University of Alabama Press, 1999.

Feldman, Lynne B. *A Sense of Place: Birmingham's Black Middle-Class Community, 1890–1930*. Tuscaloosa: University of Alabama Press, 1999.

Fogelson, Raymond D. "The Ethnohistory of Events and Non-events." *Ethnohistory* 36 (1989): 133–47.

Fosl, Catherine. "Life and Times of a Rebel Girl: Jane Speed and the Alabama Communist Party." *Southern Historian* 18 (1997): 45–65.

Friend, Craig Thompson, ed. *Southern Masculinity: Perspectives on Manhood in the South since Reconstruction*. Athens: University of Georgia Press, 2009.

Garrett, Paul W., and Austin H. MacCormick, eds. *Handbook of American Prisons and Reformatories, 1929*. New York: National Society of Penal Information, 1929.

Gilmore, Glenda Elizabeth. *Defying Dixie: The Radical Roots of Civil Rights, 1919–1950*. New York: Norton, 2008.

Gladney, Margaret Rose, ed. *How Am I to Be Heard? Letters of Lillian Smith*. Chapel Hill: University of North Carolina Press, 1993.

Goldsby, Jacqueline. *A Spectacular Secret: Lynching in American Life and Literature*. Chicago: University of Chicago Press, 2006.

Goodman, James. *Stories of Scottsboro*. New York: Pantheon, 1994.

Hale, Grace Elizabeth. *Making Whiteness: The Culture of Segregation in the South, 1890–1940*. New York: Vintage, 1998.

Hall, Jacquelyn Dowd. "The Mind That Burns in Each Body." In *Powers of Desire: The Politics of Sexuality*, edited by Ann Snitow, Christine Stansell, and Sharon Thompson, 328–49. New York: Monthly Review Press, 1983.

Hall, Jacquelyn Dowd. *Revolt against Chivalry: Jessie Daniel Ames and the Women's Campaign against Lynching*. New York: Columbia University Press, 1979.

Harding, Vincent. *There Is a River: The Black Struggle for Freedom in America*. New York: Harcourt Brace Jovanovich, 1981.

Harris, Carl V. *Political Power in Birmingham, 1871–1921*. Knoxville: University of Tennessee Press, 1977.

Harris, Carl V. "Reforms in Government Control of Negroes in Birmingham, Alabama, 1890–1920." *Journal of Southern History* 38, no. 4 (1972): 567–600.

Harris, Lashawn. "Running with the Reds: African American Women and the Communist Party during the Great Depression." *Journal of African American History* 94, no. 1 (2009): 21–43.

Herndon, Angelo. *Let Me Live*. New York: Random House, 1937.

Hine, Darlene Clark. "Rape and the Inner Lives of Black Women in the Middle West." *Signs* 14, no. 4 (1989): 912–20.

Holden-Smith, Barbara. "Lynching, Federalism, and the Intersection of Race and Gender in the Progressive Era." *Yale Journal of Law and Feminism* 8, no. 1 (1995): Article 3.

Howard, Walter T., ed. *Black Communists Speak on Scottsboro: A Documentary History*. Philadelphia: Temple University Press, 2008.

Hubler, Angela. "From Margin to Center of Civil Rights History: Black Women and Anti-rape Activism." *Against the Current* 27, no. 6 (2013): 18–19.

Ifill, Sherrilyn A. "Legacies of Lynching, an Interview with *On the Courthouse Lawn* Author Sherrilyn Ifill." *Public Eye Magazine* 22, no. 3 (2007). http://www.publiceye.org/magazine/v22n3/lynching.html.

Ifill, Sherrilyn A. *On the Courthouse Lawn: Confronting the Legacy of Lynching in the Twenty-First Century*. Boston: Beacon, 2007.

Ingalls, Robert. "Antiradical Violence in Birmingham during the 1930s." *Journal of Southern History* 47, no. 4 (1981): 521–44.

Janken, Kenneth Robert. *White: The Biography of Walter White, Mr. NAACP*. New York: New Press, 2003.

Jones, Jacqueline. *Labor of Love, Labor of Sorrow: Black Women, Work, and the Family from Slavery to the Present*. New York: Basic Books, 1985.

Jones, Pam. "Alabama Mysteries: Williams/Wood Murders." *Alabama Heritage*, no. 79 (winter 2006): 4–6.

Jordan, Emma Coleman. "Crossing the River of Blood between Us: Lynching, Violence, Beauty, and the Paradox of Feminist History." *Georgetown Law Faculty Publications* (2000): 546–80.

Kaufman-Osborn, Timothy V. "Capital Punishment as Legal Lynching?" In Ogletree and Sarat, *From Lynch Mobs to the Killing State*, 21–54.

Kelley, Robin D. G. "'Comrades, Praise Gawd for Lenin and Them!': Ideology and Culture among Black Communists in Alabama, 1930–1935." *Science and Society* 52, no. 1 (1988): 59–82.

Kelley, Robin D. G. *Hammer and Hoe: Alabama Communists during the Great Depression*. Chapel Hill: University of North Carolina Press, 1990.

Kelley, Robin D. G. "A New War in Dixie: Communists and the Unemployed in Birmingham, Alabama, 1930–1933." *Labor History* 30, no. 3 (1989): 367–84.

Kelley, Robin D. G. "Resistance, Survival, and the Black Poor in Birmingham, Alabama, 1929–1970." Institute for Research on Poverty, University of Wisconsin–Madison, Discussion Paper no. 950–91, 1991.

Kelly, Brian. "Birmingham District Coal Strike of 1908." In *Encyclopedia of Alabama*, May 13, 2011. http://www.encyclopediaofalabama.org/article/h-1478.

Kelly, Brian. "Policing the 'Negro Eden': Racial Paternalism in the Alabama Coalfields, 1908–1921, Part I." *Alabama Review* 51, no. 3 (1998): 163–83.

Kelly, Brian. *Race, Class, and Power in the Alabama Coalfields, 1908–21*. Urbana: University of Illinois Press, 2001.

King, Gilbert. *Devil in the Grove: Thurgood Marshall, the Groveland Boys, and the Dawn of a New America*. New York: Harper, 2012.

Kinshasa, Kwando Mbiassi. *The Man from Scottsboro: Clarence Norris and the Infamous 1931 Alabama Rape Trial in His Own Words*. Jefferson, NC: McFarland, 1997.

Kolchin, Peter. *First Freedom: The Responses of Alabama's Blacks to Emancipation and Reconstruction*. Westport, CT: Greenwood, 1972.

Lee, Chana Kai. "Civil Rights History Reframed." *Reviews in American History* 40, no. 1 (2012): 122–27.

Lee, Harper. *To Kill a Mockingbird*. Philadelphia: Lippincott, 1960.

Lewis, David Levering. *W. E. B. DuBois: The Fight for Equality and the American Century, 1919–1963*. New York: Henry Holt, 2000.

Lewis, W. David. *Sloss Furnaces and the Rise of the Birmingham District: An Industrial Epic*. Tuscaloosa: University of Alabama Press, 1994.

Linder, Douglas. "Before Brown: Charles H. Houston and the Gaines Case." SSRN, 2008. https://ssrn.com/abstract=1109108.

Loveland, Anne C. *Lillian Smith: A Southerner Confronting the South: A Biography*. Baton Rouge: Louisiana State University Press, 1986.

Lumpkin, Katherine Du Pre. *The Making of a Southerner*. Athens: University of Georgia Press, 1991. First published 1946 by Alfred A. Knopf.

March, Ray A., ed. *Alabama Bound: Forty-Five Years Inside a Prison System*. Tuscaloosa: University of Alabama Press, 1978.

Martelle, Scott. "Educators Take a Hard Look at 'To Kill a Mockingbird.'" *Los Angeles Times*, June 21, 2000.

McGuire, Danielle L. *At the Dark End of the Street: Black Women, Rape, and Resistance: A New History of the Civil Rights Movement from Rosa Parks to the Rise of Black Power*. New York: Alfred A. Knopf, 2010.

McGuire, Danielle L. "'It Was Like All of Us Had Been Raped': Sexual Violence, Community Mobilization, and the African American Freedom Struggle." *Journal of American History* 91, no. 3 (2004): 906–31.

McKiven, Henry M., Jr. *Iron and Steel: Class, Race, and Community in Birmingham, Alabama, 1875–1920*. Chapel Hill: University of North Carolina Press, 1995.

McNeil, Genna Rae. *Groundwork: Charles Hamilton Houston and the Struggle for Civil Rights*. Philadelphia: University of Pennsylvania Press, 1983.

McWhorter, Diane. *Carry Me Home: Birmingham, Alabama: The Climactic Battle of the Civil Rights Revolution*. New York: Simon and Schuster, 2001.

Miles, Tiya. *Tales from the Haunted South: Dark Tourism and Memories of Slavery from the Civil War Era*. Chapel Hill: University of North Carolina Press, 2015.

Miles, Tiya. *Ties That Bind: The Story of an Afro-Cherokee Family in Slavery and Freedom*. Berkeley: University of California Press, 2005.

Mjagkij, Nina. *Light in the Darkness: African Americans and the YMCA, 1852–1946*. Lexington: University Press of Kentucky, 1994.

Montgomery, Ben. "Spectacle: The Lynching of Claude Neal." *Tampa Bay Times*, October 20, 2011.

Moos, Malcolm C. *State Penal Administration in Alabama*. University: Bureau of Public Administration, University of Alabama Press, 1942.

Morales, Aurora Levins. *Medicine Stories: History, Culture, and the Politics of Integrity*. Cambridge, MA: South End Press, 1998.

Nelson, Linda J. "To the Serving of Our Brethren: Origins and Early Social Ministry of the Independent Presbyterian Church of Birmingham, Alabama, 1915–1930." Master's thesis, University of Alabama at Birmingham, 1985.

"No Color Line in State Federation of Labor So Alabama Lawyer Quits." *Crisis*, July 1936, 219.

Norrell, Robert J. "Caste in Steel: Jim Crow Careers in Birmingham, Alabama." *Journal of American History* 73, no. 3 (1986): 669–94.

Norrell, Robert J. "Labor at the Ballot Box: Alabama Politics from the New Deal to the Dixiecrat Movement." *Journal of Southern History* 57, no. 2 (1991): 201–34.

Norris, Clarence, and Sybil D. Washington. *The Last of the Scottsboro Boys: An Autobiography*. New York: G. P. Putnam's Sons, 1979.

Norris, Michelle. *The Grace of Silence: A Family Memoir*. New York: Vintage, 2011.

Ogletree, Charles J., Jr., and Austin Sarat, eds. *From Lynch Mobs to the Killing State: Race and the Death Penalty in America*. Charles Hamilton Houston Institute Series on Race and Justice. New York: New York University Press, 2006.

Painter, Nell Irvin. *The History of White People*. New York: Norton, 2010.

Painter, Nell Irvin. "Hosea Hudson: The Life and Times of a Black Communist." In *Southern History across the Color Line*, 134–76. Chapel Hill: University of North Carolina Press, 2002.

Painter, Nell Irvin. *The Narrative of Hosea Hudson: His Life as a Negro Communist in the South*. Cambridge, MA: Harvard University Press, 1979.

Painter, Nell Irvin. *Southern History across the Color Line*. Chapel Hill: University of North Carolina Press, 2002.

Patterson, Haywood, and Earl Conrad. *Scottsboro Boy*. Garden City, NY: Doubleday, 1950.

Praytor, Robert E. "From Concern to Neglect: Alabama Baptists' Religious Relationship to the Negro, 1823–1870." Master's thesis, Samford University, 1971.

Raper, Arthur F. *The Plight of Tuscaloosa: A Case Study of Conditions in Tuscaloosa County, Alabama, 1933*. Atlanta: Southern Commission for the Study of Lynching, 1933.

Raper, Arthur Franklin. *The Tragedy of Lynching*. Chapel Hill: University of North Carolina Press, 1933.

Record, Wilson. *The Negro and the Communist Party*. New York: Atheneum, 1971.

Record, Wilson. *Race and Radicalism: The NAACP and the Communist Party in Conflict*. Ithaca, NY: Cornell University Press, 1964.

Rickard, Marlene Hunt. "An Experiment in Welfare Capitalism: The Health Care Services of the Tennessee Coal, Iron and Railroad Company." *Journal of Economic History* 45, no. 2 (June 1985): 467–70.

Ring, Natalie. "The 'New Race Question': The Problem of Poor Whites and the Color Line." In Cole and Ring, *The Folly of Jim Crow*, 91–123.

Ritterhouse, Jennifer. *Growing Up Jim Crow: How Black and White Southern Children Learned Race*. Chapel Hill: University of North Carolina Press, 2006.

Ross, Nat. "The Communist Party in the Birmingham Strikes." *Communist*, July 1934, 687–99.

Rossi, Faust. "The Scottsboro Trials: A Legal Lynching." *Cornell Law Faculty Publications*, no. 948 (2002). http://scholarship.law.cornell.edu/facpub/948.

Schipper, Martin. *A Guide to the Microfilm Edition of Papers of the NAACP: Part 6. The Scottsboro Case, 1931–1950*. Frederick, MD: University Publications of America, 1986.

Schwabauer, Barbara A. "The Emmett Till Unsolved Civil Rights Crime Act: The Cold Case of Racism in the Criminal Justice System." *Ohio State Law Journal* 71, no. 3 (2010): 653–98.

Shuman, Howard, and Jacqueline Scott. "Generations and Collective Memories." *American Sociological Review* 54, no. 3 (1989): 359–81.

Smith, Lillian. *Killers of the Dream*. New York: Norton, 1949.

Sosna, Morton. *In Search of the Silent South: Southern Liberals and the Race Issue*. New York: Columbia University Press, 1977.

Stevenson, Bryan. *Just Mercy: A Story of Justice and Redemption*. New York: Spiegel and Grau, 2014.

Suggs, Henry Lewis, ed. *The Black Press in the South, 1865–1979*. Westport, CT: Greenwood, 1983.

Sullivan, Patricia. *Lift Every Voice: The NAACP and the Making of the Civil Rights Movement*. New York: New Press, 2010.

Taft, Philip. *Organizing Dixie: Alabama Workers in the Industrial Era*. Revised and edited by Gary M. Fink. Westport, CT: Greenwood, 1981.

Terrell, Mary Church. "Lynching from the Negro's Point of View." *North American Review*, no. 178 (1904): 853–68. Reproduced in *Digital History*, 2012. http://www.digitalhistory.uh.edu/disp_textbook.cfm?smtid=3&psid=3615.

Thornton, J. Mills, III. *Dividing Lines: Municipal Politics and the Struggle for Civil Rights in Montgomery, Birmingham, and Selma*. Tuscaloosa: University of Alabama Press, 2002.

Tindall, George Brown. *The Emergence of the New South: 1913–1945*. Baton Rouge: Louisiana State University Press, 1967.

Verney, Kevern, and Lee Sartain, eds. *Long Is the Way and Hard: One Hundred Years of the NAACP*. Fayetteville: University of Arkansas Press, 2009.

Waldrep, Christopher, ed. *Lynching in America: A History in Documents*. New York: New York University Press, 2006.

Watson, Elbert L. "J. Thomas Heflin." In *Encyclopedia of Alabama*, September 26, 2016. http://www.encyclopediaofalabama.org/article/h-2952.

Wexler, Laura. *Fire in a Canebrake: The Last Mass Lynching in America*. New York: Scribner, 2003.

Wexler, Laura. "A Sorry History." *Washington Post*, June 19, 2005.

White, Walter. *A Man Called White: The Autobiography of Walter White*. New York: Viking, 1948.

Whiting, Marvin Yeomans. *The Bearing Day Is Not Gone: The Seventy-Fifth Anniversary History of Independent Presbyterian Church of Birmingham, Alabama, 1915–1990*. Birmingham, AL: Independent Presbyterian Church, 1990.

Whiting, Marvin Yeomans, with Linda J. Nelson. *An Enduring Ministry: A Biography of Henry Morris Edmonds, 1878–1960*. Birmingham, AL: William F. Edmonds and Joan McCoy Edmonds, 2007.

Wilkerson, Isabel. *The Warmth of Other Suns: The Epic Story of America's Great Migration*. New York: Vintage, 2010.

Wood, Amy Louise. *Lynching and Spectacle: Witnessing Racial Violence in America, 1890–1940*. Chapel Hill: University of North Carolina Press, 2009.

Woodrum, Robert. "The Rebirth of the UMWA and Racial Anxiety in Alabama, 1933–1942." *Alabama Review* 58, no. 4 (October 2005): 243–81.

Woodward, C. Vann. *The Strange Career of Jim Crow*. 3rd rev. ed. New York: Oxford University Press, 1974.

Zangrando, Robert L. *The NAACP Crusade against Lynching, 1909–1950*. Philadelphia: Temple University Press, 1980.

side in, 55, 56; steel industry in, 18, 19, 25, 26, 27, 123, 186; white elites living in, 2, 10, 18–19, 23, 25–27, 46, 185; Williams/Wood murders in, 3, 7–10, 11, 25, 47, 82, 91; Woodlawn neighborhood in, 56, 58, 92, 194; zoning in, 27. *See also* Jefferson County Jail (Birmingham); manhunt, Shades Mountain assailant; Mountain Brook, AL; Redmont (neighborhood); Shades Mountain murders

Birmingham Age-Herald (newspaper): on black Communists, 31; on crime scene, 45; on death of Jennie Wood, 45; on death of Willie Peterson, 190; on manhunt violence, 39; Miller lauded by, 179; on Miller's commutation, 179; on Nell Williams's engagement, 139–40; photos in, 45, 139; Tuscaloosa declaration in, 144

Birmingham Bar Association, 137

Birmingham City Commission, 36, 37

Birmingham City Jail, 41, 193

Birmingham News (newspaper), 31, 32; "Alabama Is Disgraced by a Heinous Crime" editorial in, 145; assailant described in, 20–21; on criminal anarchy ordinance, 211n12; crime scene details in, 20, 75; Dent Williams described in, 74; Dent Williams's obituary in, 190; editor Chappell of, 138, 155–56, 183; editor Childers of, 183; Hawkins letter lauded by, 155; Irondale letter and, 50–51; "Lynch Law" editorial and, 144; on manhunt violence, 34–35, 39, 46; McDuff repudiation in, 158–59; on Peterson's commutation, 155, 180; Peterson description in, 65; Tuscaloosa lynching decried by, 144, 145, 148; victim photographs in, 20; white supremacy condemned in, 144

Birmingham Police Department, 16, 18, 38, 95, 104, 158; assailant manhunt by, 39–40; Chief McDuff of, 16, 20, 39; and Jefferson County Sheriff's Department, 39

Birmingham Police Red Squad, 186

Birmingham Post (newspaper): on Dent Williams, 74; on manhunt violence, 37;

on murder investigation, 18, 31, 46; on Nell Williams, 16–17; on Scottsboro trials, 122

Birmingham Public Library, 8

Birmingham Reporter (newspaper), 110, 141; on Peterson's repudiation of ILD, 132; Roach and Johnson's statement in, 90

Birmingham-Southern College, 19, 139, 199, 230–31n2

black community: bias against, 169; in Birmingham, 9, 18, 57, 123; communism and, 28, 31, 36, 41, 49, 83, 124; doubts about Nell Williams's story surface in, 22–24; employment in, 23, 26, 56, 215n3; Jim Crow attitude toward, 26–27, 98; newspapers and, 22, 74–75, 90, 98–99, 169, 180, 190, 213n39; racially zoned neighborhoods and, 18, 27; racist stereotypes of, 22; rumors circulating in, 23–24; scapegoating of, 24, 195; social class and, 10, 18–19, 26, 30–31, 136, 139–40, 174; social inequality and, 17, 32, 63, 148; support for Peterson in, 169–71, 194–95; women in, 23, 43–44, 56, 191, 213–14n39, 215n3. *See also* churches; CIC (Commission on Interracial Cooperation); Jim Crow; lynching; manhunt, Shades Mountain assailant; NAACP (National Association for the Advancement of Colored People); segregation

Bradford, James, 175

Brandon, John, 157, 172, 176, 178

Brown v. Board of Education, 194

Bryan, Brother (preacher), 71, 77

Buckner, Nina, 164

Burge, W. M., 61, 68, 81, 104

Burrs, J. J., 160

Burton, Mrs. B. B., 117

California Eagle (newspaper), 213n39

Camp Hill, AL, 30–31, 41, 49

capital punishment, legal lynching and, 191

Cardwell, Oscar L., 91

Carter, Dan, 209n4

CFWU (Croppers' and Farm Workers' Union), 30

grand jury (Willie Peterson): indictment from, 82–83, 174; Knight and, 157; Nell Williams's testimony to, 76–80, 95, 101, 174; Peterson and, 76, 174, 198; racism and, 174; transcripts from, 10, 198, 216n1; Wood and Williams slayings and, 76, 79

Graves, David Bibb, 183

Great Depression. *See* Depression

Great Southern Insurance Company, 110

Hammer and Hoe (Kelley), 8

Hanna, Walter, 186, 187, 188, 189

Harden, A. T., 142–47

Harding, Vincent, 194

Harris, Carl V., 26–27

Harris, Walter, 156

Harvard Law School, 135, 151

Harvard University, 86

hat, gray, 22, 40; found in Willie Peterson's house, 65, 104, 176; Nell Williams's description of, 20–21, 78, 65, 95, 170–71; Officer Nollner's testimony about, 95

Hawkins, James F.: Alexander met, 137; black TCI employees and, 38; communists and, 31, 36; Dent Williams grand jury testimony by, 82, 116; evidence about Peterson gathered by, 65; Houston interviewed, 137; impeachment of, 72–73, 74, 87; Kilby Prison and, 153–54; letters to, 50–51; letter to Governor Miller by, 154–56, 174; Long's interrogation and, 69, 70; manhunt and, 31, 51; McDuff repudiated, 158–59, 163, 166–67; at pardon board, 174, 176, 178; Peterson protected by, 61, 67, 72–74; on Peterson's innocence, 137–38, 153–55, 158, 163, 174, 178; warrant issued by, 65

Haynes, Orville, 81–82

Hays, Arthur Garfield, 220n23

Heflin, H. P., 100–103, 107–8, 119–20, 198

Heflin, J. Thomas (Cotton Tom), 100

Herndon, Angelo, 41–43, 124, 173

Highland Park, 104

Highlands Methodist Church, 19, 38

Hill, Anna, 56, 106, 181, 189. *See also* Peterson, Henrietta (second wife)

Hillman Hospital, 37, 40; National Guard and mob at, 72, 85, 89; Peterson treated at, 72–73, 85, 88–89, 92, 93, 104, 116

Hine, Darlene Clark, 213–14n39

Hollums, E. L., 68, 70, 80–81

Horton, Charlie, 37, 39

hospital: Nell Williams in St. Vincent's, 17, 35, 38, 79; Peterson in Kilby prison, 180, 189. *See also* Hillman Hospital

Houston, Charles Hamilton: Alexander communication with, 136, 140–41, 181–82; Altman and, 152–53, 159, 163–64, 166; American Civil Liberties Union and, 146; at Amherst College, 135; appeals by, 164, 165; Attorney General Cummings met, 146; Birmingham investigative trip by, 136, 137–38, 142; Birmingham welcomed, 151; black lawyers mentored by, 135; Communist Party and, 136; confidential memo by, 138–39; as Crawford counsel, 165; free Peterson campaign and, 134; as Harvard Law School graduate, 135, 151; as Howard Law School dean, 134, 135, 151, 163; ILD and, 135, 136, 145; Jim Crow dismantling and, 135, 136; legal lynching and, 88; McDuff repudiation and, 159, 166–67; military service of, 135; as NAACP lawyer, 134, 136, 145–46, 181, 191, 194, 200; Nell Williams testimony questioned by, 138; Peterson case and, 134–37, 140–41, 182; Peterson clemency and, 178; on Peterson's innocence, 138–39; on Scottsboro case, 136; Supreme Court appeal and, 150; Tuscaloosa lynchings and, 145–46, 191; Walter White, friendship with, 134–35, 136, 152, 162, 164; Washington trip of, 145–46

Houston, Sam, 117

Howard Law School, 88, 134, 135, 151, 165

Howard University, faculty, 135

Howell, J. T., 186

Hudson, Hosea, 83, 123, 124, 194

ILD (International Labor Defense), 124; as American Communist Party legal arm, 29, 87–88, 142; attorneys and, 82–83,